2nd
Edition

Developing
PORTFOLIOS
in EDUCATION

To all future portfolio architects:
May this text enlighten and guide you through your portfolio journey.

**2nd
Edition**

Developing
PORTFOLIOS
in EDUCATION

A Guide to Reflection, Inquiry, and Assessment

Ruth S. Johnson
California State University, Los Angeles

J. Sabrina Mims-Cox
California State University, Los Angeles

Adelaide Doyle-Nichols
California State University, Los Angeles

Los Angeles | London | New Delhi
Singapore | Washington DC

For information:

SAGE Publications, Inc.
2455 Teller Road
Thousand Oaks, California 91320
E-mail: order@sagepub.com

SAGE Publications Ltd.
1 Oliver's Yard
55 City Road
London EC1Y 1SP
United Kingdom

SAGE Publications India Pvt. Ltd.
B 1/I 1 Mohan Cooperative Industrial Area
Mathura Road, New Delhi 110 044
India

SAGE Publications Asia-Pacific Pte. Ltd.
33 Pekin Street #02-01
Far East Square
Singapore 048763

Printed in the United States of America

Library of Congress Cataloging-in-Publication Data

Johnson, Ruth S.
Developing portfolios in education: A guide to reflection, inquiry, and assessment / Ruth S. Johnson, J. Sabrina Mims-Cox, Adelaide Doyle-Nichols.—2nd ed.
    p. cm.
Includes bibliographical references and index.
ISBN 978-1-4129-7236-9 (paper w/cd)

   1. Portfolios in education—United States. 2. Portfolios in education—United States—Evaluation. 3. Teachers—Rating of—United States. 4. Teachers—Training of—United States. I. Mims-Cox, J. Sabrina. II. Doyle-Nichols, Adelaide. III. Title.

LB1029.P67J656 2010
370.71'1—dc22   2009005424

Printed on acid-free paper

09   10   11   12   13   10   9   8   7   6   5   4   3   2   1

Acquiring Editor:	Diane McDaniel
Associate Editor:	Deya Saoud
Editorial Assistant:	Ashley Conlon
Production Editor:	Sarah K. Quesenberry
Copy Editor:	Marilyn Power Scott
Proofreader:	Gail Fay
Indexer:	Marilyn Augst
Typesetter:	C&M Digitals (P) Ltd.
Cover Designer:	Tony Lemos
Marketing Manager:	Christy Guilbault

Brief Contents

Detailed Contents

PART II: A GUIDE FOR DEVELOPING PORTFOLIOS   85

5 Your Portfolio Journey: Ten Steps for Organizing, Managing, and Completing the Process   87

6 Contents of the Portfolio   108

PART III: THE FUTURE OF YOUR PORTFOLIO   199

10 After the Credential Program, Now What? Keeping the Portfolio Alive   201

Appendixes A—F may also be found at www.sagepub.com/portfolios2e.

CD Contents

Chapter 1: Why Develop the Portfolio?

PowerPoint Slides
Sample Permission Form
Activities
    Activity 1.1 What Might Be Some Visions for Your Portfolios?
    Activity 1.2 Preparing for Success in Your Portfolio Development

Chapter 2: Portfolio Development as Action Research

PowerPoint Slides
Activities
    Activity 2.1 Questions and Activities for Beginning Action Research
    Activity 2.2 Questions and Activities for the First Level of Planning
    Activity 2.3 Questions and Activities for the Second Level of Planning
    Activity 2.4 Activities for the Third Level of Planning
    Activity 2.5 Activities for the Fourth Level of Planning
    Activity 2.6 Activities for the Fifth Level of Planning
    Activity 2.7 Activities for the Sixth Level of Planning
    Activity 2.8 Questions and Activities for Reflection and Application

Chapter 3: Using Portfolios as Tools for Authentic Assessment and Evaluation

PowerPoint Slides
Table 3.6 Portfolio Assessment Planner
Classroom Management Plan Guidelines
Sample Classroom Management Plan
Sample Rubric: Classroom Management Plan
Sample Rubric: Elementary Credential Portfolio
Sample Rubric: Counselor Candidates
Sample Rubric: Scoring a Summative Portfolio
Activities
    Activity 3.1 Questions and Activities for Matching Portfolio Forms and Functions
    Activity 3.2 Exploring Assessment and Categories of Learning Targets
    Activity 3.3 Question and Activities for Exploring Assessment Options
    Activity 3.4 Question and Activities for Designing and Using Rubrics

Chapter 4: Reflective Inquiry: A Tool for Giving Voice to the Portfolio

PowerPoint Slides
Table 4.4 Ten Ways Reflections Transform Artifacts Into Evidence
Table 4.6 The Multifaceted, Cyclical Nature of Portfolio Reflection
Sample Rubric: Elementary Credential Portfolio
Sample Rubric: INTASC Principle 1
Sample Rubric: INTASC Principle 2
Sample Rubric: ISLLC
Activities
> Activity 4.1 Questions and Activities Exploring Reflective Inquiry
> Activity 4.2 Activity for Reflective Inquiry About Your Portfolio Process
> Activity 4.3 Activity for Focus Questions to Guide Initial Reflective Inquiry
> Activity 4.4 Activities for Writing Reflections and Reflective Statements
>   That Transform Artifacts Into Evidence
> Activity 4.5 Activities for Writing Structured Reflections on Past Assignments

Chapter 5: Your Portfolio Journey: Ten Steps for Organizing, Managing, and Completing the Process

PowerPoint Slides
Table 5.5 Sample Portfolio Checkpoint Time Line (for Programs One Year or Less)
Sample Program Portfolio Checkpoint Time Line (for Programs Two or More Years)
Sample Portfolio Checklist for Teaching Credential Candidates
Sample Portfolio Checklist for Administrative Credential Candidates
Sample Portfolio Checklist for Counseling Credential Candidates
Sample Rubric for Teaching Credential Candidates
Sample Rubric for Master of Arts in Instructional Technology
Activities
> Activity 5.1 Forging a Vision for Your Portfolio
> Activity 5.2 Exploring Sample Rubrics and Sample Scoring of Portfolios

Chapter 6: Contents of the Portfolio

PowerPoint Slides
Table 6.1 Sample Cover Page or Title Page
Sample Cover Page
Table 6.3 Sample Sections for End-of-Program Portfolio Contents
Table 6.4 Sample Elementary Teacher Candidate Portfolio Table of Contents
Table 6.5 Sample Secondary Teacher Candidate Portfolio Table of Contents
Table 6.6 Sample Administrator Candidate Portfolio Table of Contents
Table 6.7 Sample School Counselor Portfolio Table of Contents
Figure 6.1 Sample Portfolio Introduction or Executive Summary
Links to Resume Formats

Table 6.9 The Three Dimensions of Competence and Their Corresponding
  Learning Domains, With Sample Artifacts
Sample Case Study
Sample Classroom Management Plan: Elementary
Sample Classroom Management Plan: Secondary
Sample End-of-Course Reflection
Sample End-of-Course Portfolio
Sample Rubric: Elementary Credential Portfolio
Sample Rubric: INTASC Principle 1
Sample Rubric: ISLLC
Sample Rubric: Master of Arts in Instructional Technology
Activities
  Activity 6.1 Activity for Developing a Personal Vision
  Activity 6.2 Develop a Resume
  Activity 6.3 Selecting Artifacts
  Activity 6.4 Write a Summative Reflection on a Completed
    Project, Course, or Program

Chapter 7: Presenting and Sharing the Portfolio

PowerPoint Slides
Table 7.1 Sample Portfolio Presentation Outline
Table 7.2 Sample Scoring Rubric for Portfolio Presentation
Table 7.3 Sample Scoring Rubric for Portfolio Presentation
Sample Rubric: INTASC Principle 1
Sample Rubric: ISLLC
Sample Rubric: Master of Arts in Instructional Technology
Activities
  Activity 7.1 Key Questions for Preparing Portfolio Presentations
  Activity 7.2 Portfolio Presentation Planner
  Activity 7.3 Portfolio Presentation Planning Worksheet
  Activity 7.4 Checklist for Developers and Audiences for a Digital Portfolio

Chapter 8: An Overview of Electronic Portfolios: Exploring the Options

PowerPoint Slides
Sample Permission Form
Sample Electronic Portfolio: Master of Arts Instructional Technology
Sample Electronic Portfolio: Elementary Teaching Credential (Template)
Sample Electronic Portfolio: Single Subject Credential (Template)
Activities
  Activity 8.1 Exploring Your Options and Preferences
    for Creating an Electronic Portfolio

Appendix A: Web Links to National and Professional Standards

Appendix B: Leadership Standards for Cultural Proficiency

Appendix C: Sample Portfolio Checklist and Time Line for Teaching Credential Candidates

Appendix D: Sample Scoring Rubrics

Appendix E: Instructional Activities for Microsoft Word 2003 and PowerPoint 2003

Appendix F: Sample Permission Form for Use of an Artifact

Appendixes A–F may also be found at www.sagepub.com/portfolios2e.

Preface

PURPOSE OF THE TEXT

As instructors in higher education, we realized that using portfolios with our students was increasingly transforming the way in which we interacted with and engaged them in the learning process. Infusing reflective practice and designing fundamentally different ways to evaluate work required changes in practice. We sought out resources to assist us and found that there was a large body of print and electronic materials on various aspects of portfolio development, assessment, and evaluation. However, we felt the need for a comprehensive text that would serve as a resource throughout a professional's career.

Our purpose in writing the first edition was to develop a text that would be useful for both candidates and instructors—one that would provide a conceptual and research framework about the usefulness of portfolios, suggest some ways to organize the process, and provide long-term, useful tools that could be used at various stages of a professional's career, including professional and academic advancement.

PEDAGOGICAL FEATURES OF THE TEXT

- **Chapter-Opening Scenarios** provide "real-life" situations that readers may experience in their own portfolio development and makes the experience of developing the portfolio more relevant.
- **"Let's Practice!" Activities** provide directed questions and hands-on exercises including prompts for students and instructors to discuss.
- **Examples and Samples** help to create a concrete representation of the material for the learner by providing hands-on tools.
- **Useful Resources** provide Web-based material students can access for more information about the chapter topics.
- **For Further Reading** suggestions direct students to books and journal articles for more information.

CHANGES TO THE SECOND EDITION

The second edition reflects the comments for improvement from outside reviewers and our personal teaching experiences in using the book with our students.

- The book's audience is preservice and professional educators and teachers, administrators, and counselors who will be developing portfolios. The book can also serve as a teaching tool for instructors.
- All chapters now have directed questions and hands-on exercises embedded, including prompts and exercises for students and instructors to discuss.
- A new chapter on action research (Chapter 2) has been added. It is designed for readers to understand the cyclical nature of the action research process, and the chapter fully develops the link between action research and portfolio development.
- Chapter 3, on authentic assessment and evaluation, has been expanded to incorporate more material on other forms of assessment. There is additional material on rubrics and scoring criteria and information on the various categories of portfolios and when each would be appropriate.
- Chapter 4, on reflective inquiry, has been enhanced to include more specific practical material on how to be reflective and a section on structured reflection that includes sample questions to reflect on and examples of written reflections.
- Additions to Chapter 5 include how to build a rubric and a step-by-step process for developing a portfolio.
- Chapter 6 contains more specific directions for developing a good teacher resume, along with more information on the development of vision and philosophy statements.
- Chapter 7 has been retooled to focus on those who will be presenting portfolios, rather than on institutional planning.
- The material in Chapters 8 and 9 have been updated to be more in line with current technology and educational trends. In Chapter 8, discussion on options and preferences for creating an electronic portfolio, a discussion on which program to use when creating an online portfolio, and information on online portfolio applications and commercial options, such as Live text are now featured. In Chapter 9, we've included updated instructions using Microsoft Word 2007 and PowerPoint 2007 in addition to Microsoft Word 2003 and PowerPoint 2003 and "how to" documents with various technology skills (all included on the CD).
- Chapter 10 has been revised to add more emphasis on how the portfolio and the skills learned in the process of its creation can be used for ongoing professional development and more information on how administrators view and use portfolios for hiring decisions.
- References have been updated and appendices have been added to improve readability by shifting some tables and charts from the chapters.

ANCILLARY FEATURES

This book includes a CD-ROM, which includes PowerPoint presentations, Web resources, hyperlinks, portfolio models and templates, implementation guidelines, additional exercises, and research information. The CD icon included in the text refers directly to material included on the CD-ROM. In order to better navigate the CD, there is a detailed CD Table of Contents immediately following the table of contents for the book.

For easy access, we've provided the book's appendixes at www.sagepub.com/portfolios2e. You can access and print the following directly from the website (the material is also included on the CD-ROM):

- Appendix A: Web Links to National and Professional Standards
- Appendix B: Leadership Standards for Cultural Proficiency
- Appendix C: Sample Portfolio Checklist and Time Line for Teaching Credential Candidates
- Appendix D: Sample Scoring Rubrics
- Appendix E: Instructional Activities for Microsoft Word 2003 and PowerPoint 2003
- Appendix F: Sample Permission Form for Use of an Artifact

Acknowledgments

Many people helped us in shaping the contents, format, and organization of the first and second editions of this book. Their guidance, time, and emotional support were invaluable.

Our current and former students and colleagues at California State University, Los Angeles, inspired much of the work in this book. Professors Ann Hafner, Darlene Michener, John Schindler, Penelope Semrau, A. Dee Williams, and former professor Fawn Ukpolo contributed research, instructional, and assessment documents. John Schindler also opened his classroom and generously allowed for taping of portfolio presentations. The Curriculum and Instruction Directed Teaching Committee members, Dolores Beltran, Rebecca Joseph, Andrea Maxie, Sabrina Mims-Cox, Rosario Morales, and Kimberly Persiani-Becker, developed and provided draft portfolio rubric samples for the final multiple-subject and single-subject portfolio presentation sessions. These guided much of our work for rubrics in Chapters 5, 6, and 7 in terms of portfolio organization, contents, and evaluation. We are especially grateful for the materials and guidance that C. D. and Sharon Johnson shared with us based on their extensive work with results-based portfolios for counselors. We also appreciate Kathy Reilly's contribution in the counseling area.

Samples of student work, photos, and portfolio presentations for the CD were contributed by the following teacher and administrator candidates: Karin Aguilar, Jean Ammon, Adrienne Balcazar, Violet Medina Bartolini, Hedy Bravo-Juarez, Tara Bultema, Helen Simmons Conroy, Antonio Cova, Gudiel Croswaite, Constantino Duarte, James Eder, Stephan Franklin, Stephanie Frederick, Flavio Gallarzo, Michael Garcia, Karen Gilmartin, Matthew Ginsberg, Stacy Griffin, John Glaister, Kisha Griggs, Myriam Islas, Lesly Lespinasse, Denise Likong, Trish Luckeroth Lockhart, Brenda Loh, Karen D. Magana, Ysenia Mancilla, Yasmin Martinez, Brenda Loh, Lusine Martinzyan, Alma Moran, Ambler Moss, Hipolito Murillo, Kirk Nichols, Margaret Olivares-Gilkyson, Leticia Orozco, Rosa Paredes, Judy Peng, Kathleen Perez, Laura Perez-Vesquez, Pamela Perkins, Consuelo M. Rodriguez-Garcia, Greg Runyon, Brenda Sanchez, Dinorah Sanchez, Luis Sanchez, Mareda Sandoval, Brooke Schufreider, Odell Scott, Eugene So, Alicia Stanco, Bernice Suen, Sylvia Torres, Soon-Ya Chang, and Josefina Zacarias-Ayala.

We thank Beth Cornell, Director of Fine Arts and Humanities from the Pennsylvania Department of Education, Division of Evaluation and Reports, for her consultation and guidance in the use of the Portfolio Implementation Guide (Pennsylvania Assessment Through Themes [PATT], 2000). We also appreciate the advice and assistance of Kirk Nichols, who reviewed parts of the manuscript and helped out with videotaping for the CD and other technical matters, Shawn Johnson-Witt, who reviewed parts of the manuscript, and Ellen Stein, who read our manuscript and provided us with insightful and useful editorial comments. Many thanks are given to Helen Quon, Instructional Designer at Cal State LA.

Our families and significant others had to delay together times and provide support for us during our writing journey. Adelaide would like to thank Kirk and Stephanie, her daughter, for their love, understanding, and support. She would also like to thank Stephen and Adelaide for their guidance and for instilling in her a desire to achieve. J. Sabrina would like to thank her mother, Willie Mae Mims, and her husband, Woodrow Cox, for their love, patience, and support throughout this process. She would also like to thank her siblings, Wayne, Wyatt, Willis, and Salimu, for their constant encouragement. Ruth would like to thank her daughters, Shawn Johnson-Witt, who reviewed many of the chapters, and Cathy Payne, for their patience, love, and support and her grandchildren, Glenn and Shawn II, who serve as an inspiration and motivation to improve the educational enterprise.

Our SAGE editors, Diane McDaniel and Deya Saoud, have provided us with guidance and support. We thank them.

We would also like to thank the peer reviewers who aided us in shaping the text so that it would best serve our readers:

From the second edition:

Cindy F. Altomari, University of New England

Rhonda Bonnstetter, Southwest Minnesota State University

Amity Smith Currie, Marist College

Christine Kolar, California State Polytechnic University, Pomona

Ochieng' K'Olewe, McDaniel College

Margaret Olson, St. Francis Xavier University

Pamela Smith, Eastern Michigan University

Lorraine Spickermann, University of Texas of the Permian Basin

Sonni Svejcar, Heritage Institute

Catherine Tannahill, Eastern Connecticut State University

Jeanne Tunks, University of North Texas

From the first edition:

Carrie E. Chapman, Indiana University

Kimberly Kinsler, Hunter College of the City University of New York

Ann M. Rule, Saint Louis University

Shawn J. Witt, University of La Verne

Kevin S. Sherman, Auburn University

Patricia A. Parrish, Saint Leo University

Natalie B. Milman, George Washington University

PART I

The Rationale for Requiring Portfolios

CHAPTER 1

Why Develop the Portfolio?

The development of portfolios by students has been lauded by teachers and principals as especially useful in graphically portraying academic and creative abilities and in enhancing learning.

—Brown and Irby (2001, p. 3)

CHAPTER OBJECTIVES

Readers will be able to

- ❏ describe the current trends and uses of portfolios in kindergarten through postsecondary education,

- ❏ describe a portfolio and its purposes,

- ❏ explain the need for documents that authentically assess learning outcomes for aspiring and **practicing educators,** and

- ❏ discuss some of the benefits and challenges of portfolio development.

SCENARIO

The College of Education at Sunshine University recently instituted portfolio assessment as a requirement for evaluating competency in professional standards of their teacher, administrative, and school counselor candidates. In three years, the college is scheduled for a visitation from state and national accrediting agencies. There is some concern about how the college will perform. The state accreditation agency requires multiple assessments for candidate certification, and the portfolio is one of the required assessments. Most of the candidates in the teacher education programs are familiar with portfolio use, as the professors in their methodology courses have instructed them on how to develop portfolios for their students. However, the students are uncertain about how to develop and organize their work for their own assessment. The candidates in the educational administration and school counseling programs have only recently been introduced to portfolio development. Their programs have relied exclusively on comprehensive exams and grade point averages to determine competency for graduation.

Even though it requires more effort to develop and score portfolios, the accreditation requirement presents an opportunity to implement a change that can potentially improve the preparation and assessment of aspiring education candidates. Students also have been informed that administrators and other hiring personnel in districts are requesting that candidates bring their portfolios to their final interviews. Many districts are gearing up for the use of e-portfolios for hiring purposes and ongoing professional development.

Sunshine University students have begun to understand the usefulness and benefits of portfolios, but they need more time and instruction on the purposes of different types of portfolios, the structuring of a portfolio, how the portfolios will be evaluated, and how to manage their time. Many of the syllabi and classes do an inadequate job of addressing the required standards. Moreover, there are major inconsistencies in how performance is measured, the quality and quantity of work expected, and the levels of rigor required to demonstrate competency. Since the college began the process of portfolio implementation, instructors and students have realized that portfolio development is a complex process that requires study and evaluation. Overall, the college and its students are willing to embrace the process, as portfolio development and assessment have been viewed as good opportunities to demonstrate how students and the college perform on important professional standards.

OVERVIEW

The foregoing scenario describes some of the expectations and dilemmas regarding the use of portfolios faced by schools, agencies, and colleges of education to assess students' competency in meeting professional **standards**. Professional educators are now teaching in an era of **standards-based reforms.** Forty-nine states have adopted standards for a variety of subjects at K–12 levels of education. There is mounting evidence that clear goals, high standards, and high expectations contribute to improved student performance.

Similarly, the standards movement is having a profound effect on colleges and schools in higher education. States are rapidly requiring that preparation and credential programs meet national or state standards or both and that students are assessed for competency in meeting those standards. Portfolios are being selected as a major way to measure those **competencies**. According to Georgi and Crowe (1998), portfolios are commonplace in today's schools and universities. Likewise, Salzman, Denner, and Harris (2002; as cited in Wilkerson & Lang, 2003) report that nearly 90% of schools, colleges, and departments of education use portfolios in evaluating their students, and about 40% use portfolios as a certification or licensure requirement. Until recently, portfolios in higher education were used primarily in preservice teacher education programs (Bartell, Kaye, & Morin, 1998a, 1998b; Campbell, Cignetti, Melenyzer, Nettles, & Wyman, 2001, 2004; Campbell, Melenyzer, Nettles, & Wyman, 2000; Stone, 1998), but to a lesser extent in leadership and other preparation programs, such as school counseling (Barnes, Clark, & Thull, 2005; Barnett, 1992; Brown & Irby, 2000, 2001).

The No Child Left Behind Act (2002) requires that districts hire and retain "highly qualified teachers." National Board Certified (NBC) teachers are recognized by the law as highly qualified (Montgomery & Wiley, 2008). The **National Board for Professional Teaching Standards** (NBPTS; 1999) requires the submission of portfolios as a major component in selecting NBC Teachers. These current demands assign portfolios an important role in pre-K–12 schools and colleges of education.

Use of portfolios in job searches is increasing (Strawhecker, Messersmith, & Balcom, 2007). Portfolios are emerging as a component for hiring, career advancement, and professional evaluation in schools and districts (Brown & Irby, 2000; Campbell et al., 2001; Dietz, 2008; Hartnell-Young & Morriss, 2007; Mosely, 2004–2005; NBPTS, 1999; Wyatt & Looper, 2004). Chapter 10 of this book provides detailed information on this aspect of portfolio use.

The remainder of this chapter describes portfolios and their use as assessment and evaluation tools, including the benefits and challenges of portfolio use. The chapter concludes with a summary.

WHAT IS A PORTFOLIO?

Initially, a portfolio may appear as simply a collection of work that has been compiled over a period of time. Portfolios are sometimes compared with **scrapbooks** (Burke, 1997). Although both may contain artifacts that are selected over time, portfolio contents can be organized to assess competencies in a given standard, goal, or objective and focus on how well the learner has achieved in that area. Portfolios have the potential to make learning concrete and visible, thereby providing faculty, hiring agents, and students with the opportunity to focus on new ways of learning (Mosely, 2004–2005; Yancey, 2001). Through the use of **artifacts**, which are concrete examples of the student's work, **portfolios** contain evidence of knowledge, skills, and dispositions (Brown & Irby, 2001). Artifacts of knowledge show what a student knows, such as exams; artifacts of skill show what a student is able to do, such as creating lesson plans; and artifacts of **dispositions** reveal the student's attitudes, beliefs, or values, such as a philosophy of education. (Samples of appropriate artifacts for each of these learning domains are found in Chapter 6, Table 6.9, The Three Dimensions of Competence and Their Corresponding Learning Domains, With Sample Artifacts.)

A portfolio used for assessment and evaluation requires a student to engage in higher levels of thinking through the use of inquiry and reflection. **Inquiry** involves a process of collecting, sorting, selecting, describing, analyzing, and evaluating evidence to answer questions about how well the evidence represents the student's accomplishment of a standard, goal, or objective. The student is involved in a personal type of action research that entails continual **reflection** or questioning and resorting of the selected work. The student is also questioning how he or she can improve personal practice. Hartnell-Young and Morriss (2007) suggest that the portfolio serves the experienced professional in meaningful ways. They state,

> Experienced teachers and administrators are finding that the benefits of
> developing a portfolio include the opportunity for professional renewal through

mapping of new goals and planning for future growth. Many people discover that one of the most important and long-lasting outcomes of producing a portfolio is the self-esteem that comes from recording and reflecting on achievements and career successes, and clarifying who they are as a professional and a person. (p. 7)

These processes are more fully described in Chapters 2, 3, 4, and 10.

PURPOSES FOR PORTFOLIOS

Portfolios serve a variety of purposes. For example, they may be used for developmental and culminating assessments, to showcase or display outstanding work, and to measure levels of competency for certification, graduation requirements, and career advancement. Barton and Collins (1997) have highlighted the fact that portfolios are

- another method to evaluate the success of a graduate,
- a way to give students and faculty the opportunity to reflect on student progress,
- a method to translate the learning from instructors to students, and
- a way to allow instructors to evaluate a variety of specific evidence when making global determinations about learner competency.

The purpose for which the portfolio is designed should determine its organization, content, and presentation style. There are a variety of portfolio styles described in the literature, each with a specific purpose. Hartnell-Young and Morriss (2007) suggest three broad categories: (1) **formative** portfolios, which are developmental; (2) **summative** portfolios, which are cumulative and include final assessments, products, or both; and (3) **marketing portfolios,** which are focused on job attainment and career advancement. Tables 1.1, 1.2, and 1.3, although not exhaustive, present information about the features of different kinds of portfolios, under these three broad categories. Some types have similar or overlapping uses or address two specific categories at once, as Table 1.2 displays.

LET'S PRACTICE!

Activity 1.1   What Might Be Some Visions for Your Portfolios?

Closely review Tables 1.1, 1.2, and 1.3 and consider the following questions:

- Can you envision the types of portfolios that can serve you now and in the future? Which types? Describe the types.
- How might these portfolios be useful for your educational and career development?
- What are the major personal benefits that might result from developing portfolios?

TABLE 1.1   Formative–Developmental

Type	Purpose or Goals	Unique Features	Use
1. Comprehensive (Johnson, Mims-Cox & Doyle-Nichols, 2006)	To store a myriad of artifacts to be used for career and academic advancement	Contains an up-to-date resource file with organizational features	To select specific artifacts to develop different types of focus portfolios
2. Resource (Taskstream, www.taskstream.com, a commercial Web site)	To store a myriad of artifacts	Contains an ongoing, systematic collection of work over time	To select specific artifacts to develop the presentation portfolio
3. Working (Campbell et al., 2001)	To show professional growth	Contains an ongoing, systematic collection of work over time	For self-assessment and goal setting
4. Growth (Mueller, 2008)	To show growth and change over time	Looks at development over time; includes strengths and weaknesses	For evaluation and goal setting
5. Web-Based Portfolios (Johnson et al., 2006)	To store resources electronically for e-portfolios	Assists in the organization and linking of artifacts	For storage, presentations, and retooling the portfolio

TABLE 1.2   Formative and Summative–Assessment and Evaluation

Type	Purpose or Goals	Unique Features	Use
1. Academic (Brown & Irby, 2001)	To assess and evaluate students, and for in-program evaluation	Contains artifacts and reflections based on academic classes, projects, field experiences, and programs	To show academic and experiential growth for credentials, certification, and graduation
2. Educational Assessment (Wyatt & Looper, 1999; Bartell, Kaye, & Morin, 1998a, 1998b)	To assess and evaluate students and programs	Contains artifacts and reflections based on academic classes, projects, field experiences, and programs	To show academic and experiential growth for credentials, certification, and graduation
3. Learning and Teaching (Bartell, et al., 1998a, 1998b)	To promote the student's reflection and ownership of the learning process	Contains personalized collections of a student's work, emphasizing ownership and self-assessment	To explore, extend, showcase, and reflect on personal learning
4. Developmental (Wyatt & Looper, 1999)	To show the stages of growth and development of the individual over time	Contains an individual's selection of work that demonstrates sequential development (growth) over time	To evaluate a student's developmental work

TABLE 1.3   Marketing

Type	Purpose or Goals	Unique Features	Use
1. Career Advancement, Employment, and Hiring (Brown & Irby, 2001; Bartell et al., 1998a, 1998b; Satterthwaite & D'Orsi, 2003; Strudler & Wetzel, 2005)	To provide information on experiences relevant to professional advancement	Contains evidence of career accomplishments; showcases best work	For employment interviews, professional advancement, and follow-up after interviews
2. Focus (Johnson et al., 2006)	To present in academic and career advancement settings	Focuses on a specific area related to academic and career advancement	For preparation and presentation in job or higher-education interviews
3. Interview (Mosely, 2004–2005)	To present when requested by an employer and in final interviews	Is usually presented in an e-portfolio using a CD, DVD, or Web-based format, which may contain video clips and scanned documents	For a final interview, prepared in formats that employers can access
4. Presentation (Campbell et al., 2001)	To present an easy-to-read display of competence	Contains samples of the best work from a portfolio collection	For presentations to an audience
5. Showcase (Wyatt & Looper, 1999)	To showcase and demonstrate achievement to impress others	Dynamically showcases the best work to demonstrate a competency and is kept current	For presentation to an audience (e.g., professor, employer, evaluator)

USING PORTFOLIOS FOR ASSESSMENT AND EVALUATION

One might ask, What are the incentives to use portfolios for assessment and evaluation? Portfolios require much more time on the part of the learner to develop and organize and much more time on the part of the instructor or other evaluator to score. When portfolios are described as an assessment tool for individuals, programs, and institutions, **assessment** is defined as an ongoing, developmental process to measure growth and change and provide information on areas that need further development. **Evaluation** usually describes a final, summative process that includes multiple assessments and is akin to a high-stakes test or a recommendation for credentials, promotion, or graduation (Campbell et al., 2004; Sewell, Marczak, & Horn, 2005; Wilkerson & Lang, 2003). (These topics are described more completely in Chapter 3.) There is ample literature supporting the notion that a collection of well-organized, real-world concrete artifacts in a portfolio offers the potential to assess in powerful ways how a student has developed and applied what was learned. It is important to assess whether students are capable of applying knowledge to real-world situations (Barton & Collins, 1997; Mueller, 2008; Sewell et al., 2005; Shaklee, Barbour, Ambrose, & Hansford, 1997).

Portfolios have been viewed historically as one of the most comprehensive and effective forms of authentic assessment since the late 1980s (Barton & Collins, 1997; Sewell et al.,

2005; Shaklee et al., 1997), as they provide a systematic way to organize and document real-life evidence of a person's performance. For many years, portfolios have been used in areas such as architecture, art, and the performance fields, in which concrete demonstrations of competencies are critical. The contents of portfolios include multiple ways to assess complex knowledge and problem-solving skills. Instruments such as videos, graphics, audio recordings, field documents, and other concrete forms of information can be used to demonstrate competency toward standards or goals and objectives.

Moreover, portfolios need not be the sole assessment tool. We advocate that they serve as enhancements to more traditional academic models, such as comprehensive exams, field observations by supervisors, and licensure exams. Portfolios provide alternative ways for students to demonstrate and document their level of achievement and competency toward meeting or exceeding a standard, goal, or objective (Barton & Collins, 1997; Pennsylvania Assessment Through Themes, 2000; Sewell et al., 2005; Shaklee et al., 1997). Chapter 3 provides a more robust discussion of this topic, including examples of how artifacts are transformed into evidence.

BENEFITS OF PORTFOLIOS

The development of a portfolio encourages learners to shift from playing a passive role in assessment and evaluation—in which they are pressed to focus on external issues, such as what questions the instructors are going to ask and what they should be studying—to an active role, in which they must engage in more complex thinking and self-evaluation in choosing representations of what they learned. This route thus requires students to reflect on and demonstrate their competencies with real-world artifacts.

Portfolio development ideally evolves as a dynamic interaction among instructors, learners, and mentors. This interaction fosters a more interpersonal approach to teaching and learning, an approach that is responsive to all students but particularly to African American, Hispanic, and Native American students (Irvine, 1990; Ladson-Billings, 1994). Portfolios also offer another way of measuring competencies for those who do not score well on traditional exams (Astin, 1993; Dollase, 1996; Steele, 2002). The process can encourage peer evaluation whereby students collaborate with and assist each other in selecting artifacts, critiquing the evidence, organizing the portfolio, and providing general support.

Zeichner and Wray (2001) comment that administrators reported that portfolios can provide important information about the talents and beliefs of teachers. Portfolios provide concrete evidence of skills and abilities. They offer the opportunity to assess how effectively education students are responding to racially, ethnically, and linguistically diverse student groups.

Our nation is experiencing demographic shifts, and these changes are reflected in our public school enrollments. Many states have high percentages of students with a primary language other than English. Brown and Wolfe-Quintero (1997) report that the University of Hawaii at Manoa used portfolios as part of ESL and EFL teacher evaluation. Some studies are finding that video clips in electronic portfolios are desirable to assess relational skills in how teachers and other professionals engage and interact with diverse student groups (Painter & Wetzel, 2005). Other pertinent factors involve the cultural, environmental, and economic contexts in which educators, students, and families interact. The National Commission on Teaching and America's Future (1996) report, *What Matters Most: Teaching for America's Future,* argues that teacher content knowledge and pedagogical strategies have a powerful effect on student achievement, particularly for students in low-achieving, low-income urban and rural schools.

The Interstate New Teacher Assessment and Support Consortium (INTASC) is a consortium of more than 30 states operating under the Council of Chief State School Officers (CCSSO) that has developed standards and an assessment process for initial teacher certification (Campbell et al., 2000). Many INTASC principles—such as Principle 3, Adapting Instructions for Individual Needs; Principle 5, Classroom Motivation and Management; Principle 7, Instructional Planning Skills; and Principle 8, Assessment of Student Learning—should be measured in ways that demonstrate how knowledge is transformed into practice to meet the needs of diverse student groups. Indicators of dispositions that reflect beliefs, values, and expectations for diverse groups of children are critical areas to assess. Richer sources of evidence can be required and provided through the effective use of case studies, videos, lesson plans, and instructional strategies; observations of student and parent interactions and student responses; reflection on lessons; and other means. A body of work is emerging in the area of **culturally responsive** classrooms and schools that can serve as a resource in this area (Banks, 2006; Johnson, 2002; Johnson & Bush, 2005; Ladson-Billings, 1994, 2003; Lee, 1997; Lindsey, Robins, & Terrell, 2005; Robins, Lindsey, Lindsey, & Terrell, 2002; Shade, Kelly, & Oberg, 2004; Villegas & Lucas, 2002). Salend (2001) emphasizes the role that portfolios can play for special education teacher candidates by providing information on a candidate's ability to use a variety of assessments to evaluate student needs. Evidence of the development of individualized education programs, as well as instructional techniques, can be included.

At the program and institutional levels, the potential for feedback to instructors for professional improvement is immense. Student reflections, when made part of the portfolio development process, provide assessment information about what was learned in courses and about program strengths, weaknesses, and levels of implementation. Because each student's voice can be heard during portfolio presentations and reviews of written documentation, program instructors, mentors, and supervisors may gain valuable insights about the efficacy of their instruction and programs. Reflection can provide program developers with vital information about how well learners have integrated the values, knowledge, and meaning from their instruction and mentoring (see video clips included in the PowerPoint presentation for Chapter 7, Presenting and Sharing the Portfolio, on the CD).

For specific information related to this concept, see the Chapter 1 resources on the CD.

CHALLENGES IN PORTFOLIO DEVELOPMENT

A former candidate described his challenges with portfolio development:

> I have begun in earnest to review the stack of documents and artifacts that will comprise my portfolio, and I have a few concerns. Mostly, I feel confused

because so much of the jargon and other stuff [is] new to me. It's not clear to me that my coursework prepared me specifically for this particular task. (To this end . . . I would like to suggest that the department make the portfolio an integral part of each class, rather than a separate component to be assembled at the end of all coursework.) Were it not for my being a pack rat, I probably would not have kept any of my "old work," since no one prompted me to do so. (Candidate reflection)

The scenario describes some of the challenges that must be confronted in portfolio development on the part of both students and evaluators. The portfolio process is more labor intensive, compared to scoring a multiple-choice or essay exam. Some challenges include (1) the need for new organizational structures, (2) technology skills, (3) time, (4) professional development, and (5) agreed-upon rubrics for scoring work. We offer some strategies for meeting these challenges throughout this book.

Another area that portfolio developers will need to familiarize themselves with is the legal requirements in the use and inclusion in the portfolio of photographs, artifacts, and electronic material from students, parents, community, and educational professionals (Hartnell-Young & Morriss, 2007). A sample permission form is on the CD.

For specific information related to this concept, see the Chapter 1 resources on the CD.

In the area of assessments, Wilkerson and Lang (2003) offer compelling arguments about the need to understand the psychometric implications of portfolio assessments, particularly if these are used to make decisions about a student's credential, licensure, or graduation. In our view, such arguments should be heeded. If not, issues of whether portfolio assessments can be considered a worthy measure of a student's professional competency are liable to come under question at some point, thus potentially undermining the credibility of programs and evaluation. Such issues are more fully presented in Chapter 3.

For students to meet these challenges, we offer the following guidelines:

1. Be thoroughly familiar with the expected goals, outcomes, **criteria**, and rubrics used for evaluation and time lines related to portfolio development.

2. Study the literature on portfolio development.

3. Find out about and use the resources and support available to you during the portfolio development process.

4. Align coursework with the portfolio purposes.

5. Seek out critiques about the portfolio from peers, supervisors, and instructors.

6. View a portfolio requirement not as a one-time event or activity but as an ongoing, valuable tool for career growth and advancement.

LET'S PRACTICE!

Activity 1.2   Preparing for Success in Your Portfolio Development

1. Review portfolio guidelines and checkpoints.

   If any of your current classes or programs requires a portfolio, review the guidelines with them in mind. Place a copy of the guidelines in your comprehensive portfolio for easy reference.

2. Create a draft portfolio calendar or time line.

   If you are able to locate portfolio time lines for your program, create and add them to a portfolio calendar. A recommended portfolio time line appears in Chapter 5 and on the CD. List important portfolio planning, collection, and assessment activities on your calendar.

3. Align your coursework with the portfolio process.

   Review your course or program documents to determine if they have a carefully articulated portfolio process. If so, add it to your comprehensive portfolio for easy reference.

4. Consult other completed portfolios as examples.

   If possible, review other portfolios completed by program alumni. Determine how coursework was integrated into the portfolio process.

5. Repeat these steps throughout your portfolio development process as an ongoing reference for updating and refinement.

SUMMARY

Portfolios are becoming a popular method for assessment and evaluation of students in schools and colleges of education. In some institutions, portfolios are used along with other assessment measures, but in others, they may be the sole criterion for judging competency. Many external agencies, such as state credentialing agencies, currently require portfolio assessment. Many school districts are also requiring portfolios for hiring and career advancement purposes.

Portfolios can provide evidence of knowledge, dispositions, and skills. A large body of information maintains that well-organized, reflective portfolios can offer authentic information about how students have progressed and what levels of competency they have achieved. Portfolios can be used for a variety of purposes, including showcasing work, measuring competency, establishing certification and graduation requirements, and pursuing career advancement.

Although we know of many benefits of portfolio use, there are also some challenges. To meet the challenge of being accepted as authentic assessments for candidate evaluation, portfolios need to be carefully designed and evaluated. In Chapter 2, we show how action research links to organizing and developing portfolios.

CHAPTER 2

Portfolio Development as Action Research

The main difference between action research and other types of inquiry is the commitment to bring about change as a result of the research. . . . The world can only be understood through trying to change it. . . . Action researchers are doers.

—Brydon-Miller, Greenwood, and Maguire (2003, p. 15)

CHAPTER OBJECTIVES

Readers will be able to

❑ define action research as a valuable tool for setting and accomplishing professional goals and objectives,

❑ describe action research as a viable process for portfolio development and identify the levels of action research as they relate to portfolio development,

❑ discuss the benefits of portfolios as both action research and authentic assessment,

❑ conduct action research by planning initial goals for their portfolios and starting a personal archive of artifacts, and

❑ find additional resources for understanding and doing action research.

SCENARIO

As Jennifer and Omar went over the course syllabus for their Introduction to the Teaching Profession course, they made several comments regarding a growing list of course requirements: "Wow, this looks like a lot of stuff!" exclaimed Jennifer. "The standards, the field work, the technology requirements, and the portfolio seem overwhelming. How are we supposed to do all of this, and still find time to study?" "I don't know," replied Omar, "but it makes you think twice about what it means to become a teacher. Teachers have to handle a lot of things, and they really have to be organized. Maybe these classes will help us to find out if we are really cut out for the job."

"I know I want to teach," Jennifer responded, "but what will help me the most, at this point, is help getting organized and seeing how all of these pieces fit together. I need to see the big picture and know where I'm going. Then I can relax and concentrate on getting there." "Me too!" replied Omar. "I'm pretty good at technology already, and I've learned how to use it to help me get organized. Maybe the portfolio will be the same way in helping us to be more organized and seeing how all of the program pieces fit together."

At that point, the professor, Dr. Ozley, greeted the students with the following comments: "Hi everyone! I'm Dr. Ozley, and I want to welcome each of you future teachers to your first course on your path to becoming a teacher. And no, I'm not trying to scare any of you off with the syllabus or the long list of portfolio requirements, as the expressions on your faces seem to suggest. We want and need you in our schools as highly qualified and motivated teachers! In our last faculty meeting, all of the professors in the credential program agreed that we would each include a list of portfolio requirements for the overall credential program in our syllabi. We would then discuss the specific requirements our course is designed to address. Even though there was some fear that such a list may overwhelm you at first, our goal is to give you the big picture and to help you see how all of the pieces fit together in preparing you to become teachers. Since this is your first course, my job is to help you get organized and begin the dynamic process of conducting action research as part of your journey. Developing your portfolio will be the major focus of your action research. The portfolio will allow you to see how the standards, the field work, and the other assignments fit together to provide evidence that you have what it takes to be a successful teacher. Are you ready to get started?" After hearing Dr. Ozley's explanation, Omar and Jennifer both breathed a sigh of relief.

OVERVIEW

The aspiring teacher candidates in the scenario are still unsure of the portfolio process and how it fits into their overall credential program. Initially, it appears to be one of a growing list of seemingly unrelated requirements whose benefits still need to be proven. Their professors, on the other hand, are taking extra steps to ensure that the portfolio requirements are communicated in a consistent manner in all of the courses so that its purpose becomes transparent as the students progress through their courses. They are doing this by continually mentioning the portfolio in their course syllabi and showing how their course assignments add to the student's professional preparation. The completed portfolios will be used to demonstrate their professional qualifications and their related achievements along the way. The professors are also using the portfolio process as a type of action research, where the goals of the research are to become successful teachers skilled in inquiry and reflection and to provide the supporting evidence.

Since we have discussed the rationale for developing portfolios in Chapter 1, we devote this chapter to expanding on the benefits of portfolio development by comparing it to action research as a process to both plan for and accomplish professional growth and development (Johnson et al., 2006; Reason, 2006; Strijbos, Meeus, & Libotton, 2007). As indicated in the scenario, the goal of this chapter is to show how action research helps all of the pieces in the credential program and the portfolio process fit together. The chapter begins with a brief definition of action research and inquiry as tools for continuous learning and improvement. The chapter continues by showing how action research is a valuable process for systematically organizing and developing the portfolio. Next, the cyclical nature of action research is described as it relates to the portfolio process. From there, we explore the levels of action research in portfolio development and the many benefits of action research as a strategic process for authentic assessment. The chapter concludes with questions and exercises for reflection and discussion. A list of pertinent resources is also included.

DEFINING ACTION RESEARCH AND INQUIRY

A common question among educators is, What exactly is action research and what role does it play in portfolio development and authentic assessment? The main difference between action research and other kinds of inquiry is the commitment to bring about change as a result of the research (Brydon-Miller, Greenwood, & Maguire, 2003). **Action research**, in the most general sense of the term, is researching one's actions or simply asking questions about one's actions for the purpose of learning from them in order to improve upon them and grow. Action research is defined as a systematic approach used to improve one's own practice (McNiff, 2003; Mertler, 2009; Reason & Bradbury, 2004; Sagor, 2003). Action research is practitioner research designed to clarify and improve professional practice. This means that those doing the research are those who are trying to improve their practice. A key value is that actions can only be understood and changed if those doing the actions are themselves involved in asking questions about those actions. This reinforces a respect for people's own knowledge and for their ability to understand and address the issues confronting them. Action research draws power from the belief that "we can know (and learn) through doing" (Sagor, 2003, p. 14). Two essential aims of action research are to improve and to involve (Dickens & Watkins, 1999). The goal of improvement is directed in three areas: (1) practice (defining what we do), (2) the understanding of practice by practitioners (explaining why we do what we do), and (3) the improvement of the situation (knowing how to improve the overall situation by changing or modifying what we do).

Therefore, action research is viewed in this context as any systematic questioning conducted by teachers, principals, and school counselors to gather information with the purpose of gaining insight about what they are doing, developing reflective practice, and making positive changes. Psychologist Kurt Lewin is often cited as originating action research when he used this methodology in 1944. His goal in conducting action research was to encourage people to see themselves as the resources for improving their own situations by systematically questioning, observing, and setting up strategies and interventions to change their behaviors and outcomes in positive ways. As an example, the students in the opening scenario are learning the skills involved in teaching by taking courses where they develop the skills they need to teach, such as writing lesson plans. As they begin to ask questions about why they are writing the lesson plans they are writing, they can begin to improve on the lesson plans by making changes to make their lessons stronger, such as using different strategies to get their students' attention or building their lessons around the backgrounds of their students. These types of changes appear over time as they continue to explore ways to improve their lessons. Once these plans are added to a teaching portfolio, they can demonstrate how the aspiring teacher has grown over time in the area of instructional planning.

Riding, Fowell, and Levy (1995) point out that action research has evolved into many forms, each involving an interactive approach, including problem identification; action planning to improve the problem; implementation of the action plan; and intervention, evaluation, and reflection. The following activity allows you to practice the early stages of action research.

LET'S PRACTICE!

Activity 2.1   Questions and Activities for Beginning Action Research

Who Am I? Creating a Comprehensive Portfolio or Personal Archive
(Montgomery & Wiley, 2008)

As a first step in using action research, let's begin by creating a *comprehensive portfolio* or *personal archive,* where you collect artifacts that represent who you are. The purpose is to help you to learn more about yourself as a result of what you put into it. Another purpose is to help others learn more about who you are. A third purpose is to begin to collect artifacts that provide evidence of your knowledge, skills, and attitudes, which can be added later to a professional or showcase portfolio. (Please note that adding new material becomes an ongoing activity as you develop your portfolios.)

1. Answer the following focusing questions: Who am I? What is my story?
   - What items would you put into your comprehensive portfolio or personal archive and why?
   - What items demonstrate your current knowledge, skills, and attitudes?
   - What is the story you want the items to tell about you?
   - How will you limit the kinds of items you put into the archive and why?
   - Where will you go to collect materials for your personal archive?

2. Start collecting items for your comprehensive portfolio. Consider where you will go to find materials to add to your personal archive (i.e., personnel files, such as resumes, vitas, letters of recommendation, awards, degrees, transcripts; past assignments, such as reports written, projects completed, fieldwork; hobbies and pastimes; professional organizations; community service; professional accomplishments; educational records; pictures; news articles; videos; valued treasures).

3. Once you have collected 10–20 items for your personal archive, think about how you can give them voice by adding captions or statements to explain what they are and how they help to tell your story.
   - What is the source of the item and how does it add to your story?
   - What does the item reveal about you in terms of your knowledge, skills, or attitudes?
   - What does the item provide evidence of?

4. Evaluate the quality of the items you have collected in terms of their ability to tell your story.
   - Do they tell your full story?
   - Is there balance in the story that they tell in terms of your knowledge, skills, and attitudes? (Do you find evidence of all three areas?)
   - What do the items you selected say about you so far?
   - In what areas would you like to add more items and why?
   - Do the items provide the best evidence of your knowledge, skills, and abilities?
   - How could you improve this collection?

5. If you were to begin an achievement portfolio, what items would you include from your personal archive and why?

You are now ready to begin developing a more specific or focused portfolio by using this same process to identify the items you will include in it.

ACTION RESEARCH AS A VIABLE PROCESS FOR PORTFOLIO DEVELOPMENT

To recap, in the simplest terms, action research is a process of learning from an activity by doing that activity and asking important questions about one's actions along the way in order to improve or make positive changes in the activity. In the case of portfolio development, action research involves compiling information and material into a portfolio while continually deciding what should be included and why. Going back to our opening scenario, as a result of each professor referring to the portfolio in his or her specific course, the students would be better able to see how each course and its assignments fits into the entire credential program. Knowing how each course and its assignments address credential program goals would help students decide how they might organize those assignments in their portfolios. They would always have a sense of the big picture and how all of the pieces fit together. Action research also involves deciding on the best way to present the material in the portfolio and to whom it will be presented.

The primary purpose of action research is to develop behaviors based on an ongoing cycle of goal setting, inquiry, reflection, and evaluation for growth and improvement (Bargal, 2006; Bradbury & Reason, 2003; McNiff & Whitehead, 2006). The goal of action research is to connect action and reflection for the purpose of learning. According to Kitchen and Stevens (2008), action research encourages inquiry and reflection by connecting theory (what we learn) to practice (what we do). Likewise, a portfolio is a vehicle for connecting theory to practice by collecting practical evidence related to professional growth and development. As an example, the portfolio can include vision statements that describe a person's beliefs and values about education and artifacts that demonstrate a person's competencies and abilities, such as field reports, video clips, presentations, or work samples (Hartnell-Young & Morriss, 2007). Still, the portfolio alone is simply a tool to provide evidence of professional development and learning. By itself, the portfolio does not describe or define the process for that professional development. Therefore, action research complements portfolio development by outlining a process in which learning can and does occur (Bargal, 2008; Baskerville & Myers, 2004; Cassell & Johnson, 2006; Levin & Rock, 2003; Miskovic & Hoop, 2006). Dehler and Edmonds (2006) suggest that people learn best when working on real, relevant problems that are grounded in their own work or experiences. What results from action research is an approach designed to generate new ideas from actual work. In a sense, action research allows people to tell their own stories, in much the same way as a portfolio does. The portfolio, in essence, is a product that can result from the action research process.

MATCHING PURPOSE WITH AUDIENCE IN ACTION RESEARCH: WHO BENEFITS?

The continual sorting and selecting of artifacts to include or withdraw from the portfolio to demonstrate the student's knowledge, skills, and dispositions is action research involving ongoing self-assessment and evaluation. In portfolio development, as in action research and inquiry, students are continually seeking **authentic,** concrete, real-life examples of their own practices. They are continually asking whether or not particular artifacts best demonstrate their growth and transformation throughout the credential program, as well as in their professional careers. They are constantly trying to perfect their skills and to document those skills and knowledge through the portfolio process.

A major aspect of action research is that it intentionally begins with questions of purpose and audience: Who is the research for and for what purpose? Bradbury and Reason (2003) outline three modes of action research, to include first person, second person, and third person. These are described in Table 2.1.

TABLE 2.1 Matching Audience to Purpose in Action Research

Mode of Action Research	Audience: Who Is Involved? Who Benefits?	Purpose	Example
First person	Me	Self-assessment, reflection, and growth	Working independently on portfolio
Second person	You and me	Collaboration, mutual benefit, face-to-face interaction, and dialogue	Working with a peer on portfolios and learning from each other
Third person	All of us; an entire group or community	Improvement benefits us all	Implementing guidelines that clarify the portfolio process for an entire group, such as referring to it in all courses and having it in the syllabi

First-person action research addresses the ability of researchers to apply an inquiry approach to their own lives or situations in order to act intentionally and with awareness. It entails self-observation and reflection. Second-person action research addresses the ability to ask questions face to face with another on issues of mutual concern and to interact with another productively. Third-person research builds upon practices of first and second person to create a wider community of inquiry involving a whole organization.

The most effective types of action research are those that involve at least two modes. First-person inquiry is the foundation for all effective action research, yet second-person inquiry is the area in which occurs the highest degree of energy and practical opportunity for truly impacting what happens. Still, third-person inquiry and actions turn out to be the most important, as they affect the conditions that ultimately shape the future settings in which first-and second-person interactions and work can occur. Going back to our scenario, Jennifer and Omar were each conducting first-person action research when they developed their individual portfolios. It becomes second-person action research when they begin to collaborate on how they can both improve their portfolios together, and they begin to share their process with each other so that they both benefit from their discussions and exchanges. Third-person action research results when the professors agree that they will each refer to the portfolio in their courses and show how their course and assignments relate to the entire program. In this way, the professors and all of the students in the credential program benefit because a systematic change has occurred to improve the process for everyone involved.

Burgess (2006) expands on this notion of the three modes of action research to include First Person action research as work done for oneself or on one's own behalf, Second Person action research as work done with a partner that is mutually beneficial, and Third Person action research as work done for the people in the wider context. Action research begins in the personal, inner work that enhances relational, interpersonal practice, and expands to the Third Person, leadership skills necessary for fostering organizational change and transformation. For the purposes of the portfolio process, much of the action research will be in the First Person, promoting self-reflection and self-awareness, while linking theory to practice in the creation of knowledge. However, when the portfolio is shared with others, its benefits can expand into the Second and Third Person. More will be discussed regarding sharing the portfolio in later chapters.

THE CYCLICAL NATURE OF ACTION RESEARCH AND PORTFOLIO DEVELOPMENT

Like action research, the portfolio process is cyclical in nature, as Figure 2.1 demonstrates. Where possible, action research projects go through several cycles or spirals, each involving some form of inquiry or questioning. The primary question—How do I improve my work?—includes a social focus (Bargal, 2008; Drummond & Themessi-Huber, 2007; Ferrance, 2000; Huxham & Vangen, 2003; McNiff, 2003; Mills, 2003; Nielsen, 2006; Sankaran, 2005; Whitehead & McNiff, 2006). That is, improving one's work is meant not only for personal benefit but also for the benefit of others. If individuals can improve what they are doing, they can likely influence situations related to this work, whether it be in teaching, serving as an administrator, or school counseling. Coghlan and Brannick (2004) describe the action research cycle as having four main steps. These include (1) diagnosing or defining what the issues are, (2) planning action based on the diagnosis, (3) taking action where one implements the plan, and (4) evaluating action to observe the outcomes of the actions that were taken. Figure 2.2 reflects the spiraling effect of the action research cycles, where each cycle builds on the previous one. It further describes the traditional round clock as a metaphor for the action research cycles. Imagine the face of the clock as a demonstration of the concurrent cycles of action research.

The hour hand, which takes 12 hours to complete its full cycle, may represent the entire credential or degree program, which could encompass 1 to 2 years. The minute hand, which takes an hour to complete its full cycle, may represent a course in the credential or degree program, which lasts only a semester. At the smallest level, the second hand, which takes a minute to complete its full cycle, could represent an assignment or project in a course. An example might be planning an interactive bulletin board to support a unit on "Working With Parents." As with the clock, the hands complete their cycles simultaneously, with each hand supporting the other in completing its full cycle or revolution. Each assignment is necessary to pass a given course. Similarly, each course is necessary to complete the credential or degree program. To summarize, action research is viewed as a type of ongoing inquiry or investigation into strategies that can improve one's practice on multiple levels.

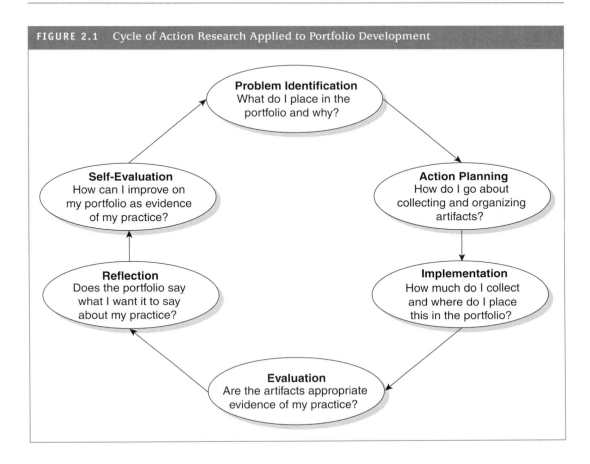

FIGURE 2.1   Cycle of Action Research Applied to Portfolio Development

LEVELS OF ACTION RESEARCH IN PORTFOLIO DEVELOPMENT

According to McNiff (2003), there are six action research levels. These six levels parallel the same cycles identified by a number of other researchers, although different terms may be used (Mertler, 2009; Mills, 2003; Stringer, 2004). Figure 2.1 demonstrates the cycle of action research as it applies to portfolio development. At the first level, Problem Identification, the question involves deciding what to place into the portfolio and why, asking yourself what artifacts or assignments provide accurate assessments and evidence for each standard. This will be very useful to you when you begin to select the contents of the portfolio. More is said about this in Chapter 6. Activities for practicing the first level of planning appear in Activity 2.2.

FIGURE 2.2   Cycle of Action Research Applied to Portfolio Development

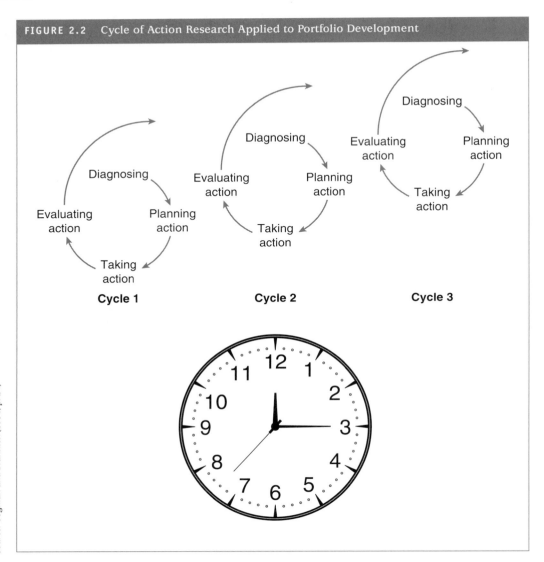

Source: Coghlan and Brannick (2004. p. 24)

LET'S PRACTICE!

Activity 2.2   Questions and Activities for the First Level of Planning

1. Begin familiarizing yourself with the standards for your program. Ask yourself the following:
   - What are the standards for my specific credential or degree program?

- How are the standards categorized?
  - Knowledge: What do I need to know?
  - Skills: What do I need to be able to do or demonstrate?
  - Attitudes or beliefs: What beliefs motivate my actions and why?
- What assignments go with the different standards?

2. Determine your personal and professional goals for pursuing your credential or degree.
   - What do you want the portfolio to communicate about you?
   - What are your personal and professional goals in creating this portfolio?

At the second level, Action Planning, the inquiry is focused on deciding how to go about collecting and organizing authentic evidence for each standard. It involves laying out a plan for collecting and organizing artifacts. It further involves clarifying the standards and determining authentic experiences in the credential program through which the knowledge, skills, and dispositions are developed. This helps make each course more relevant in the overall credential preparation and each assignment more authentic in shaping overall professional development. This process of organizing the portfolio is discussed in more detail in Chapter 5. Practice with the following activity:

LET'S PRACTICE!

Activity 2.3   Questions and Activities for the Second Level of Planning

1. Carefully review the standards, courses, and requirements for your specific credential or degree program, and answer the following questions:
   - In what courses are the different standards emphasized?
   - What are the course goals and objectives, and how do they support your professional growth?
   - What are sample course requirements, and how do they address the standards?
     - Course readings, textbooks
     - Fieldwork
     - Research assignments, projects
     - Course journals
     - Exams

2. What additional experiences outside of the course may address the standards?
   - Work experience, community service
   - Conference attendance
   - Professional memberships

3. Are there standards that need more clarification at this time?

At the third level, Implementation, you actually go about collecting the evidence according to the plan, all the while asking yourself how much to collect and where to place it in the portfolio for the best display of evidence for each standard. The following activity allows you to practice third-level planning.

LET'S PRACTICE!

Activity 2.4   Activities for the Third Level of Planning

1. Create an outline or template for your credential portfolio, based on the standards. (Some programs already have a sample outline listing the contents of the expected portfolio, as seen in Chapter 6. This can be done in hard copy in a three-ring binder, electronically, or both. Details for creating **electronic portfolios** are discussed in Chapter 9. Separate tabs could be used for each standard.)

2. Sort sample course requirements by standard. (Please note: Some requirements may address multiple standards.)

   - Course readings, textbooks (knowledge, theories)
   - Fieldwork (skills, application)
   - Research assignments, projects (knowledge, skills, beliefs, behaviors)
   - Course journals (attitudes, beliefs, reflections)
   - Exams (knowledge, skills, beliefs, behaviors)

3. Sort additional experiences outside of the course by standards.

   - Work experience (knowledge, skills, beliefs, behaviors)
   - Conference attendance (knowledge, skills, beliefs, behaviors)
   - Professional memberships and so on (knowledge, skills, beliefs, behaviors)

Moving on to the fourth level, Evaluation, you reflect on the items placed in the portfolio and decide whether or not they provide appropriate evidence for the standards or if other artifacts would be more effective to demonstrate the desired competencies and characteristics. You also reflect on the process used to collect and organize the artifacts. Is the plan working? How can it be modified, if necessary? More will be said about evaluation in Chapter 3. The following activity allows you to practice planning at the fourth level.

LET'S PRACTICE!

Activity 2.5   Activities for the Fourth Level of Planning

1. Review what has been sorted so far to see if artifacts reflect the standards.

2. Determine if all standards have been addressed or if there are any gaps.

3. Ask for feedback from a peer or instructor on the progress of the portfolio and what is being collected.

4. Repeat this process for each course throughout the program.

At the fifth level, Reflection, you reflect on the original purpose of the portfolio and decide if it lives up to its purpose. Ask, Does the portfolio say what I want it to say about my practice as a teacher, administrator, or counselor? If not, why not? The following activity allows you to practice fifth-level planning.

LET'S PRACTICE!

Activity 2.6   Activities for the Fifth Level of Planning

1. Return to the original portfolio goals and objectives to see if they have changed.

2. Determine if all standards have been addressed or if there are any gaps or omissions.

3. Decide how to address any gaps or omissions.

4. Review feedback from peers or instructors and apply, if appropriate.

At the sixth level, Self-Evaluation, you ask how the portfolio can be improved to provide the best evidence of your knowledge, skills, and dispositions. In answering these questions, the systematic process begins again in the form of a spiral, with each cycle introducing a higher level of questioning and perfecting the portfolio (McNiff, 2003; Mills, 2003; Stringer, 2004). The action research process as applied to portfolio development can also be done collaboratively, as the student receives feedback from peers, instructors, and mentors. Collaborative feedback on the portfolio is valuable at both the formative and summative assessment levels. The following activity allows you to explore the sixth level of portfolio planning.

LET'S PRACTICE!

Activity 2.7   Activities for the Sixth Level of Planning

1. Revise goals and objectives as you develop deeper understanding of program standards.

2. Determine the best ways to address the revised goals and objectives through courses, and so forth.

3. Continue to collects artifacts and refine the portfolio with each step.

4. Repeat each level until the portfolio is completed to your satisfaction.

When action research is applied to the portfolio process, authentic examples of students' practice or coursework become the data or products of their research. These products are authentic examples of their knowledge, skills, and dispositions. They are then compiled into their portfolios as artifacts. As the students research their own practice and performance

or specific
formation
lated to
is
oncept,
e the
hapter 1
sources
n the CD.

to identify the most appropriate evidence of their abilities, understanding, attitudes, and beliefs, the portfolios become the templates for painting comprehensive portraits of the students as professionals.

As an example, a student may place samples of lesson plans into the portfolio. These artifacts demonstrate the student's ability to plan effective lessons. This is according to INTASC (1992) Principle 7, Instructional Planning Skills, which states that the teacher plans instruction based on knowledge of subject matter, students, the community, and curriculum goals (Campbell et al., 2000). Table 2.2 applies the action research steps in posing inquiry questions related to INTASC Principle 7, Instructional Planning Skills. (Please note: A full list of **INTASC Standards** is included in the CD that accompanies this text.)

TABLE 2.2   Action Research Cycle Applied to INTASC Principle 7

Action Research Step	Related Inquiry Questions on Instructional Planning
Problem Identification	What is appropriate evidence of instructional planning (e.g., lesson plans, unit plans, case studies)?
Action Planning	Where in the program can evidence of instructional planning be collected (e.g., courses, fieldwork, assignments)?
Implementation	How many examples of instructional planning should be collected, and will they demonstrate more than one standard? Where do I place them in the portfolio, and what supporting documentation should I include to explain their purpose?
Evaluation	Are the examples that I've included the best evidence of my personal skills in instructional planning? Do they show a range of my skills in instructional planning?
Reflection	Do the examples of instructional planning that I've included say what I want them to say about my professional knowledge, skills, and attitudes?
Self-Evaluation	How can I improve on my professional profile in the area of instructional planning? What additional skills do I need to grow? What other artifacts would provide stronger evidence?

Source: Adapted from McNiff (2003).

At the beginning of the credential program, the lesson plans placed in the portfolios may be rather basic, demonstrating only a fundamental understanding of how to teach academic areas, such as math or social studies. As the students continue to grow, however, the quality of their lesson planning improves; the plans begin to show greater detail of classroom organization and student interaction with the subject matter. The students can then reflect on the artifacts placed into the portfolios. They strive to assess and evaluate the value of lesson plans produced later in the program in comparison with earlier plans, in terms of which plans provide better evidence of the standard and each student's development.

The later plans may be more complex and demonstrate new interventions the students have implemented once they have had a better grasp on the subject matter, their students, and the variety of ways the subject could be taught. Examples of plan upgrades might include providing home links so that parents can participate in the lesson. For instance, parents might be encouraged to help their children recognize and remind them of environmental information in print around the home and community (e.g., food labels or packaging, fast food restaurant logos, road signs, advertising logos, and toy trademarks—the print we recognize from the colors, pictures, and shapes that surround it) as reinforcement for a literacy lesson at school. Similarly, later lesson plans may include applications of technology, such as students taking virtual tours of museums around the world as part of a world history lesson.

Later plans could also provide evidence of a variety of INTASC (1992) principles, such as Principle 3 (Adapting Instruction to Individual Needs) and Principle 4 (Using Multiple Instructional Strategies). Similarly, students may include their philosophy of education at the beginning of the credential program as evidence of Principle 9 (Professional Commitment and Responsibility). However, by the end of the program, the original philosophy may have been pulled completely and replaced with a more current one that is supported by the students' real-life experiences in the field of education. Activity 2.8 allows you to reflect on action research and to apply the principles of action research to your portfolio process.

LET'S PRACTICE!

Activity 2.8   Questions and Activities for Reflection and Application

1. What is action research, and what is its relevance to portfolio development?

2. What are key features of action research, and how do they enhance the portfolio process?

3. How can action research assist you in developing your portfolio?
   - List specific portfolio goals you currently have.
   - What do you want your portfolio to reveal about you?
   - What types of competencies will you be demonstrating and how?

4. Use the action research cycle in Figure 2.1 to clarify the tasks involved in planning your portfolio.

5. What inquiry questions will you initially address?

6. Use the artifacts collected in your comprehensive portfolio or personal archive to begin developing a portfolio.
   - What kind of portfolio will you develop and why?
   - What other kinds of portfolios can be developed from your comprehensive portfolio or personal archive?

7. In what other areas might you use action research and why?

8. Choose one or two of the questions here to discuss with a peer.
   - Were there similarities in your answers?
   - Did you gain new insights from the discussion?

SUMMARY

In this chapter, we discuss the benefits of applying action research to portfolio development as a means of *articulating a specific process and purpose* for the portfolio. The portfolio is viewed as a tool underlying a much more defined process that leads the student through activities of self-reflection, self-assessment, and self-regulation or continuous learning. Action research provides a viable process for portfolio development and at the same time, allows the student to develop greater knowledge of education through interaction with and participation in relevant educational events. Multiple approaches to action research are presented, along with a variety of modes, each with the goal of integrating theory with practice, reflecting on that practice, and transforming that practice to bring about desired outcomes.

USEFUL RESOURCES

Classroom Action Research (http://www.madison.k12.wi.us/sod/car/ carhomepage .html)

This site is maintained by Madison Metropolitan School District in Madison, Wisconsin, and has extensive action research resources for teachers.

Action Research Introduction (http://www.accessexcellence.org/LC/TL/AR)

By author Sharon Parsons of San Jose State University, this site provides an overview of action research and several examples of classroom-based action research.

Action Research for Teachers by Teachers (http://rubble.heppell.net/TforT/ default.html)

This site highlights action research projects developed by teachers, with a focus on integrating technology in the classroom.

Action Research International—Online Journal (www.scu.edu.au/schools/gcm/ar/ari/ arihome.html)

This refereed online journal of action research is edited by Bob Dick and sponsored by the Institute of Workplace Research Learning and Development (WoRLD) at Southern Cross University.

Teacher Research (http://ucerc.edu/teacherresearch/teacherresearch.html)

This site lists action research magazines and journal articles, some of which are presented in full text.

FOR FURTHER READING

Avison, D., Lau, F., Myers, M., & Nielsen, P. (1999). Action research: To make academic research relevant, researchers should try out their theories with practitioners in real situations and real organizations. *Communications of the ACM, 43*(1), 94–97.

Caro-Bruce, C., Flessner, R., Klehr, M., & Burmaster, E. (2007). *Creating equitable classrooms through action research.* Thousand Oaks, CA: Sage.

Chandler, D., & Torbert, B. (2003, October). Transforming inquiry and action: Interweaving 27 flavors of action research. *Action Research, 1,* 133–152.

Coghlan, D., & Brannick, T. (2004). *Doing action research in your own organization* (2nd ed.). Thousand Oaks, CA: Sage.

Dick, B. (2006). Action research literature 2004–2006: Themes and trends. *Action Research, 4,* 439–458.

Glanz, J. (2003). *Action research: An educational leader's guide to school improvement.* Norwood, MA: Christopher-Gordon.

Greenwood, D. J., & Levin, M. (2006). *Introduction to action research: Social research for social change* (2nd ed.). Thousand Oaks, CA: Sage.

Hendricks, C. C. (2008). *Improving schools through action research.* New York: Addison Wesley.

May, W. T. (1993, Winter). Teachers-as-researchers or action research: What is it and what good is it for art education? *Studies in Art Education, 34*(2), 114–126.

McNiff, J., & Whitehead, J. (2006). *All you need to know about action research.* Thousand Oaks, CA: Sage.

Mertler, C. (2009). *Action research: Teachers as researchers in the classroom* (2nd ed.). Thousand Oaks, CA: Sage.

Mills, G. E. (2006). *Action research: A guide for the teacher researcher.* Englewood Cliffs, NJ: Pearson Merrill Prentice Hall.

Sykes, J. A. (2002). *Action research: A practical guide to transforming your school library.* Greenwood Village, CO Libraries Unlimited.

Whitehead, J., & McNiff, J. (2006). *Action research: Living theory.* Thousand Oaks, CA: Sage.

Using Portfolios as Tools for Authentic Assessment and Evaluation

"Fairness" does not exist when assessment is uniform, standardized, impersonal, and absolute. Rather, it exists when assessment is appropriate—in other words, when it's personalized, natural, and flexible; when it can be modified to pinpoint specific abilities and function at the relevance of difficulty; and when it promotes a rapport between examiner and student.

—Funderstanding (2009)

CHAPTER OBJECTIVES

Readers will be able to

❑ define authentic assessment and evaluation,

❑ outline elements of the portfolio process as formative evaluations,

❑ identify elements of the portfolio process as summative evaluations,

❑ articulate the benefits of portfolios as both action research and authentic assessment,

❑ apply appropriate precautions in using portfolios for assessment and evaluation,

❑ use portfolios for both formative and summative evaluation, and

❑ follow guidelines for using rubrics linked to standards for portfolio assessment.

SCENARIO

As part of their course culmination, teacher credential candidates presented final portfolios to their professor and peers in formal presentations. Included in the presentations were answers to questions regarding the organization of their portfolios, the specific rationale for their selected artifacts, the value of courses and assignments in preparing them to be teachers, and the portfolio process as a tool to assess their individual growth and development throughout the program. Lisa, one of the teaching interns, reflected on her experience with the portfolio process:

"Through the assignments and other activities, such as developing unit plans to teach science and math or a classroom management plan that included my teaching philosophy and views on discipline, I saw leadership qualities in myself that I may not have taken note of before. I probably would never have saved letters of commendation from supervisors and peers or taken pictures of bulletin boards I created if I had not been forced to keep a portfolio. As I collected artifacts for each teaching standard, I gained a better understanding of what the standard was and how that standard was vital to my professional development as a teacher. Keeping a portfolio was almost like doing research on how I was becoming a teacher! Things that I thought were good lesson plans at the beginning of the program were thrown out by the end, as I learned how to plan better lessons. I had the opportunity to evaluate my own work, deciding what made the best evidence to prove I could teach and what artifacts to keep in my final portfolio.

"Keeping a portfolio also helped me to monitor my growth on a daily basis as a formative assessment for each standard. Not only did it help me to define the standard, but it also helped me use specific criteria to assess or evaluate that standard. Reflecting and presenting the final portfolio helped me to see the summative or overall growth of the standards working together in my overall development as a teacher."

Across the way, a similar conversation was taking place among a group of administrative credential candidates who were also in a final portfolio presentation session. Rogelio was among the first to comment on the portfolio process:

"When I first heard of the portfolio, I thought, 'No problem!' I'm a teacher, and I've used portfolios in my school with my elementary students. I know how helpful they are for showing growth in my students and helping them to evaluate themselves. Still, I did not really understand what I was in for as an administrative credential candidate. Portfolios are a lot of work!! The process really helped me to think about what I was doing in each class and why, and how that class or assignment would help me to grow as an administrator. The portfolio helped me to stay focused on the big picture of becoming a school principal. Having to keep and organize assignments into artifacts also helped me to think more deeply about each assignment and how that assisted me in developing skills and abilities as an administrator. I was constantly putting myself through a microscope to view and evaluate my progress. Completing an assignment was not enough until I figured out what that assignment or activity had to do with my overall profile as an administrator or educational leader. When I developed a workshop for paraprofessionals on legal issues surrounding their roles and responsibilities, I saw how this one activity addressed several administrative standards. The portfolio process helped me to clearly identify each standard and to cross-reference assignments, artifacts, and activities when appropriate. The workshop I presented addressed community outreach, instructional leadership, and technology."

OVERVIEW

What is assessment, and what significance does it have in the portfolio process? What is meant by the terms *formative* and *summative* when applied to assessment, and what role does the portfolio play in each of these? From the scenario, it is evident that students benefit from the portfolio process as a formative, developmental assessment as they are advancing through their credential program. Similarly, students benefit from collaboratively reflecting on the portfolio process as a summative, final assessment or overall evaluation of their performance at the completion of the program. The purpose of this chapter is to examine the role of portfolios in both formative and summative assessment and evaluation and to highlight the value of the portfolio for each type of assessment. In it, we expand on the concept of the portfolio as a type of action research, introduced in Chapter 2, where the portfolio serves as a magnifying lens for viewing and measuring one's own growth and professional development (Bargal, 2008; Cook, 2006; Mills, 2003; Newman, 2000). Used in this way, the portfolio is a powerful tool for self-assessment, goal setting, and future planning in how to improve.

Here is a brief roadmap of this chapter: We begin with a definition of assessment, authentic assessment, and evaluation. We continue with a description of the portfolio process and its benefits as a formative assessment, where learning stems from responsible experience linked to actions (Dehler & Edmonds, 2006; McNiff & Whitehead, 2006). Next, we present some critical issues on the role of portfolios as summative, **high-stakes assessments** for licensure and certification purposes, such as completing a teaching or other type of credential. Precautions and recommendations are presented to promote the most effective use of portfolios for authentic assessment and evaluation. We conclude the chapter with guidelines for developing and following rubrics as a means to establish consistent and specific criteria to clarify portfolio expectations and evaluate portfolios.

DEFINING ASSESSMENT AND EVALUATION

It is important to clarify what is meant by the terms *evaluation* and *assessment,* and how they are used in this book. Most dictionaries use these words interchangeably (Landau & Bogus, 1975; Morris, 1976). Often, they are used to refer to the same processes, implying that to evaluate is also to examine or judge. This involves determining the value of a person or thing in relation to others of the same kind. Similarly, to assess is also to estimate the value of something or someone, to appraise or form a judgment of worth or significance. In both cases, specific criteria need to be established as a basis for forming judgments of overall worth or value. Stiggins (2008) defines *assessment* as the process of gathering evidence of student learning to inform instructional decisions. In this book, the term *assessment* is used to refer to observing the ongoing, developmental process of growth and change. It refers to the formative, progressive nature of determining one's growth in a particular skill or area. Table 3.1 contrasts formative assessment and summative evaluations. Oosterhof, Conrad, and Ely (2008) describe formative assessments as taking place during instruction. These assessments are designed for ongoing monitoring of the learning process, followed by mentoring and further instruction. In contrast, summative evaluation occurs after all instruction is completed and is designed to measure what has been learned as a result of instruction. For example, students often do a pretest or preassessment in a class to determine their background knowledge on a particular subject or skill. Preassessments are often used to establish baseline data, or a starting point, from which to measure growth. Later, after instruction has taken place, the same test can be used as a posttest to determine what has been learned. By comparing the results on the two assessments, the instructor can see how much the student has learned as a result of instruction or course activities. A midterm exam is another type of formative assessment to determine how a student is doing at the halfway mark in a course. It is a way to give a progress report on the knowledge and skills acquired by the student midway through the course. Similarly, when someone goes to the doctor, temperature and blood pressure are taken as assessments of health. These data help the doctor determine some basic information about a patient's health before going on to determine other areas of concern. If the temperature or blood pressure is higher or lower than normal, a more severe, possibly life-threatening health situation might be indicated.

TABLE 3.1   Contrasting Formative Assessment and Summative Evaluation

Formative Assessment	Summative Evaluation
Pretest	Posttest
Posttest on assignment or activity	
Quizzes, grades on course assignments	Final exam
Attendance and participation in course	
Midterm	Final grade in a course
Peer evaluations	
Lesson plans, research reports	
Program coursework, fieldwork, and exams	Comprehensive exam
Assignment reflections	High-stakes test
Working portfolio	Showcase portfolio
Entrance interview	Exit interview

Evaluation, on the other hand, is used to describe the final or summative process of determining overall progress in attaining minimal standards in a skill or field of study. A **final grade,** unlike a midterm, represents a summative or overall evaluation of a student's performance in the course. It results from collecting information from all other data sources used to assess a student's progress and performance, such as attendance, class participation, special projects, research reports, and a midterm exam. The final portfolio presentation session, described in the opening scenario for this chapter and discussed in more detail in Chapters 7 and 9, is an example of a summative assessment or overall evaluation. In the scenario, students were sharing their completed portfolios and the impact of the portfolio process on their overall professional development in their credential programs. Evaluation usually takes place at the end and is the culminating exercise following emphasis on a series of skills and activities throughout a program or course of study. Showcase and academic portfolios may serve as summative evaluations of students' achievements and may be reviewed as partial fulfillment of the overall credential requirements. Evaluation is the final step in determining overall qualification to fulfill the responsibilities of a teacher, counselor, or principal.

Portfolios in which the student systematically demonstrates his or her completion of specific assignments, competencies, and standards over time can be used effectively for both formative and summative aspects of assessment and evaluation. To review, the working portfolio, described in Chapter 1, serves as a formative, developmental assessment, in which students select certain assignments or artifacts to include from various courses in their credential program. This working portfolio shows a student's progress up to that point in the program. As the student continues to develop knowledge, skills, and dispositions as a teacher, counselor, or principal, new artifacts are included that provide better demonstrations of more recent competencies while others are eliminated. This process of systematically selecting and refining the portfolio's contents is discussed in more detail in Chapters 4 and 6. The showcase portfolio, also described in Chapter 1, serves as a summative evaluation for the student, in which the best evidence of that student's qualifications is presented. In this chapter's opening scenario, the students were discussing their academic showcase portfolios, which they developed from their working portfolios.

PORTFOLIOS AS AUTHENTIC ASSESSMENT: A DEFINITION

Assessments are authentic when they have meaning in and of themselves, when the learning they measure has value beyond the classroom, and when learning is also meaningful to the learner (Kerka, 1995; Stiggins, 2008; Wiggins, 1999). Oosterhof, Conrad, and Ely (2008) note that authentic assessments are often referred to as **performance assessments** because they involve an activity that is a direct goal of instruction. Mueller (2008) defines **authentic assessment** as "a form of assessment in which students are asked to perform real-world tasks that demonstrate meaningful application of essential knowledge and skills" (p. 1).

According to Mueller, authentic assessment development can be viewed in terms of four guiding questions. First, what should students know and be able to do? Second, what actions or activities indicate if students have met the standards? Third, what does good or acceptable performance look like? And fourth, how do you measure or evaluate performance? Table 3.2 outlines four basic steps to develop authentic assessments along with these four guiding questions. Different forms of authentic assessment are also presented in the table. These will be expanded upon throughout the chapter.

Stiggins (2008) goes on to contrast authentic assessment with traditional assessment by the following attributes: Authentic assessment involves performing tasks in real-life situations rather than selecting from limited choices on written exams. It also entails direct **application**

TABLE 3.2   Steps in Developing Authentic Assessment With Guiding Questions

Steps in Developing Authentic Assessments	Guiding Questions
1. Identify the standards (learning targets).	What should candidates know and be able to do? • Knowledge (content standards) • Skills (process standards) • Dispositions (value or attitude standards)
2. Select authentic tasks.	What actions or activities indicate if candidates have met the standards? • Selected response (e.g., multiple choice, true–false, matching, fill in the blank, labeling a diagram) • Constructed response (productlike, e.g., concept map, flow chart, graphic organizer, journal response, short-answer essay; or performancelike, e.g., role playing, simulation, laboratory experience, performing a skill) • Product (essay, research report, thematic unit, portfolio, bulletin board, website, newsletter) • Performance (more extensive, e.g., interview, presentation, planning and implementing a field trip, organizing a conference)
3. Identify criteria to evaluate the tasks.	What does good performance on the task look like? • Establish guidelines for measuring performance. • Define what constitutes adequate performance.
4. Create the rubrics (scoring scales used to assess student performance based upon specific criteria).	How well did students perform? How do you measure or evaluate performance? What criteria and levels of performance are used? What does performance look like at each level? • For each criterion, select two or more levels of performance, ranging from weak to strong. • Choose the scoring mode: analytic (each criterion separately scored) or holistic (entire task scored).

Source: Adapted from Mueller (2008).

of knowledge rather than mere recall of facts. Last, authentic assessment provides direct evidence and examples of the knowledge and skills being evaluated rather than indirect evidence obtained through traditional quizzes or tests. Determining real-life examples and applications of competencies is the primary aim of authentic assessment. An example would be high school students' ability to formally debate an issue, such as student-centered versus teacher-centered classrooms, as authentic evidence of their understanding and implementation of persuasive writing. Authentic assessment addresses the skills and abilities needed to perform actual tasks (e.g., for teachers, writing and implementing a lesson plan; for administrators, conducting a program evaluation; and for school counselors, coordinating a mediation meeting between a student and parents). Portfolios afford students opportunities to display genuine examples of their achievements and to reflect on the value of those examples through written and other types of documentation.

For teachers, the process of setting up a supportive classroom environment where there is a social contract between students and teachers regarding appropriate behavior can be assessed in a variety of ways. A teacher could take a **traditional exam,** which asks the teacher to list or describe characteristics of effective classroom management, or as a more authentic example of INTASC (1992) Principle 5, the teacher could show a video clip of classroom interaction with students and include a sketch of the classroom floor plan, perhaps as included in a **classroom management plan.** Developing a classroom management plan is an assignment in some teacher credential courses. In it, aspiring teachers describe their rationales for proposing management systems appropriate for them. (Some sample classroom management plans, along with instructions for how to create them, are found on the CD.) These provide a more comprehensive example of a student's knowledge, skills, and dispositions in the area of classroom management than the answer to a simple test question ever could. Table 3.3 compares traditional assessment with authentic assessment by looking at their characteristics, followed by some examples.

Other examples of authentic assessment are letters of commendation and acknowledgment from principals or supervisors, written after having observed a teacher in the classroom and witnessed effective management. These examples, which become artifacts in the portfolio, provide a more comprehensive view from which to assess whether a teacher can practically apply the knowledge, skills, and dispositions measured by the standard. Rogelio, the administrative credential candidate in our opening scenario, commented on how his paraprofessional workshop on legal issues (another example of authentic assessment) addressed several administrative standards, such as the **Interstate School Leaders Licensure Consortium's** (ISLLC; Council of Chief State School Officers [CCSSO], 2007) Leadership Standard 5 (Human Resource Administration) and Leadership Standard 3 (Organizational Management). More examples of authentic assessment in the portfolio process are presented in Chapters 4 through 7.

For specific information related to this concept, see the Chapter 3 resources on the CD.

ASSESSMENT OPTIONS: MEASURING LEARNING TARGETS AND OUTCOMES

Stiggins (2008) emphasizes the importance of using assessments not only to gather accurate information about student achievement but also to benefit students by enhancing their desire to learn and their ability to achieve. In order for portfolios to be most effective in assessment, they must tell a clear story. The form or design of the portfolio follows the function or purpose it will serve in assessment. Stiggins lists four primary types of portfolios that can serve in assessment. These include (1) *celebration portfolios,* which are personal collections of favorite work; (2) *growth portfolios,* designed to measure growth in abilities or achievements over time; (3) *project portfolios,* which emphasize the steps or processes gone through in

TABLE 3.3   Traditional Versus Authentic Assessment

Traditional: Knowledge Based (seeks information)	Authentic: Performance Based (seeks demonstration)
Selecting a response (on tests or quizzes) • Multiple choice • True–false • Matching • Fill in the blank	Performing a task • Conducting an experiment • Researching an issue or topic • Writing a report or lesson plan • Creating a presentation
Artificial, made up, contrived circumstances • Grades, GPA • Transcripts • Checklists • Report cards • Standardized test scores	Real-life circumstances • Video clips • Field notes, observation reports, reflections • Pictures of bulletin boards • Workshop agendas and evaluations • Assignment reflections • Supervisor evaluations with reflections
Recall, recognition (on tests or quizzes) • Matching • Fill in the blank	Construction, application of information • Conducting a workshop • Designing an organizational chart
Indirect evidence • Grades, GPA • Transcripts • Report cards • Written tests and quizzes	Direct evidence • Examples of K–12 student work • Letters, cards from students, parents • Letters of commendation • Classroom management plans with reflections • Exit interviews • Focus groups • Rubrics • Portfolios and conferences
Teacher structured • Tests and quizzes	Student structured • Assignment reflections • Philosophy of education • Self-evaluations • Peer evaluations • Portfolios • Student-led conferences

completing a project over time; and (4) *achievement portfolios,* designed to measure the fulfillment of specific achievement or learning targets. Table 3.4 outlines the major attributes of each type of portfolio in terms of who sets the learning targets, who is involved in the assessment, and guiding questions to consider when collecting artifacts for the portfolio.

TABLE 3.4 Functions of Portfolios in Assessment (What story do we want to tell?)

Portfolio Format	Primary Purpose or Function	Driving Questions	Main Assessors
Celebration portfolio, showcase portfolio	Used as a keepsake; personal collection of favorite work	• What do I think is really valuable about my work and why? • What am I most proud of and why?	Self-evaluation and self-selection of criteria; candidate identifies what constitutes good or important work
Growth portfolio or time sequence–developmental portfolio	Used to highlight or document growth or accomplishments over time • Provides multiple indicators of the same proficiency • Evaluation criteria held constant over time	• How have my abilities changed or improved over time? • How do I measure or document my progress toward my goals?	Candidate Instructors Mentors Peers
Project portfolio	Used to highlight completion of steps in a project in a timely manner; emphasis is on the process	• How do I break down large projects into smaller, manageable units? • What steps are key to my completion of this project? • What time lines can I set to guide the completion of the project?	Candidate Instructors Mentors Peers
Achievement status portfolio, academic portfolio	Used to demonstrate meeting academic or achievement standards; valuable as summative evaluations	• What academic standards do I need to fulfill? • What criteria will be used to measure or evaluate my performance?	Candidate Instructors Mentors Peers Program evaluators Policy makers

What is most important to remember is that portfolios serve different purposes and can be retooled or reorganized to accomplish numerous goals. Chapter 10 discusses ways to retool the portfolio to keep it alive, once certain goals are met. Activity 3.1 allows you to practice matching portfolio forms with their purpose or functions.

LET'S PRACTICE!

Activity 3.1   Questions and Activities for Matching Portfolio Forms and Functions

- Reflect on your current classes or credential program. What would you place in a celebration portfolio at this time and why?
- What do you believe is the true value of a celebration portfolio?
- Create a celebration portfolio and write a reflection describing its contents.
- Determine the types of portfolios that would best serve you in your program. Remember that a single portfolio can have multiple functions and that the functions may overlap at times.
- What types of artifacts would you place in the portfolio and why?
- What type of assessments would these portfolios provide and for whom?

So far, we've addressed *why* assessment is important and how the portfolio is used to guide assessment. Other questions that must also be addressed are *what* to assess and *how* to assess it. In answering what to assess, we begin by defining the learning targets. What is it that we want students to know and be able to do in a specific area or discipline? Standards, goals, and objectives are used to define learning targets in education. As we have mentioned, some categories of learning targets are (1) *knowledge, reasoning* (e.g., recalling information, understanding concepts, being able to explain rationale); (2) *performance skills* (e.g., conducting a parent–teacher conference, assessing student achievement), producing various products (e.g., lesson plans, case studies, workshops); and (3) *dispositions* (e.g., attitudes, interests, motivational intentions). Table 3.5 presents a Sample Teacher Portfolio Planner to guide the collection of assessments to address the various learning targets. The table further answers the questions of *where* and *when* to collect the assessments by listing specific courses or activities where these assessments are required and when they are scheduled in the program.

Activity 3.2 allows you to practice identifying learning targets for your specific program or course.

LET'S PRACTICE!

Activity 3.2   Exploring Assessment and Categories of Learning Targets

- Carefully review the standards and objectives in your current courses or credential program.
- Identify the categories of learning targets that are being assessed (knowledge, performance skills, products, dispositions).
- Identify the types of assessments that are used to demonstrate proficiency for each of the learning targets or standards.

- Are there other types of assessments that can demonstrate the same proficiency in a different way? This may give you hints about the types of artifacts you may collect for each standard. (Examples of different types of assessment appear in Chapter 6, Contents of the Portfolio.)
- Use Table 3.6: Sample Portfolio Assessment Planner Template to begin listing specific learning targets for your course or program and identifying what assessments you will start collecting for your portfolio as evidence.

TABLE 3.5   Sample Teacher Portfolio Assessment Planner

Standards to Be Addressed (learning targets: what)	Types of Assessment Collected (how)	Source of Assessment (where)	Assessment Calendar, Time Line (when)
INTASC Principle 1: Knowledge of Subject Matter	Essay • Philosophy of education • Autobiography Transcripts Product or process • Lesson plans (all content areas) • Course research project: Math Facilitation for Primary Students Through Games Fieldwork and directed teaching logs	Class: EDCI 300: Introduction to Teaching, Initial credential program application All methods courses	Spring 2009 2009–2011
INTASC Principle 5: Classroom Motivation and Management	Product or Process • Classroom management plan • Video of student engagement • Fieldwork and directed teaching logs Supervisor evaluations	Class: EDCI 402: Classroom Management, Assessment, and Instructional Strategies	Fall 2009
INTASC Principle 8: Assessment of Student Learning	Product or Process • Literacy case study • Thematic science unit • Essay, journal • Introductory statement, reflection on standard	Class: EDEL 415: Teaching Reading in the Elementary School EDEL 417: Teaching Elementary Science EDEL 403C: Directed Teaching Seminar	Fall 2010 Spring 2011 Summer 2011

TABLE 3.6   Sample Portfolio Assessment Planner Template

Standards to be Addressed (learning targets: what)	Types of Assessment Collected (how)	Source of Assessment (where)	Assessment Calendar, or Time Line (when)

Because there are a variety of standards, goals, and objectives that can become learning targets, many options become apparent as we consider how to assess these targets. Researchers agree that traditional assessments serve an important purpose and often complement performance or authentic assessments by measuring a student's knowledge and understanding of key concepts (Mueller, 2008; Oosterhof, Conrad, & Ely, 2008; Stiggins, 2008). Authentic assessments still provide greater flexibility in directly measuring a student's ability to apply that knowledge in appropriate ways. Some assessment options include selected response tests, essays, performance assessment, personal communication, and various products. Table 3.7 gives examples of the types of assessments that may be included in the portfolio as evidence of the standards. Activity 3.3 allows you to practice exploring assessment options by identifying the types of assessments used in your current course or program.

BENEFITS OF PORTFOLIOS AS AUTHENTIC ASSESSMENTS

Portfolios have still more benefits as authentic assessments. First, as noted in Chapter 1, they provide greater equity in evaluation of culturally and linguistically diverse students than do more traditional forms of testing. Portfolios can provide evidence of equity by aligning authentic real-world examples of knowledge, skills, and dispositions to specific standards. Well-designed portfolios provide a rich array of what students know and are able to do. They display both the products of learning (e.g., lesson plans and case studies) and the processes or reflections associated with each artifact. Portfolios are also able to accommodate different learning styles as well as to acknowledge multiple ways to demonstrate competence, unlike tests or other traditional assessments.

Second, portfolios provide an internal, student-centered focus on artifacts and specific criteria. These criteria are thus aligned with the standards in which students are actively involved, such as the collection and documentation of their own achievement data linking theory to practice. This action research approach, as mentioned in Chapter 2, helps students to become more aware of their process and encourages ownership of their programs (McNiff, 2003; McNiff & Whitehead, 2006; Mills, 2003; Strijbos et al., 2007). They see the benefits of a systematic process to help them to evaluate and assess their own strategies. In addition,

TABLE 3.7   Assessment Options, With Examples

Selected Response: Exam, Quiz	Essay	Performance Assessment (process)	Personal Communication	Product
Multiple choice	Philosophy of education	Writing reports	Journals	Unit plan
True–false	Short-answer essays	Conducting workshops	Learning logs	Bulletin board
Matching	Relating theory to practice	Developing an Individualized Education Plan	Writing reflections	Parent newsletter
Fill in the blank	Letter of intent	Evaluating a school	Conferences and interviews	Assessment plan
	Comprehensive exam	Interviewing a teacher or administrator	Oral examinations	Interview protocol
		Videotaping performance	Focus groups	Multimedia presentation
		Organizing an assembly	Letters	Portfolio

LET'S PRACTICE!

Activity 3.3   Questions and Activities for Exploring Assessment Options

1. Carefully review the assignments in your current courses or credential program.
   - How many of them involve performance or authentic assessment? How many of them represent traditional written assessments? Indicate whether they are formative (developmental) or summative (final evaluations).

2. Do a draft time line of your assessment schedule. This can be inserted into your initial portfolio planning, along with the standards you will address in your portfolio.
   - Is there a balance in the assessment options currently used in your courses or program? Do they provide a comprehensive profile of your knowledge, skills, and dispositions? If not, where do you see a need to provide more evidence of your abilities?

3. What is the most valuable concept you have learned so far in this chapter in terms of assessment and planning your portfolio? Write a short reflection on questions or concerns you have regarding the assessments you will include in your portfolio.

students are encouraged to collaborate with peers for deeper insight into how to improve their portfolios and the documentation of their professional performance. This collaboration affords multiple opportunities for self-evaluation and improvement.

Third, portfolios allow for ongoing collaboration and reflection among the authors, the assessors, and the evaluators, entailing a more relational process. Portfolios provide a tool that can ensure communication and accountability to a range of audiences. This type of interactive, dynamic process among instructors and learners is again more appropriate, equitable, and culturally responsive for students from diverse cultural and linguistic backgrounds (Johnson, 2002; Robins et al., 2005; see the CD for further standards on cultural proficiency). Furthermore, the overall portfolio process encourages ongoing and sustained dialogue among program instructors and students as they continue to refine the process and clarify the criteria used to measure success and effective completion of program standards and requirements. Evaluation standards must be clear, concise, and openly communicated.

For specific information related to this concept, see the Chapter 3 resources on the CD.

Fourth, portfolios allow for multiple levels of assessment and evaluation over extended periods of time, including self, peer, mentor, and supervisor or evaluator assessments. Because most portfolio assessment is longitudinal and emphasizes the process of change or growth at multiple points in time, it may be easier to see patterns (Sewell et al., 2005). The feedback resulting from such a process allows all participants to consider the next steps to improve both teaching and learning (Kerka, 1995). To be most effective, portfolios as authentic assessments need to be an integral part of the whole program, linked to all its courses. The portfolio process is thus a dynamic process that constantly goes through dialogue, revision, and modification. (Organizing and implementing the portfolio process is discussed further in Chapter 5.)

CHALLENGES OF PORTFOLIOS AS AUTHENTIC ASSESSMENTS

Although numerous advantages accompany the use of portfolios as authentic assessments, there are several drawbacks or challenges that must be mentioned; the three most prevalent are (for consistency with earlier lists)

1. managing the time-intensive nature of portfolio development,
2. ensuring curriculum validity and reliability, and
3. minimizing evaluator bias and inconsistency.

There is no doubt that portfolios are time-consuming both to prepare and to evaluate because they require clarity in goals, outcomes, criteria, and expectations and the assurance that all stakeholders understand these elements in the same way (Mueller, 2008; PATT, 2000; Stinger, 2008; Wilkerson & Lang, 2003). To ensure that students and their instructors have the necessary time to manage the portfolios, the portfolio process must be emphasized throughout the program. This means spelling out careful guidelines and benchmarks that are understood and agreed upon by all stakeholders, along with building in support for meeting the standards and criteria. To ensure curriculum validity and reliability, both assessment and instruction should be planned concurrently to make certain that they are linked

(Kerka, 1995; Wiggins, 1999). Grant Wiggins, in his *Understanding by Design* program (Wiggins & McTighe, 2000), referred to this process as "backwards planning." In backwards planning, one begins with the standards or the outcomes, then works backward to determine indicators or assessments for those outcomes, and last, plans instruction that will lead to those indicators and outcomes.

In addition, to ensure that evaluation standards are applied consistently, instructors and other raters or evaluators of the portfolios need careful training and collaboration on the process. Staff development and ongoing dialogue regarding evaluation criteria must be part of the full portfolio implementation process. At the course level, instructors must present clear definitions of program and course expectations to students in their syllabi. They also must indicate how these expectations relate to assignments in the course and to meeting program standards. This is a good time also to describe which assignments may be used as possible portfolio artifacts, along with how each assignment will be evaluated. Rubrics should be provided to add further clarity of expectations and grading criteria. (Rubrics are discussed more fully later in this chapter.)

PORTFOLIOS AS FORMATIVE (DEVELOPMENTAL PROCESS) ASSESSMENTS

There are numerous aspects of portfolios that make them extremely desirable and effective as developmental assessments over time (Campbell et al., 2004). Such portfolios are often viewed as *process* or *working portfolios,* described in Chapter 1, which document growth over time toward a goal. Documentation includes statements of the end goals, criteria, and plans for the future. The process or working portfolio, as a formative assessment, is most useful for the internal information of the students and instructors as they plan for the future. It is an excellent tool to reinforce learning and make formative decisions about student knowledge, skills, dispositions, and growth, as well as the programs that prepare them (Sewell et al., 2005; Wilkerson & Lang, 2003). Individual course assignments are usually targeted for inclusion in the working portfolio as demonstrations of course goals and objectives and of overall credential program outcomes. In a teacher credential course, for example, aspiring teachers must demonstrate their ability to tailor their teaching styles to the individual needs and learning styles of their students, as in INTASC (1992) Principle 3 (Adapting Instruction for Individual Needs) and Principle 4 (Multiple Instructional Strategies). They must also demonstrate a value and sensitivity to diversity, as in INTASC Principle 2 (Knowledge of Human Development and Learning). For instance, completing a case study as an assignment (e.g., the student not only diagnoses oral-language and reading ability of an elementary or middle school student but also plans appropriate reading and oral-language interventions to support that student's growth) addresses all three INTASC principles. Such an assignment is a natural fit for inclusion in the working portfolio. McNiff (2003) describes a five-tiered action research approach, which can be applied to the portfolio development process. This approach best illustrates how the actual portfolio process has inherent advantages in the formation and development of any program, as outlined in Table 3.8.

TABLE 3.8   Five-Tiered Approach to Program Development and Portfolio Assessment

Tier 1: Program Definition	Clarifying program goals, standards, and desired outcomes
Tier 2: Accountability	Agreeing on appropriate forms of evidence and how they will be collected and evaluated consistently in the portfolio process
Tier 3: Understanding and Refining	Conducting ongoing assessment of the program and candidates at regular portfolio checkpoints to refine, modify, and align outcomes with the program vision
Tier 4: Progress Toward Outcomes	Collecting and reviewing evidence in portfolios at regular intervals throughout the program in the form of dialogues among program participants, to ensure consistency and reliability
Tier 5: Program Impact	Cumulatively collecting a broad band of evidence through the portfolio process to form a summative evaluation of overall program impact

Source: Adapted from McNiff (2003).

Tier 1, Program Definition, establishes portfolio criteria to assist in clarifying program goals, objectives, and desired outcomes. It can also assist in forging a vision and purpose for the program.

At Tier 2, Accountability, the portfolio is considered an assessment practice that informs all constituents about appropriate forms of evidence that serve as criteria for accountability. The process of identifying and selecting evidence involves ongoing dialogue and feedback among all stakeholders involved in developing the portfolio. When students and instructors agree on expectations and goals, there is greater acceptance and satisfaction with program activities because the purpose is clear.

At Tier 3, Understanding and Refining, the portfolio provides a means of conducting ongoing assessments of the program, the participants, or both as the program addresses evolving needs and assets of those involved. This process of refining helps to maintain a focus on program outcomes, the steps needed to attain these outcomes, and assurance that the program implementation is in line with the vision.

At Tier 4, Progress Toward Outcomes, it is most effective to select and provide evidence of progress toward specific outcomes at regular intervals throughout the program, in the context of conferences and dialogues among program participants. These intervals can be scheduled at the end of courses, midway through the program, and at the conclusion of the program. (These types of regular portfolio checkpoints and time lines are discussed more fully in Chapter 4.) The use of checkpoints reinforces the collaborative nature of the portfolio process and supports consistency and reliability of the evidence.

At Tier 5, Program Impact, all of the earlier levels work together to communicate overall program impact to those outside the program. Through portfolios, a broad range of evidence has been collected over time to determine (1) if the program has met its goals and (2) what the overall effect of the program and goals have been for the participants involved. This type of evidence, including successes of individuals or programs, can be very persuasive and influential for policy makers, funders, community members, and agencies for accreditation and licensing (Sewell et al., 2005; Wilkerson & Lang, 2003).

PORTFOLIOS AS SUMMATIVE (FINAL PRODUCT) EVALUATIONS

Some of the main concerns regarding portfolios surface when they are used in summative, high-stakes evaluations (Bateson, 1994; Sewell et al., 2005; Wilkerson & Lang, 2003). High-stakes evaluations are those in which tests or other devices, such as portfolios, are used to make high-stakes decisions.

For example, students may be granted or denied diplomas, certificates, or licenses based on the results of the evaluation. Summative product portfolios (also known as *showcase* or *employment* portfolios) include final evidence, or items that demonstrate attainment of the end goals.

Wilkerson and Lang (2003) caution that portfolios could be used as appropriate and safe vehicles to make summative decisions in a certification context only so long as the contents are rigorously controlled and systematically evaluated. When decisions are standards based, summative, and meant to result in initial certification, minimal competency must be established. In licensure, the state must ensure that candidates are qualified to enter the profession and can effectively carry out its responsibilities. Summative product portfolios must contain evidence that demonstrates the candidates' ability to fulfill their responsibilities in the profession. Portfolio assessments, when used as summative evaluations to make licensure decisions, must stand the tests of validity, reliability, fairness, and absence of bias.

PRECAUTIONS AND RECOMMENDATIONS FOR EFFECTIVE PRACTICE IN PORTFOLIO EVALUATION

In light of the earlier discussion of the role of portfolios in both formative and summative evaluation, it is important to outline a few precautions and recommendations. Wilkerson and Lang (2003) recommend eight requirements for the construction of portfolios as summative evaluations used for certification in a school, college, or department of education. These are summarized in Table 3.9.

As with any other qualitative assessment, care must be taken in collecting, evaluating, and reporting the results. Methods of analysis will vary, depending on the purpose of the portfolio and the types of data collected. This information needs to be clear and specific at the beginning of the portfolio process. When goals and criteria are clearly defined, it is relatively easy to demonstrate that a student has moved from a baseline level of performance to achievement of particular goals. To reduce subjectivity of judgments, portfolios should be assessed and rated periodically and independently. This provides a check on reliability, which can be simply reported. For example, a local programmer could say, "To ensure some consistency in assessment standards, every fifth portfolio (or 20%) was assessed by more than one instructor. Agreement between raters, or interrater reliability, was 88%" (Sewell et al., 2005, p. 6).

TABLE 3.9 Requirements for Portfolio Use in Certification Testing

1. Knowledge, skills, and dispositions must be essential and authentic representations of job-related behaviors.

2. Portfolios must be representative of, relevant to, and proportional to the profession, and criteria used to evaluate the portfolios must be relevant to the job.

3. Candidates must be provided in advance with adequate written guidelines and procedures for compiling the portfolios. These guidelines must include how and when to prepare it, how it will be reviewed, who is allowed to help them, and how much help they can receive. They must also be notified of the consequences of failure, the opportunities for remediation, and their due-process rights and procedures, should they wish to challenge the review results. In addition, candidates must be notified on the appeals process and assured of its fairness in design and implementation.

4. Instructional time must be built into the program for candidates to succeed in meeting the portfolio requirements and to remediate when performance is inadequate. The portfolio process should be embedded into the entire instructional program, and all instructors need to buy into and support the portfolio preparation activities.

5. Scoring rubrics used to guide the portfolio process must be realistic in determining acceptable performance. A specific score, or set of characteristics, needs to differentiate between those candidates who are competent, or demonstrate proficiency in the knowledge skills and dispositions to enter the profession, and those who are not.

6. Options and alternatives must be provided to candidates who cannot successfully complete specific portfolio requirements, or, in the case where there is no alternative, the SCDE must be able to demonstrate why no alternatives exist. Options and alternatives must be equitable and relate to specific artifacts in the portfolio. The institution must ensure that alternatives are also representative of, relevant to, and proportional to the profession.

7. Portfolio evaluation (scoring) in terms of equity of outcomes for protected populations (i.e., with differences based on culture, language, ability, gender) should be monitored.

8. The portfolio process must be designed, implemented, and monitored to ensure reliable scoring and to provide for necessary candidate support. Regular portfolio assessment checkpoints should be established for collaboration, with tests of reliability performed and samples of candidates' work and instructors' scoring reviewed regularly to ensure that they remain valid and consistent, and that measurement error is minimized. Portfolio scorers need to receive professional development in scoring and be updated on a regular basis. Directions should be clear and consistent.

Source: Adapted from Wilkerson and Lang (2003).

RUBRICS FOR PORTFOLIO ASSESSMENT

A **rubric** is a tool used in authentic assessment to assess or establish criteria that are complex and subjective (Goodrich, 1997; Lazear, 1998; Popham, 1997; Wiggins, 1999). The rubric is designed to simulate real-life activity, to engage students in solving problems such as classroom management or lesson planning. Effective rubrics also help to define and quantify successful levels of performance. According to Wiggins (1999), rubrics show

or specific
information
related to
his
concept,
see the
Chapter 3
resources
in the CD.

levels of performance on a standard or skill over a continuum, ranging from high or expert level of performance to low or ineffective performance. Sample rubrics are available later in this chapter and on the CD. A rubric is a formative type of assessment because it becomes an ongoing part of the entire teaching and learning process, as criteria are defined and quantified from high to low. Students can be actively engaged in the rubric design process: as they become more familiar with rubrics, they can assist in their design. This involvement empowers students to become more focused and self-directed in their own learning. As a result, they have a much clearer idea of what is expected of them. Tables 3.10 and 3.11 describe the characteristics of rubrics, as well as the advantages of using them in portfolio assessment, based on prominent research findings (Goodrich, 1997; Popham, 1997; Wiggins, 1999).

TABLE 3.10   Characteristics of Rubrics

Rubrics are tools for

- communicating specific expectations and grading criteria based on examples,
- measuring or quantifying a stated objective or standard (e.g., performance, behavior, skill, or quality),
- assigning levels or using a range to score performance, and
- describing the degree or amount to which a standard has been met, based on ascending levels.

TABLE 3.11   Advantages of Effective Rubrics in Portfolio Assessment

Effective rubrics

- build more objectivity and consistency in assessment and evaluation,
- allow instructors to clarify grading criteria in specific terms with examples,
- demonstrate to students how their work will be evaluated and explain what is expected of them,
- provide students with clear targets in specific, measurable terms,
- assist students in being more self-directed and reflective,
- promote student awareness of the criteria to use in assessing peer performance,
- give useful feedback to instructors regarding the effectiveness of the instruction,
- outline benchmarks for measuring and documenting progress,
- offer students a greater sense of ownership for their learning, and
- provide the opportunity to assess more student outcomes than traditional assessment does.

specific
ormation
ated to
s
acept,
the
apter 3
ources
the CD.

Table 3.12 provides an example of a rubric used to evaluate a thematic English language development (ELD) unit in a teacher credential program. In it, the instructor lays out specific criteria of the assignment and how they will be scored. The unit could later be placed in the portfolio as an example of INTASC (1992) Principle 3 (Adapting Instruction for Individual Needs). Figures 3.1, 3.2, and 3.3 provide examples of holistic and analytic rubrics. More sample rubrics are also provided in Chapter 4 and on the CD.

TABLE 3.12   Sample Thematic English Language Development Unit Assessment Rubric

Criteria	Excellent	Satisfactory	Needs Improvement
Overview	3 points. Conveys purpose clearly. Notes target grade level. Introduces why topic is of interest to English-language learners. Notes length of unit.	2 points. Conveys purpose. Notes target grade level and length.	1 point. Introduces unit but not grade level. Purpose or relevance is vague.
Unit goals	2 points. Goals clearly written. Goals cover a range of outcomes. State standards are cited, including ELD and related content standards.	1 point. Goals are written.	0 points. No goals are stated.
Assessment instrument	4 points. A reliable scale is developed (i.e., detailed, concrete, well designed). Scale is appropriate for task. Task is explained clearly. Usage and data collection is explained clearly.	3 points. A reliable scale is developed (i.e., detailed, concrete). Scale is appropriate for task. Usage and data collection is explained.	2 points. A usable scale is developed. Scale is somewhat appropriate for task. Usage is explained.
Lesson plans	12 points. At least *five* plans are developed. Plans are clearly explained so that another could use them. Plans state *three* objectives written in correct format. Assessment is addressed. Plan format fits the proposed learning activities and is modified (i.e., differentiated) for each ELD level.	9 points. At least *four* plans are developed. Plans are clearly explained so that another could use them. Plans state *three* objectives written in correct format and are modified (i.e., differentiated) for each ELD level.	6 points. At least *three* plans are developed. Plans are clearly explained. Plans state *two* objectives and are modified (i.e., differentiated) for each ELD level.
Home connection and technology applications	2 points. There is a clear home connection in the unit as well as applications of technology.	1 point. There is a home connection in the unit.	0 points. There is no home connection.
Resource and reference list	2 points. There is a reference list at the end of the unit identifying all references and resources used to develop the unit, including related Web sites. Complete references are also stated on individual lesson plans where appropriate.	1 point. Complete references are stated on individual lesson plans where appropriate.	0 points. There is no reference list.

FIGURE 3.1   Sample Oral Presentation Rubrics

Oral Presentation: Analytic Rubric (Assigns levels of performance for each criterion)

Criteria	Level 3	Level 2	Level 1
Organization	Very well organized; logical sequence of information	Fair organization, slight sequence of information	Poorly organized; no sequence of information
Subject knowledge	High comfort with and mastery of subject matter; able to answer questions with elaborations	Some mastery of subject with few inaccuracies; able to answer basic questions	Little to no mastery of subject matter, lots of inaccuracies, unable to answer questions
Multimedia	Strong use of multiple forms of media and technology	Slight use of different media or technology	No integration of other media or technology
Audience appeal	Audience interested and able to follow presentation; high interaction and appeal	Audience somewhat able to following presentation; slight interest and interaction	Audience unable to understand or follow presentation; no interest or interaction

Oral Presentation: Holistic Rubric
(Assigns a level of performance across multiple criteria as a whole)

Level 3: Excellent Presenter

- Well organized; presents information in logical sequence
- High comfort with and mastery of subject matter; able to answer questions with elaborations
- Strong use of multiple forms of media and technology in presentation
- High audience interest and appeal with lots of interaction

Level 2: Fair Presenter

- Fair organization; presents information in somewhat logical sequence
- Some comfort with and mastery of subject matter; able to answer basic questions
- Slight use of different media and technology in presentation
- Some audience interest and appeal, with moderate interaction

Level 1: Poor Presenter

- Disorganized; presents information in no logical sequence
- Low comfort with and mastery of subject matter; unable to answer questions
- No use of multiple forms of media or technology in presentation
- No audience interest or appeal, with no interaction

FIGURE 3.2	Samples of Analytic Rubrics (Assign levels of performance for each criterion)

Oral Presentation: Analytic Rubric A

Criteria	Level 3	Level 2	Level 1
Organization	Very well organized; logical sequence of information	Fair organization; slight sequence of information	Poorly organized; no sequence of information
Subject knowledge	High comfort with and mastery of subject matter; able to answer questions with elaborations	Some mastery of the subject with few inaccuracies; able to answer basic questions	Little to no mastery of subject matter lots of inaccuracies; unable to answer questions
Multimedia	Strong use of multiple forms of media and technology	Slight use of different media or technology	No integration of other media or technology
Audience appeal	Audience interested and able to follow presentation; high interaction and appeal	Audience somewhat able to follow presentation; slight interest and interaction	Audience unable to understand or follow presentation; no interest or interaction

Reflective Journal: Analytic Rubric B

Criteria	5	3	1	0
Topic relevance	All or almost all of the reflections have a connection to the topic.	Most reflections have a connection to the topic.	Few reflections have a connection to the topic.	None of the reflections have a connection to the topic.
Attitudes and beliefs	Attitudes and beliefs are revealed in all or almost all of the reflections.	Attitudes and beliefs are revealed in most reflections.	Attitudes and beliefs are revealed in few of the reflections.	No attitudes or beliefs are revealed in any of the reflections.
Format	The recommended format has been followed for all of the reflections.	The recommended format has been followed for most of the reflections.	The recommended format has been followed for few of the reflections.	The recommended format has not been followed for any of the reflections.

(Continued)

(Continued)

Criteria	5	3	1	0
Mechanics	All or almost all of the reflections use correct punctuation and spelling.	Most reflections use correct punctuation and spelling.	Few reflections use correct punctuation and spelling.	None of the reflections use correct punctuation or spelling.
Completion	All reflections are included in order and together.	All reflections are included, but are either not together or in order.	Not all reflections are included, but they are together or in order.	Not all reflections are included nor are they together or in order.

Designing Authentic Assessments: Analytic Rubric C			
Criteria	**Level 3**	**Level 2**	**Level 1**
Learning targets	All learning targets are clearly identified.	Some learning targets are clearly identified.	Learning targets are not clearly identified.
Real-life activities	Learning targets are directly linked to real-world knowledge, skills, and dispositions.	Some learning targets are directly linked to real-world knowledge, skills, and dispositions. At least two assessments are included. Analytic or holistic rubrics are used appropriately.	Learning targets are not directly linked to real-world knowledge, skills, and dispositions. Only one assessment is included. Neither analytic nor holistic rubrics are used.
Defined criteria with rating scale	Specific criteria are listed as performance outcomes for each learning target. A rating scale is used to measure three or more levels of performance.	Criteria are listed as performance outcomes for some learning targets. A rating scale is used to measure two levels of performance.	Criteria are not listed as performance outcomes for learning targets. A rating scale is not used to measure levels of performance.
Variety of assessments	A variety of assessments is included.	At least two assessments are included.	Only one assessment is included.
Rubrics	Analytic and holistic rubrics are used appropriately.	Analytic or holistic rubrics are used but not always appropriately.	Neither analytic nor holistic rubrics are used.

FIGURE 3.3   Samples of Holistic Rubrics (Assign levels of performance across multiple criteria as a whole)

Oral Presentation: Holistic Rubric A

Level 3: Excellent Presenter

- Well organized; presents information in logical sequence
- High comfort with and mastery of subject matter; able to answer questions with elaborations
- Strong use of multiple forms of media and technology in presentation
- High audience interest and appeal, with lots of interaction

Level 2: Fair Presenter

- Fair organization; presents information in somewhat logical sequence
- Some comfort with and mastery of subject matter; able to answer basic questions
- Slight use of different media and technology in presentation
- Some audience interest and appeal, with moderate interaction

Level 1: Poor Presenter

- Disorganized; presents information in no logical sequence
- Low comfort with and mastery of subject matter; unable to answer questions
- No use of multiple forms of media or technology in presentation
- No audience interest or appeal, with no interaction

Reflective Journal: Holistic Rubric B

Level 3: Excellent Reflections

- All or almost all of the reflections have a connection to the topic.
- Attitudes and beliefs are revealed in all or almost all of the reflections.
- The recommended format has been followed for all of the reflections.
- All or almost all of the reflections use correct punctuation and spelling.
- All reflections are included in order and together.

Level 2: Good Reflections

- Most reflections have a connection to the topic.
- Attitudes and beliefs are revealed in all or almost of the reflections.
- The recommended format has been followed for most of the reflections.
- Most reflections use correct punctuation and spelling.
- All reflections are included, but are either not together or in order.

Level 2: Fair Reflections

- Few reflections have a connection to the topic.
- Attitudes and beliefs are revealed in few of the reflections.
- The recommended format has been followed for few of the reflections.
- Most reflections use correct punctuation and spelling.
- Not all reflections are included, but they are together or in order.

(Continued)

(Continued)

Level 1: Poor Reflections

- None of the reflections have a connection to the topic.
- No attitudes or beliefs are revealed in any of the reflections.
- The recommended format has not been followed for any of the reflections.
- None of the reflections use correct punctuation or spelling.
- Not all reflections are included, nor are they together or in order.

Designing Authentic Assessments: Holistic Rubric C

Level 3: Excellent Assessments

- All learning targets are clearly identified.
- Learning targets are directly linked to real-world knowledge, skills, and dispositions.
- Specific criteria are listed as performance outcomes for each learning target.
- A rating scale is used to measure three or more levels of performance.
- A variety of assessments is included.
- Analytic and holistic rubrics are used appropriately.

Level 2: Fair Assessments

- Some learning targets are clearly identified.
- Some learning targets are directly linked to real-world knowledge, skills, and dispositions.
- Criteria are listed as performance outcomes for some learning targets.
- A rating scale is used to measure two levels of performance.
- At least two assessments are included.
- Analytic or holistic rubrics are used appropriately.

Level 1: Poor Assessments

- Learning targets are not clearly identified.
- Learning targets are not directly linked to real-world knowledge, skills, and dispositions.
- Criteria are not listed as performance outcomes for learning targets.
- A rating scale is not used to measure levels of performance.
- Only one assessment is included.
- Neither analytic nor holistic rubrics are used.

LET'S PRACTICE!

Activity 3.4   Questions and Activities for Designing and Using Rubrics

- Review some of the standards in your present course or program. Determine if they are accompanied by rubrics that specify how the learning targets will be evaluated.
- Think of a skill or learning target that is important or essential in your present course or program. If you were to evaluate this skill, what criteria would you use and why?

Write out the criteria in separate categories. Determine levels of performance for each criterion, ranging from high to low. Compare your answers with those of your peers.

- Visit some of the recommended Web sites for sample rubrics and rubric makers. Use the samples shown on the Web sites for designing rubrics for assignments that you have given.
- Which types of rubrics do you prefer, analytic or holistic, and why?
- Use the Designing Authentic Assessments Rubric to guide and evaluate your development of rubrics.

SUMMARY

Portfolios offer excellent tools for authentic assessment by providing real-life evidence of completion of program standards. They further expose students to a type of action research that is focused on helping them improve their own practice in both formative, developmental assessment and summative evaluation. Still, despite the benefits, portfolios are not a panacea and require careful guidelines and collaboration to avoid pitfalls such as inconsistencies in definitions and expectations. The contents of portfolios must be rigorously controlled and systematically assessed. There must also be ongoing tests of validity, reliability, and fairness in scoring, particularly when portfolios are used as summative evaluations for licensure or degree decisions. The use of rubrics helps the portfolio process to be more objective, consistent, and reliable.

USEFUL RESOURCES

The following resources are useful in viewing grading criteria and designing sample rubrics for the portfolio.

Assessing Student Outcomes: Performance Assessment Using the Dimensions of Learning Model (http://www.amazon.com/exec/obidos/ISBN = 0871202255/kathyschrocksguiA)

A textbook by Manzano, R. Pickering, D., and McTighe, J. (1993).

Assessment Rubrics (http://edtech.kennesaw.edu/intech/rubrics.htm)

Simple definitions and examples of rubrics from Kennesaw State University.

Association for Supervision and Curriculum Development (ASCD; http://www.uwstout.edu/soe/profdev/rubrics.shtml)

From the University of Wisconsin–Stout, an assortment of rubrics for assessment.

Authentic Assessment Toolbox created by Jonathan Mueller (http://jonathan.mueller.faculty.noctrl.edu/toolbox/rubrics.htm)

This site contains information and resources. Excellent resource with practical examples and guidelines.

The Dumb Test (http://www.quizrocket.com/dumb-test/6)

A fun link for conversation and assessment

Full Text Journal Articles
(http://pareonline.net/pdf/v10n3.pdf)

Andrade, H., & Du, Y. (2005). Student perspectives on rubric-referenced assessments. *Practical Assessment Research and Evaluation.*

(http://www.smallschoolsproject.org/PDFS/coh0103/using_rubrics.pdf)

Andrade, H. (2000). Using rubric to promote thinking and learning. *Educational Leadership, 57* (5).

Kathy Schrock's Guide for Educators from Discovery School's (http://school.discov eryeducation.com/schrockguide/assess.html)

This site contains assessment and rubric information.

Northwest Regional Laboratory Assessment Resources and Toolkit (http://www .nwrel.org/assessment/toolkit98.php)

Full Toolkit may be purchased.

Rubistar (http://rubistar.4teachers.org/index.php)

A site for developing a variety of rubrics.

Stone Middle School, Melborne, Florida (http://stone.web.brevard.k12.fl.us/html/com prubric.html)

A Web page on automating authentic assessments with rubrics.

Sue LeBeau (http://www.suelebeau.com/assessment.htm)

Assortment of texts and Web links related to assessment and the development of rubrics, including rubric makers, compiled by Sue LeBeau.

FOR FURTHER READING

Campbell, V. M., Cignetti, P. B., Melenyzer, B. J., Nettles, D. H., & Wyman, Jr., R. M. (2004). *How to develop a professional portfolio: A manual for teachers* (3rd ed.). Boston: Allyn & Bacon.

Hebert, E. A. (2001). *The power of portfolios: What children can teach us about learning and assessment.* San Francisco: Jossey-Bass.

Mueller, J. (2008). *Authentic assessment toolbox.* Retrieved August 24, 2008, from http://jonathan .mueller.faculty.noctrl.edu/toolbox/rubrics.htm

Oosterhof, A., Conrad, R., & Ely, D. (2008). *Assessing learners online.* Columbus, OH: Merrill/Prentice Hall.

Sagor, R. (2003). *Action research guidebook: A four-step process for educators and school teams.* Thousand Oaks, CA: Sage.

Stiggins, R. (2008). *An introduction to student-involved assessment for learning* (5th ed.). Columbus, OH: Merrill/Prentice Hall.

Stiggins, R. J., Arter, J. A., Chappuis, J., & Chappuis, S. (2004). *Classroom assessment for student learning: Doing it right—Using it well.* Portland, OR: Educational Testing Service.

CHAPTER 4

Reflective Inquiry

A Tool for Giving Voice to the Portfolio

> *More than anything else, the portfolio process should inspire reflection—alone and in the company of others. . . . Reflective commentaries by the portfolio owner are essential companion pieces to artifacts. Writing reflections pushes teachers to more deeply examine their practice and allows others to examine the thinking behind the teaching documented in the portfolio. . . . With reflection, the portfolio can become an episode of learning.*
>
> —Wolf and Dietz (1998, p. 14)

> *We do not learn from experience. We learn from reflecting on experience.*
>
> —John Dewey

CHAPTER OBJECTIVES

Readers will be able to

❑ define reflection and reflective inquiry;

❑ use structured reflections as a key component of action research;

❑ view reflections as the glue bonding the portfolio to a purpose;

❑ identify 10 ways reflections transform artifacts into evidence;

❑ recognize the multifaceted, cyclical nature of reflections; and

❑ state the outcomes and benefits of reflective inquiry in portfolio development.

SCENARIO

Irma and Matt, two teaching credential candidates, have just entered their science methods course for the first time. As the syllabi are distributed and the professor begins to give an overview of the course, including the ongoing portfolio requirement, the following exchange occurs between the two:

Matt begins, "I've heard portfolios are just a waste of time; nobody looks at them anyway! I can't understand why we're required to do them. To me, it's just more busywork that gets in the way of real, practical activities. What can a portfolio teach me about working in school?"

Irma responds, "My portfolio has taught me a lot about myself and my values when it comes to teaching because I explain in my reflections why I put in the different items. My portfolio has really helped me to see how much I've changed since I began this program. It also helped me to focus! It was a lot of work at first, but now I'd be lost without it. The most important thing is that my portfolio helped me to get organized. When I first started, it seemed like I was just collecting a lot of 'stuff,' and I didn't see how it all related. Then some of my professors explained different ways to set it up so that it told a story. They helped me to explain why I had put certain things into the portfolio and what I wanted the portfolio to say about me through my portfolio reflections. Once I became clear about my purpose for having a portfolio, then it took on a life of its own. I also began to realize that you don't have to save everything and that there are different kinds of portfolios. You can set them up in different ways depending on your goals, and you can use reflections to explain the different artifacts you put in."

Later in the quarter, Irma and Matt participated in a portfolio exchange conducted in the class, in which students exchanged portfolios with peers. Once Matt saw the variety of ways portfolios could be organized, he began to realize how he could modify his own to present a clearer picture of who he was as a teacher. He noted the extra care with which Irma had developed her portfolio, such as her table of contents outlined by the standards; careful reflection on each artifact; and use of pictures, parent letters, and more. Her portfolio definitely had a clear purpose and told a story, unlike his.

OVERVIEW

A major goal of ours for this book is to make the experience of developing and maintaining a portfolio one that is positive, relevant, and rewarding. Yet the two contrasting viewpoints in the foregoing scenario indicate the possible range of responses to the requirement to keep a portfolio. The students' statements also indicate the range of reactions instructors receive when they announce the portfolio requirements for the courses they teach.

The questions become, How does one transform negative statements and experiences about portfolios into affirming ones? What enables the portfolio process to become a valuable and meaningful experience for students, leading to a lifelong practice of documentation and reflection? How can students be supported in the process of developing professional portfolios in a way that can guide them throughout their education and subsequent careers? The answers to these questions lie in the use of carefully articulated reflections.

In this chapter, we describe the central role that reflections play in the portfolio process by linking isolated artifacts to specific purposes, thereby increasing the relevance of the portfolio (Barrett, 2001; Bartell, Kaye, & Morin, 1998a, 1998b; Burke, 1997; Cook, 2006;

Greenwood & Levin, 2007; Mueller, 2008; Wolf & Dietz, 1998). We illustrate how reflections breathe life into the portfolio by giving voice to the supporting action research, as discussed in Chapter 2. We also describe the process of reflective inquiry, or guiding reflections through questioning, to further clarify the rationale for each artifact and transform it into evidence of the students' professional knowledge, beliefs, and abilities (Burke, 1997; Coghlan & Brannick, 2004; Dollase, 1996; McNiff & Whitehead, 2006; Southwest Educational Development Laboratory [SEDL], 2000). As indicated by numerous researchers, students must take ownership of their portfolios by relating them to their own personal and professional goals. These goals may be

1. formative or developmental, for showing areas of growth and levels of achievement;

2. summative, where the portfolio serves as a final evaluation that indicates completion of program, course, or certification requirements; or

3. for marketing, where the portfolio is used as part of applying for a job or as a preliminary introduction prior to an interview.

Setting clear goals is necessary for students to see a personal benefit to portfolios (Dietz, 2008; Grant & Huebner, 1998; Hartnell-Young & Morriss, 1988; McKinney, 1998; Schmuck, 1997; Strijbos et al., 2007; Wolf & Dietz, 1998). Each of these goals or purposes reinforces the concept of reflection as an essential component of the portfolio process.

REFLECTIVE INQUIRY: PROVIDING A GLOBAL, BIRD'S EYE VIEW OF THE PORTFOLIO

We begin by asking, What is **reflective inquiry,** and how is it used to support the portfolio process? In simple terms, reflective inquiry is a process of tracking or examining our actions by constantly asking questions about why we are doing them in order to learn from our actions. It involves asking the following questions: *What* actions or activities are we doing? *Why* we are doing them? *How* are we doing them? *When* are we doing them? *Where* are we doing them? *Who* is doing them with us or *who* is responsible for us doing them? These questions repeat themselves at every level of inquiry and are continually being reexamined for new insights and clarity. An analogy of reflective inquiry would be the act of peeling an onion. Once you have peeled through the outer layer, a new layer is revealed. This process is continued until you have peeled through each layer and arrived at the core. Mueller (2008) reminds us that the portfolio is a tool created by the student and for the student. Because reflections are designed to connect inquiry with actions, the reflective phase of the portfolio has the most promise for promoting growth.

Mid-Continental Research for Education and Learning (MCREL; 2008) defines reflection as "a thinking process through which individuals examine their experiences to better understand the assumptions and implications of events and actions in their lives" (p. 1). *Inquiry* is defined as a close examination or investigation of a matter for information or truth.

Combining these two, we define *reflective inquiry* as asking penetrating questions, challenging assumptions, and carefully examining the implications of an individual's actions and choices. Reflective inquiry addresses the Why of the portfolio process by helping to establish a purpose for compiling the portfolio as well as a guide through the various artifacts contained in the portfolio. It provides a means to step away from specific activities or actions in order to get a broader perspective, or global, bird's eye view of the situation. The goal is to enable the individual to see the big picture underlying certain activities or actions. As stated in Chapter 2, both reflection and inquiry are pivotal components in the action research cycle, aimed at learning through our actions to improve our practice (Dehler & Edmonds, 2006; Reason, 2006; Strijbos et al., 2007). Reflective inquiry involves making the right choices about doing what we are doing and, like action research and learning, it evolves over time. True learning occurs when understanding, insights, and explanations are connected with actions. Therefore, quality in reflective inquiry comes from an awareness of and transparency about the choices open to an individual that are made at each level of inquiry through their actions. The following activity allows you to practice reflective inquiry.

LET'S PRACTICE!

Activity 4.1   Questions and Activities for Exploring Reflective Inquiry

Bring to mind an important activity you have recently been involved in (i.e., a purchase you have made, a trip you have taken, a phone call you made, a letter you have written, an application you have filled out, an event you participated in, a statement you made to someone, a conversation you have had). Describe the activity.

Write a reflection about the activity or events by answering the following reflective inquiry questions:

1. What was the event or activity, and why did you consider it important?
   - What was the purpose behind the event or activity? Why did you do it? What were your goals?
   - What did you specifically do? What actions were involved? What enabled you to accomplish the activity?
   - What choices, if any, did you make during the activity?
   - What assumptions did you make about the event before doing it?
   - What, if anything, did you learn from the event or activity? What were the results or outcomes of the activities? Did you accomplish your goals? Why or why not?

2. If you were to do the activity again, what, if anything, would you change about it and why?

3. What, if anything, did you learn by reflecting on this activity or event?

4. How could applying what you learned through this activity benefit you in future activities?

Share your reflections with a peer or small group.

- What is your reaction to this experience of reflective inquiry?
- Was there value in having a global, bird's eye view of the activity or event? Why or why not?
- When, if ever, would you recommend using reflective inquiry and why?

Mertler (2009) reinforces the idea that action research is, by nature, full of choices. Through inquiry, we are able both to view and dissect our choices. The key to reflective inquiry is to enable us to become aware of our choices and the consequences of them and subsequently to make the best choices possible for our particular situations. This entails asking probing questions before, during, and after undertaking any actions in order to explore the possible options and consequences. Reflections help us to take a step back from our activity to weigh our options before making choices and decisions (Fisher & Phelps, 2006; Greenwood & Levin, 2007; Mueller, 2008; Strijbos et al., 2007; Stringer, 2004). This, in essence, allows us to regulate our own learning by the choices we make before taking action. Our actions become focused and intentional rather than random and spontaneous or unplanned. In this way, reflective inquiry leads to self-regulated learning, where we have a choice in what, where, how, when, and why we learn. Quality in reflective inquiry comes from asking, What is important in a particular situation? How well are we doing? How can we demonstrate to others how well we have done? What are the choices we are making and are they the best choices? In the following two activities, we use guiding questions to help you practice reflective inquiry as you plan for your portfolio process.

LET'S PRACTICE!

Activity 4.2 Activity for Reflective Inquiry About Your Portfolio Process

First, consider why you are reading this textbook and what you are gaining or learning from the experience. The goal of this text is to make the portfolio process a rewarding experience that enables you to

1. *define* your learning goals,

2. *evaluate* your progress toward your learning goals, and

3. *demonstrate* accomplishment of your learning goals in a variety of ways for the appropriate audience.

(Continued)

(Continued)

Through reflective inquiry, another goal is to make you aware of the variety of choices you have in designing your portfolio to

1. *tell your own story,* thus allowing you to regulate your own learning, and

2. *communicate* with others about your learning.

The following questions will guide you in an initial reflective inquiry about your portfolio process.

- What are *your* specific reasons for reading this text (being in the class, taking this course, etc.)? What do you hope to accomplish as a result of reading the text, being in this class, or taking this course?
- What are the learning goals involved in creating your portfolio? What benefits or value does the portfolio potentially have for you? What specific questions do you want the portfolio to answer about you and why? What story do you want the portfolio to tell about you and why?
- How will you evaluate or measure your progress toward your goals? What criteria will you use?
- In what ways will you use your portfolio to demonstrate your progress to different audiences (i.e., instructors, peers, supervisors, self, mentors)?
- What are some of the choices you will make in designing your portfolio so that it tells your own story?

Discuss your responses with an instructor, mentor, or peer. Add whatever feedback they provide from your discussion and place your responses to these questions in your portfolio and refer back to them as you add your artifacts. (This may later become part of the Introduction to your portfolio, which is discussed more fully in Chapter 6.)

You can review these same questions with regard to future artifacts or assignments you consider adding to the portfolio.

(See Focus Questions for Initial Reflective Inquiry About Artifacts in Activity 4.3.)

LET'S PRACTICE!

Activity 4.3   Activity for Focus Questions to Guide Initial Reflective Inquiry About Artifacts

Identify the selected artifact and its source. Respond to the focus questions

Artifact: _____ Date: _____

Source of Artifact: _____

Focus Questions for Initial Reflective Inquiry About Artifacts:

1. What are the learning targets or goals?

2. How will the learning targets be evaluated? What criteria will be used (e.g., best work, evidence of growth, evidence of standard)?

3. What ways will you use to demonstrate progress toward your goals? What options are available (e.g., performance of skills, demonstrations of knowledge, such as written exams, essays, projects, products)?

4. How does this artifact add to your story? What does it tell about you and what you have learned? How does it relate to the big picture of what you want the portfolio to do?

5. What is the best way to communicate about this artifact in the portfolio?

6. What additional considerations did you make in selecting this artifact for your portfolio, if any?

ENHANCING LEARNING THROUGH STRUCTURED REFLECTIONS

Research continues to prove that learning is greatly enhanced through **structured reflections** (ARC CAS, 2008; Campus Compact, 2008; Danielson & McGreal, 2000; Mueller, 2008). *Structured reflection* is the term used to refer to a thoughtfully constructed process that challenges and guides students in (1) examining critical issues related to their coursework and related activities; (2) connecting their activities to coursework, professional standards, and program goals; (3) enhancing the development of civic and ethical skills and values; and (4) assisting students in finding personal relevance in their work.

Throughout this chapter, a variety of structured reflections are used to give purpose and voice to the items placed in your portfolio. As a result of such reflections, the value of each learning experience is amplified as it becomes an essential building block for your portfolio and the demonstration of your professional competencies. Structured reflections facilitate critical thinking skills, such as the ability to identify issues, be open and receptive to new or different ideas, and foresee the consequences of your actions and choices. Structured reflections promote a range of other competencies that are essential to your ethical development and civic responsibility, such as communication and teamwork skills, leadership and self-awareness, and problem solving. A variety of reflective activities are listed in Table 4.1 that are valuable for writing structured reflections.

REFLECTIONS AS AN ESSENTIAL COMPONENT OF ACTION RESEARCH

Reflective inquiry is an aspect of action research in which the reflective process is guided by specific inquiry questions aimed at identifying only the most effective evidence to

TABLE 4.1   Sample Assignments and Activities to Promote Structured Reflection

Types of Assignments	Related Reflective Activities
Case studies	Describe the processes you went through in completing the case study. What were the initial goals? Who was involved and why? What did you learn through the process? How does it relate to the big picture in your credential program?
Journals	Set up a journal at the beginning of a course, project, or assignment, in which you regularly add entries conveying your thoughts, feelings, observations, and questions. A journal can also be set up at the beginning of your portfolio process to record your activities in compiling your artifacts. Suggestions for setting up a portfolio journal are shared in Chapter 5.
Team journals	Create a conversational team journal for a collaborative project you are working on to promote greater communication and interaction among team members. Team members take turns recording shared and individual experiences, observations, and responses to other team members' entries.
Portfolios	Create one of the types of portfolios described in Chapters 1, 3, and 4. Think of ways to structure portfolios to communicate different purposes, such as a celebration portfolio, a growth portfolio, a working portfolio, a course portfolio, and a showcase portfolio. Be sure to identify the learning targets or goals for each type of portfolio and organize the artifacts or evidence by the standards or learning targets.
Paper	Write a paper where you describe a project, program, assignment, or course. Describe how it fits into your learning goals. Journals and other products can serve as building blocks upon which to construct the final paper.
Discussions	Record your thoughts, observations, and opinions before, during, or after discussions. Many discussions are stimulated by question prompts. Generate topics you want to discuss with your peers or instructors regarding an assignment, course, or activity. Introduce the discussion topic at an appropriate time during the course. Describe what you learn from the experience. Which opinions do you most agree with and why? Which opinions are most different from your own?
Presentations	Present your findings on a project or activities to your peers. What are the most important aspects to share about the experience? What are strategies you will use to interact with your peers during the presentation? How can you make the presentation interesting and relevant for your peers? How does this presentation relate to your overall learning goals?
Interviews	Interview someone who has already completed your credential program and is now a practicing professional. Think of questions you want to explore regarding that person's credential program and how well it prepared the person for his or her current position. What are the most rewarding aspects of that person's profession and why? What are the most challenging aspects and why? What, if anything, could have prepared him or her better for the first year in the new profession?

Source: Categories adapted from Campus Compact (2008).

demonstrate growth and development toward learning targets (Coghlan & Brannick, 2004; McNiff, 2003; McNiff & Whitehead, 2006). Many artifacts, therefore, are eliminated before they ever reach the portfolio. In order to know which artifacts to keep in a portfolio, we must have a clear vision of what story we want the portfolio to tell. As Stephen Covey (1990) stated in his book, *The 7 Habits of Highly Effective People,* the first two steps toward effectiveness in any endeavor are (1) being proactive and (2) beginning with the end in mind. This means taking the initiative to set clear goals before beginning your work. In portfolio development, reflections work much the same way as taking these initial steps. Even before the first artifact is collected, you need to reflect on the reasons for developing the portfolio and the nature of the desired outcomes—what would make the portfolio be of value to you in your professional or personal life or both? Your answers will determine what types of artifacts will be collected, what will be written about them, and how they will shape the overall portfolio (Campbell et al., 2000; Dietz, 2008; Hurst, Wilson, & Cramer, 1998). Reflections and reflective inquiry, therefore, involve *thinking about what* to put into the portfolio and *why,* as well as providing *the actual written statements* that accompany and explain the artifacts. In the next section, we discuss four different types of portfolio reflections as statements or explanations.

FOUR TYPES OF PORTFOLIO REFLECTIONS

Our next goal is to introduce a broader definition of reflections by asking, How does one define *reflections* in the portfolio process? Our previous definition referred to them as a way of thinking deeply about an item or event. It involved the *action* of thinking. In this section, we expand on that definition to include reflections as statements that result from thinking about an item or event. In this way, reflections become the result, or the *products,* of those thoughts. Reflections can become captions or small statements and explanations that are used to give voice to the various artifacts collected in the portfolio (Barrett, 2001; Burke, 1997; Dietz, 2008; Mueller, 2008; Wolf & Dietz, 1998).

There are four general types of portfolio reflections or statements, namely,

1. goal-setting statements,
2. reflective statements,
3. caption statements, and
4. assessment and evaluation statements.

These reflections or statements are attached to each artifact, explaining what it is, why it is evidence, and what it is evidence of. They are the result of reflective inquiry to determine the absolute value of each artifact to the portfolio (Grant & Huebner, 1998; McKinney, 1998; Stiggins, 2008; Taggart & Wilson, 2005). Samples of each type of statement are listed in Table 4.2.

TABLE 4.2 Samples of Four Types of Portfolio Reflections

Goal-Setting Statements

I am submitting this portfolio in partial fulfillment of my teaching credential.

One of my professional goals in creating this portfolio is to secure a position as a school administrator.

This portfolio demonstrates my competencies as a school psychologist, and it lays the foundation for my desire to enter the PhD program in counseling.

One of my primary goals in completing this activity was . . .

Reflective Statements

I learned a great deal about myself through this assignment because . . .

When I met with my supervisor after this field assignment, I discovered . . .

This activity not only demonstrated my use of technology but also addressed . . .

The feedback I received from my peers on this assignment was . . .

Caption Statements

This is my resume, which shows my background in . . .

This is a copy of my credential, which I included because . . .

This is an award I received from . . .

This is a letter of recommendation from . . .

Authentic Assessment and Evaluation Statements

My growth is demonstrated by . . .

In the area of classroom management, I have grown in the following ways, as demonstrated by . . .

I use this artifact as evidence of my skills in educational leadership in the area of leading individuals and groups toward common goals.

I received the highest points possible in the multimedia presentation, which fulfilled both the technology and the community outreach standards.

Source: Adapted from PATT (2000)

Goal-setting statements refer to educational or professional goals that can be clearly articulated (i.e., career ladder, professional advancement, education). They further outline the purpose behind the portfolio.

Reflective statements can be the result of either personal reflection or collaborative reflection resulting from communications with mentors, supervisors, peers, professors, and so forth. Reflective statements provide general reactions or responses to the artifact as well as a context for it, clarifying its purpose in the portfolio. They further demonstrate the interactive nature of the portfolio: the individual interacting with the artifact, the process, and others during the portfolio process.

Caption statements usually include explanations and identification that further provide a rationale for the inclusion of certain artifacts. They fall more in the category of labels, definitions, or explanation of artifacts. Captions can also state the source of the artifact, such as a course and its purpose in the overall credential program.

Authentic assessment and evaluation statements are formative and summative evaluative statements that indicate growth or accomplishment in the targeted criteria or standards. These statements often make reference to the standards and discuss growth in comparison with the original goal of the portfolio.

There may be some overlap in the purpose of the statements. Most important is the value of the statement in giving life and meaning to the artifacts. Reflections take on many forms, from simple captions of two or three sentences that are used to identify an artifact, its source, and its purpose, to more elaborate explanations and definitions of the artifact's role in the portfolio. Table 4.3 provides examples of artifacts and their corresponding reflections.

TABLE 4.3   Sample Artifacts and Corresponding Reflections

Artifact	Reflections
Philosophy of education statement	This is my philosophy of education (EDUC 300), written in the first semester, which continued to evolve throughout the program.
Parent letter	This is a letter I wrote to the parents of my middle school students to encourage greater parental support in my literacy unit. As a result, I increased parental involvement by 50% (EDSE 415).
Paraprofessional workshop on testing	This is a workshop I conducted to help paraprofessionals understand the new testing procedures in our district. I developed a digital slideshow presentation to explain new procedures and laws regarding testing. Evaluations of the workshop are also attached (EDAD 420).
Samples of student work	These are samples of student work resulting from the sample lesson plan I wrote and taught. I used them to assess the students.
Lesson plans (English language)	This lesson plan demonstrates my ability to work with special populations in the area of English-language development.
Lesson plans (math)	This is my first attempt at a math lesson. Notice how subsequent plans show much more variety in the use of manipulatives, higher-order thinking, and classroom organization.
Pictures of bulletin boards	These are pictures of bulletin boards I created to reinforce my lessons and enhance the classroom environment.
Science learning center	I developed this exploratory center on sound to help my elementary students have a hands-on experience in discovering how sound travels. The learning center helped me to individualize instruction and foster greater student responsibility.
Resume	This is a copy of my resume, which I include to show my previous experience as a tutor and teaching assistant.
Workshop flyers	These are workshops I attended as evidence of INTASC Principle 9 (Professional Commitment and Responsibility).

The author of a portfolio may explain what he or she has learned as demonstrated by the artifact and how this information has enhanced the overall portfolio process. For instance, the parent letter mentioned in Table 4.3 was used to support a middle school literacy program. It resulted in a 50% increase in parent participation. This is strong evidence of INTASC (1992) Principle 10 (Partnerships). Similarly, a math lesson plan can show various details involving multiple instructional strategies (INTASC Principle 4), such as manipulatives and higher-order questioning. These artifacts are much more powerful with the reflections to support them. The author of a portfolio may also simply identify an artifact, such as a resume or credential, without any further explanation other than the origin or date. It is best, however, to include the overall reflection and rationale for why those artifacts were selected for inclusion and how each adds texture to the author's professional profile.

Reflections require careful and serious thought and consideration. They are presented in written form in order to articulate or explain each artifact's purpose or value in the portfolio. Thus reflections, in a general sense, are a way of constructing meaning around past events for the purpose of informing actions in the present. Kay Burke (1997) further explains in her work, *Designing Professional Portfolios for Change,* that without reflections or written commentaries, the portfolio is no more than a scrapbook, with no insight into the criteria used to collect the artifacts. Kenneth Wolf and Mary Dietz (1998) go even further to emphasize the importance of reflections in their article, "Teaching Portfolios: Purposes and Possibilities," when they state,

> More than anything else, the portfolio process should inspire reflection—alone and in the company of others. . . . Reflective commentaries by the portfolio owner are essential companion pieces to artifacts. Writing reflections pushes teachers to more deeply examine their practice and allows others to examine the thinking behind the teaching documented in the portfolio. . . . With reflection, the portfolio can become an episode of learning. (p. 14)

REFLECTIONS AS GLUE: BONDING THE PORTFOLIO TO A PURPOSE

Hurst et al. (1998) refers to reflections as the glue bonding the portfolio to a specific purpose. Greenwood & Levin (2007) expand on this concept when they describe the purpose of inquiry as linking reflections and actions, making it a useful approach for the creation of new knowledge. Reflections fall into four different categories each with its own unique objective. These categories of reflections include

1. *intentions*—where the purpose of the artifact is revealed;
2. *planning*—where the processes, steps, or strategies used to plan for the completion of the artifact are explained;
3. *actions*—where the implementation and actual performance or artifact products are described; and
4. *outcomes*—where the results and consequences related to the artifact are shared.

Because there are numerous types of portfolios, including learning or working portfolios, assessment portfolios, and showcase or employment portfolios (see Chapter 1), reflections serve a vital role in identifying the different types (Dietz, 2008; Johnson et al., 2006; Hartnell-Young & Morriss, 1999; Mueller, 2008; Wilcox & Tomei, 1999; Wolf, 1999). Furthermore, reflections throughout the portfolio enable their potential use as a living history of a teaching-learning life, beyond assessment, learning, and professional development. In the next section, we describe examples of how portfolios are used in this manner. One of the major advantages of reflections and reflective inquiry is that they promote ownership of the learning process by guiding it through goal setting, focusing, and prioritizing possibilities (Coghlan & Brannick, 2004; Danielson & Abrulyn, 1997; Gathercoal, Love, Bryde, & McKean, 2002; Stone, 1998; Strijbos et al., 2007; Taggart & Wilson, 2005; Wolf, 1999).

TEN MAJOR WAYS REFLECTIONS TRANSFORM ARTIFACTS INTO EVIDENCE

Building on the concept of reflective inquiry as a foundation, Table 4.4 describes 10 related behaviors that further demonstrate the multifaceted nature of reflections. When

TABLE 4.4   Ten Major Ways Reflections Transform "Artifacts" Into "Evidence"

1. *Project* purposes of portfolio	Set clear goals and state them in reflections. *What purpose does the artifact serve? What does it say about me?*
2. *Collect* and organize artifacts with captions	Insert labels for the rationale of artifacts—giving them voice. *How do I identify each artifact? Its source? What does it say about my knowledge, skills, or dispositions?*
3. *Select* key artifacts	Prioritize and include rationale. *Why am I including these artifacts, and what purpose do they serve?*
4. *Interject* personality	Incorporate style and tone in reflections. *How can I personalize these artifacts to show my unique style?*
5. *Reflect* metacognitively	Insert formative statements. *How does this artifact reflect my growth and development?*
6. *Inspect* to self-assess	Draw conclusions and include more formative statements. *Does the artifact say what I want it to say about me?*
7. *Perfect* and evaluate	Refine selections and include evaluative statements. *What else could I say about this artifact that would give a better demonstration of my competence?*
8. *Inject or eject* to update	Maintain currency in reflections. *Is this the best example of my performance on the standard? If not, what could I replace it with?*
9. *Connect* and collaborate	Conduct meaningful dialogue with others through reflections. *Whom could I get more feedback from regarding my portfolio?*
10. *Respect* accomplishments	Celebrate, display, and incorporate summative statements. *What finishing touches can I add to help the portfolio speak for itself?*

Source: Adapted from Barrett (2001).

one systematically builds a professional portfolio in a developmental and cyclical manner, based on these questioning practices and behaviors, artifacts are slowly transformed into evidence. In this process, each artifact is supported with a clear rationale stating its purpose in the context of the entire portfolio or explaining how it fits into the big picture.

To recap, artifacts are linked to specific purposes and goals within the portfolio through reflections. Reflections serve to clarify the portfolio documents and make the thinking process explicit. Reflective inquiry questions guide the process of collecting artifacts and documenting their purpose. The following activity allows you to practice writing reflections and reflective statements.

LET'S PRACTICE!

Activity 4.4   Activities for Writing Reflections and Reflective Statements That Transform Artifacts Into Evidence

Review some of the assignments from your credential or degree program that you are considering as possible artifacts for your portfolio. You might begin by revisiting your exercises from the earlier chapters in this text, where you identified the credential program standards or learning targets, the courses in which each standard or learning target is emphasized, and the course requirements.

1. For each assignment, list the ways that they address the program standards. How does the assignment relate to the big picture? Use Table 4.4 as a guide. Answer the reflective questions as a means of transforming your artifacts into evidence.

2. Begin to categorize the assignments by linking them to a specific purpose. Where does the artifact fit into the action research cycle? Use Table 4.5 as a guide. If you don't have the actual assignments, you may simply list them on the template that follows.

3. Compile your answers to the questions as a way of beginning your reflections about the artifact. Complete only the categories that are appropriate for your artifact, taking into account that some questions or categories may not apply.

4. If possible, try to list at least one artifact for each standard or learning target in your credential program.

Planning Template for Transforming Artifacts Into Evidence

Title or Description of Artifact:_____

Standards
Addressed: _____

Step in Transformation	Guiding Questions	Sample Statements Describing Letters of Recommendation	Category
1. Project—Setting a purpose for the artifact	What purpose does the artifact serve, and what does it say about me?	"These are letters of recommendation I included as evidence of my prior experience as a camp counselor and tutor."	1: Goal setting
2. Collect—Organizing artifacts with captions or labels	What does this artifact say about my knowledge, skills, and dispositions? How should I label this artifact?	"These letters show my ability to work in a variety of settings with diverse student populations."	
3. Select—Choosing key artifacts, prioritizing	Why am I including this particular artifact over others? Why is it the best example of my competencies?	"The authors of these letters were significant mentors to me, and I incorporated many of their ideas into my work."	5: Monitoring own actions
4. Interject—Personality	How can I personalize this artifact so that it tells my story better and shows my unique style?	"I title this section of my portfolio 'My Hall of Fame.'"	
5. Reflect—Metacognitively, inserting formative statements	How does this artifact demonstrate my growth and development?	"I became a camp counselor to increase my expertise in working with troubled teens. This letter demonstrates my growth."	1: Goal setting and 5: Monitoring own actions

(Continued)

(Continued)

Step in Transformation	Guiding Questions	Sample Statements Describing Letters of Recommendation	Category
6. Inspect—To self-assess	Does this artifact say what I want it to say about me? What more can I say or include to give a clearer demonstration?	"I've also included a letter from one of my students to indicate how I supported him in the program."	7: Evaluating others
7. Perfect—And evaluate; include evaluative statements	What else could I say about this artifact that would give a better demonstration of my competence?		
8. Inject or Eject—To update; maintain currency in your reflections	Is this the best, most current example of my performance for this standard? If not, what could I replace it with? What else could I add for a more comprehensive demonstration?		
9. Connect—And collaborate with others	Who could I collaborate with to get more feedback about my artifacts and portfolio up to this point?	"I will ask my university supervisor for feedback."	9: Next steps
10. Respect—Accomplishments; incorporate summative statements	What finishing touches can I add to allow this artifact and the portfolio to speak on behalf of my accomplishments overall?	"These letters of recommendation reinforce my overall qualifications and accomplishments as a teacher, as verified by my professors and supervising teachers who are themselves leaders in the field."	

THE MULTIFACETED, CYCLICAL NATURE OF PORTFOLIO REFLECTION

To determine the value of reflection in the portfolio process, it is first important to examine the nature of reflection as a means of comprehending the types of roles that it can play. In this book, the term *reflections* refers to the process used to give voice to each artifact, and the term *reflective inquiry* refers to the action research process of using guiding questions in the collection and documentation of artifacts. Richard Schmuck (1997) discussed 10 categories of reflective practice among educators maturing in conducting action research. These categories are listed in Table 4.5.

TABLE 4.5   Ten Categories of Reflective Practice in Action Research

Category 1	Setting clear goals
Category 2	Assessing the situation
Category 3	Creating action strategies
Category 4	Implementing action strategies
Category 5	Monitoring one's own actions
Category 6	Assessing others' reactions
Category 7	Evaluating what others have learned
Category 8	Confronting oneself with the results
Category 9	Reflecting on what to do next
Category 10	Setting new goals

Source: Adapted from Schmuck (1997).

The categories of reflective practice coincide closely with the role reflections play in transforming artifacts into evidence by linking them with a purpose. Merging the two views of reflection and adding guiding questions to better direct the portfolio reflection process at each phase results in a framework for reflective inquiry in the portfolio process. Questions also reinforce the continuous need for reflection at multiple levels. Reflective inquiry in portfolio development is actually action research guided by reflections and inquiry questions on how to identify and organize the appropriate artifacts in a portfolio. It is demonstrated in Figure 4.1 and Table 4.6.

PATT (2000) offers a list of prompts, which can be used to guide students in formulating their reflections. These are summarized in Table 4.7.

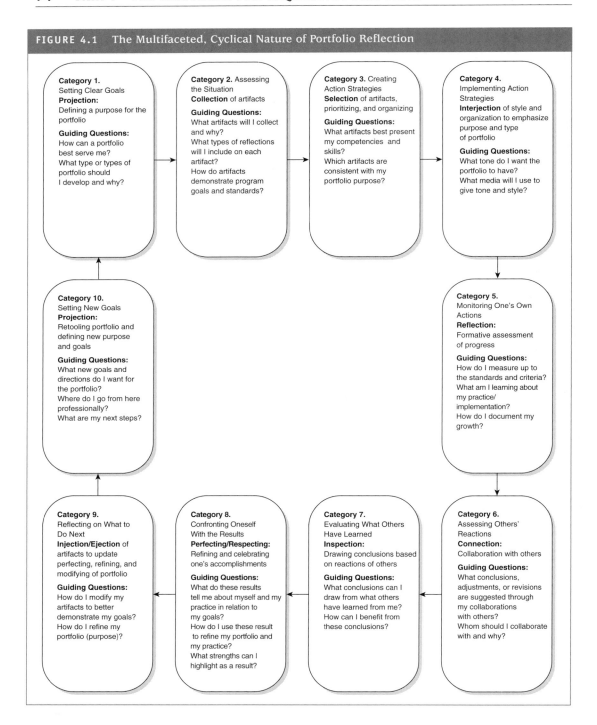

FIGURE 4.1   The Multifaceted, Cyclical Nature of Portfolio Reflection

Category 1.
Setting Clear Goals
Projection:
Defining a purpose for the portfolio

Guiding Questions:
How can a portfolio best serve me?
What type or types of portfolio should I develop and why?

Category 2. Assessing the Situation
Collection of artifacts

Guiding Questions:
What artifacts will I collect and why?
What types of reflections will I include on each artifact?
How do artifacts demonstrate program goals and standards?

Category 3. Creating Action Strategies
Selection of artifacts, prioritizing, and organizing

Guiding Questions:
What artifacts best present my competencies and skills?
Which artifacts are consistent with my portfolio purpose?

Category 4.
Implementing Action Strategies
Interjection of style and organization to emphasize purpose and type of portfolio

Guiding Questions:
What tone do I want the portfolio to have?
What media will I use to give tone and style?

Category 10.
Setting New Goals
Projection:
Retooling portfolio and defining new purpose and goals

Guiding Questions:
What new goals and directions do I want for the portfolio?
Where do I go from here professionally?
What are my next steps?

Category 5.
Monitoring One's Own Actions
Reflection:
Formative assessment of progress

Guiding Questions:
How do I measure up to the standards and criteria?
What am I learning about my practice/implementation?
How do I document my growth?

Category 9.
Reflecting on What to Do Next
Injection/Ejection of artifacts to update perfecting, refining, and modifying of portfolio

Guiding Questions:
How do I modify my artifacts to better demonstrate my goals?
How do I refine my portfolio (purpose)?

Category 8.
Confronting Oneself With the Results
Perfecting/Respecting:
Refining and celebrating one's accomplishments

Guiding Questions:
What do these results tell me about myself and my practice in relation to my goals?
How do I use these result to refine my portfolio and my practice?
What strengths can I highlight as a result?

Category 7.
Evaluating What Others Have Learned
Inspection:
Drawing conclusions based on reactions of others

Guiding Questions:
What conclusions can I draw from what others have learned from me?
How can I benefit from these conclusions?

Category 6.
Assessing Others' Reactions
Connection:
Collaboration with others

Guiding Questions:
What conclusions, adjustments, or revisions are suggested through my collaborations with others?
Whom should I collaborate with and why?

TABLE 4.6   The Multifaceted, Cyclical Nature of Portfolio Reflection

Category 1. Setting clear goals Project: Define a purpose for the portfolio.	Guiding questions: How can a portfolio best serve me? What types of portfolios should I develop and why?
Category 2. Assessing the situation Collect artifacts.	Guiding questions: What artifacts will I collect and why? What types of reflections will I include on each artifact? How do artifacts demonstrate program goals and standards?
Category 3. Creating action strategies Select artifacts, prioritize and organize.	Guiding questions: What artifacts best present my competencies and skills? Which artifacts are consistent with my portfolio purpose?
Category 4. Implementing action strategies Interject style and organization to emphasize purpose and type of portfolio.	Guiding questions: What tone do I want the portfolio to have? What media will I use to give tone and style?
Category 5. Monitoring one's own actions Reflect: Make formative assessment of progress.	Guiding questions: How do I measure up to the standards and criteria? What am I learning about my practice and implementation? How do I document my growth?
Category 6. Assessing others' reactions Connection: Collaborate with others.	Guiding questions: What conclusions, adjustments, or revisions are suggested through my collaborations with others? Who should I collaborate with and why?
Category 7. Evaluating what others have learned Inspect: Draw conclusions based on the reactions of others.	Guiding questions: What conclusions can I draw from what others have learned from me? How can I benefit from these conclusions?
Category 8. Confronting oneself with the results Perfect and respect: Refine and celebrate one's accomplishments.	Guiding questions: What do these results tell me about myself and my practice in relation to my goals? How do I use these results to refine my portfolio and my practice? What strengths can I highlight as a result?
Category 9. Reflecting on what to do next Inject or eject artifacts to update perfection, refinement, and modification of portfolio.	Guiding questions: How do I modify my artifacts to better demonstrate my goals? How do I refine my portfolio?
Category 10. Setting new goals Project: Retool portfolio and define new purpose and goals.	Guiding questions: What new goals and directions do I want for the portfolio? Where do I go from here professionally? What are my next steps?

Source: Reflective terms adapted from Barrett (2001).

TABLE 4.7 Prompts for Candidates' Self-Reflection

1. Reflection
   - I have chosen to include this work sample because . . .
   - If I did this assignment over, I would . . . because . . .
   - Completing this portfolio reflection has helped me increase my knowledge and understanding
     of . . . because . . .

2. Collaboration (for a group activity)
   - My role in the activity was . . .
   - I would give the group a grade of . . . for the activity because . . .
   - I would give myself a grade of . . . because . . .
   - I might change the way the group worked together because . . .

3. Understanding
   - I now know . . . about the topic that I didn't know before.
   - A summary of the information about the topic in this work entry would be . . .
   - Examples of accurate information and ideas about this work entry would be . . .
   - Examples of the connections among different ideas in this work entry would be . . .
   - Examples of the patterns and trends discussed in this work entry would be . . .

4. Inquiry
   - The next step of problem solving I would do is . . . because . . .
   - If I could do more research, study, experimentation (circle one) about this entry, I would choose to . . . because . . .
   - Other questions about this topic that have occurred to me are . . .

5. Communication
   - I focused and organized the information in this work entry in the following ways: . . .
   - I expressed the information in this work entry clearly by . . .

6. Personal Relevance
   - What I liked most (least) about this topic was . . . because . . .
   - I can apply this knowledge or understanding in my daily life by . . .
   - I can apply this knowledge or understanding to the controversies or issues of . . . because . . .
   - This topic is interesting to me because . . .
   - I explained how this topic is connected to other topics in these ways: . . .
   - I explained the different choices people have about this topic in these ways: . . .

Source: Adapted from PATT (2000).

SCHEDULING REFLECTIONS IN THE PORTFOLIO PROCESS

Reflections become more meaningful and manageable when they are scheduled and integrated into the entire portfolio process. One way to schedule reflections is to include them as part of assignments or regular course activities. For example, students can be asked to add a reflection after they have completed an assignment, to be considered when grading that assignment. They can also write goal statements at the beginning of a course or program or conclude their work with a course or program reflection statement. Students can be asked to provide weekly formative reflections on their activities or to prepare an executive summary of the entire portfolio at the completion of the portfolio process. Chapter 5 offers a time line that elaborates on scheduling intervals for including and updating portfolio reflections. Tables 4.8 and 4.9 give samples of prompts that can be used for weekly course reflections and end-of-course reflections. The actual scheduling of reflections is left largely up to the instructors' and students' discretion. If you are a student enrolled in a course that requires a portfolio or portfolios but has no specific reflection schedule, consider using the foregoing suggestions to develop one for yourself.

TABLE 4.8   Sample Prompts for Weekly Course Reflections

In writing your reflections, you may want to consider some or all of the suggestions that follow. You are by no means limited to these items. Please expand on these suggestions or include other thoughts and comments.

1. What has changed for you?
   - Perceptions—changed or reinforced
   - Deeper learning
   - New quandaries

2. What were this week's most powerful learning experiences?

3. Have your perceptions changed in any way?

4. What areas will you continue to develop?

5. Will you revise your vision as a result of something you learned or experienced? How?

TABLE 4.9   Sample Prompts for End-of-Course Reflections

In writing your reflections, you may want to consider some or all of the suggestions that follow. You are by no means limited to these items. Please expand on these suggestions or include other thoughts and comments. It would be helpful for you to reflect on your assignments and to review the course outline and your weekly reflections to refresh your memory about some of the topics covered in earlier class sessions.

1. What has changed for you?
   - Perceptions—changed or reinforced
   - Deeper learning
   - New quandaries

2. What were some of the most powerful learning experiences?

3. Have your perceptions about teaching (leadership, counseling) changed in any way?

4. What areas will you continue to develop?

5. Will you revise your vision as a result of this course? How?

LEVELS OF REFLECTION IN
THE PORTFOLIO PROCESS: A SAMPLE RUBRIC

How does one measure levels of reflection in portfolio development? How much reflection should be included, and how do reflections influence the overall effectiveness of the portfolio? Questions such as these are common both to students who are developing their own professional portfolios and to instructors who are guiding them through the process.

Whether one is preparing a traditional, two-dimensional portfolio or a multidimensional electronic portfolio (described in Chapters 8 and 9), lack of reflections has the same debilitating impact, rendering the portfolio ineffective and ambiguous. Table 4.10, adapted from Barrett (2001), serves as a type of scoring rubric for students and evaluators of professional portfolios to indicate how reflections can be used to strengthen and clarify the purpose of the portfolio. The table shows levels of reflection and sample artifacts by including a range from Level 0, where little or no reflection is included, to Level 5, where extensive reflection is incorporated throughout.

Portfolios at Level 0 include no reflections and are viewed as highly ineffective scrapbooks.

Portfolios at Level 1 include only an introductory reflection that states the purpose of the portfolio or a summative reflection at the end of the portfolio. These could be general statements about the overall portfolio process or summary statements about the cumulative nature of the artifacts.

At Level 2, along with an overall portfolio reflection, curriculum standards and portfolio goals are indicated. In this way, the artifacts provide evidence of meeting standards or accomplishing goals. These types of reflections would be vital in assessment and learning portfolios to measure growth and accomplishments toward those goals.

Building upon Level 2, Level 3 reflections could include explanations of how the standards or goals were met, strategies used to accomplish these goals, and what was learned through the process. In addition, Level 3 reflections indicate future goals and projections for education, professional development, or career advancement. These types of reflections are valuable in all three types of portfolios, whether learning–working portfolios, assessment portfolios, or showcase–employment portfolios.

Level 4 contains additional reflections for each artifact, explaining its purpose and reason for inclusion. An example would be an award from a particular service organization, such as the Rotary Club, commending the student for creating a "Grandparents & Books" program at various community centers. In the reflection, the student could indicate goals and standards that were met that resulted in the award, but the student may also include pictures of other national and international community events, demonstrating an ongoing commitment to service learning and community outreach through the reflections on these artifacts.

Level 5 relies on the addition of connecting statements that give evidence of collaborative reflections gathered through sharing the portfolio with a variety of audiences. These types of reflections provide the strongest evidence of the portfolio's use in the context of a learning community. The process thus incorporates feedback from multiple sources to strengthen the portfolio and support the student's professional development. Another asset

TABLE 4.10 Levels of Reflection and Reflective Inquiry in the Portfolio Process

Level 0	Level 1	Level 2	Level 3	Level 4	Level 5
• Little or no reflection or mention of standards or goals • A collection of artifacts, a scrapbook, or multimedia presentation	• Simple overall reflection on the portfolio as a whole • A general summative statement	• Level 1, plus • Standards or portfolio goals	• Level 2, plus • Reflections on achieving each standard or goal, plus • Future directions (learning goals)	• Level 3, plus • Reflections on role of each artifact in the portfolio	• Level 4, plus • Feedback from portfolio conferencing and responses from others • Self-evaluation of portfolio
Sample artifact: • Pictures	Sample artifact: • Course portfolio	Sample artifact: • Parent letter to demonstrate INTASC Standard 10 (Community Involvement)	Sample artifacts: • Parent letters • Sample assignments with home links for parents • Sample student work • Sample parent survey • Sample parent resources included with letter	Sample artifacts: • Opening statement explaining the purpose of the portfolio • Opening statement for each section of portfolio, briefly listing its contents	Sample artifacts: • Letter from university supervisor, supporting completed portfolio rubric

(Continued)

TABLE 4.10 (Continued)

Level 0	Level 1	Level 2	Level 3	Level 4	Level 5
Sample reflection: None	Sample reflection: "I completed this portfolio at the end of my first field assignment as part of the course requirement."	Sample reflection: "This is a sample of a parent letter I developed to keep the parents informed about our class activities. I would send these out at the beginning of the year and at the beginning of each new unit. They encouraged parent participation and showed parents ways of getting involved. It demonstrated INTASC Principle 10, Community Involvement."	Sample reflection: "I plan to use a variety of letters and home links in my lessons to ensure ongoing parental involvement. I will also survey my parents for additional feedback. Here is a sample of a parent survey I use at the beginning of the year. It helps me modify lessons based on parent feedback.	Sample reflection: "This is my Directed Teaching Portfolio, which was compiled to provide evidence of my successful completion of the program requirements, including the INTASC standards. This portfolio is organized according to each INTASC standard. Items in each section provide evidence of my fulfillment of the standard in a variety of ways."	Sample Reflection: "I have included this final portfolio checklist and evaluation from my University supervisor after our last portfolio conference. It shows the rubric that was used in the evaluation process. I believe my careful organization of the portfolio in telling my story helped it to receive the outstanding score it did."

Source: Adapted from Barrett (2001).

80

to Level 5 reflections is the self-evaluation statement from the student. This indicates what has been learned through the portfolio process and how the student has benefited. Level 5 portfolio reflections thus incorporate all of the types and aspects of reflections and reflective inquiry, and we therefore view them as the most effective and advantageous type. Reflections at Level 5 are also beneficial and appropriate for inclusion in all three types of portfolios, as they provide comprehensive information about the artifacts and their overall role in the portfolio. These reflections offer the student the greatest flexibility in retooling and refining the portfolio for future purposes.

OUTCOMES AND BENEFITS OF REFLECTION AND REFLECTIVE INQUIRY

In this final section, we return to our original questions: What is the value of reflection and reflective inquiry in the portfolio process? Why include reflections? Are these really necessary? The primary outcome of reflective inquiry in portfolio development is an awareness of our choices and consequences, enabling us to make the best choices possible for a particular situation. Reflection allows us to pause and step away from our activity to explore options before taking action. These pauses, which result from recording and reflecting on lessons learned, achievements, and successes, further promote professional renewal through the process of mapping new goals and planning for future growth (Campus Compact, 2001; Mueller, 2008). Such benefits exist for both students and program instructors. Just as students can see how they have progressed systematically toward their goals, program instructors can determine what students are learning from their program and whether program goals are being met. Another benefit is that reflections establish an ongoing dialogue between students and instructors, particularly when they include Level 5 reflections. The next activity prompts you to practice writing structured reflections on earlier assignments.

LET'S PRACTICE!

Activity 4.5   Activities for Writing Structured Reflections on Past Assignments

Learning to Reflect; Guiding Reflections (Adapted from Stiggins, 2008)
   Select some artifacts or assignments that you are considering for your portfolio, particularly those that do not already contain reflections. Use the following prompts to write reflections to accompany the artifacts when you place them in your portfolio.

- For each artifact or assignment representing a process (i.e., case study, research report, designing a workshop for paraprofessionals, evaluating a school site plan), describe the steps you went through to complete the assignment. Tell whether or not the process you used was effective in helping you complete the assignment. Explain any changes you would make for a similar future assignment and why.

(Continued)

(Continued)

- Select a project or an assignment where you have received feedback. Describe whether or not the feedback was helpful to you in completing the project or refining your work. Describe your response to the feedback offered—did you agree or disagree with it? Why? What was the overall outcome of the feedback you received?
- Select an assignment or artifact that you are especially proud of and that represents one of your most effective examples of performance. What are the strengths of your work on this assignment or project? What do you feel the most proud of with this assignment and why?
- Select another assignment that would represent one of your least effective demonstrations of performance. In this assignment, what areas still need more work? What kind of help or assistance is needed? Where might you get help?
- What makes your most effective work different from your least effective work? What does your best work tell you about where you have improved and where you need further guidance or support?
- Think of an assignment or project that has impacted you in some way. What impact has the assignment had on your interests, beliefs, and attitudes and in what areas?

SUMMARY

Reflections and reflective inquiry are important in the portfolio process, setting a foundation for the portfolio and aligning it to a specific purpose. Reflective inquiry enables students to have a clearer understanding of how the course activities align with the program standards and course outcomes. These activities can later become critical artifacts in the students' portfolios. Reflections are the products used to give voice to each artifact, and reflective inquiry is the action research process of using guiding questions in the collection and documentation of artifacts. A variety of strategies produce useful, structured reflections that help shape the portfolio and make it a more effective tool for professional growth and planning.

USEFUL RESOURCES

Authentic Assessment Toolbox (http://jonathan.mueller.faculty.noctrl.edu/toolbox/rubrics.htm)

Mueller, J. (2008). Web site resources retrieved on August 24, 2008.

Coaches Plus Learning Community (http://www.coachesplus.com/articles/20080502_1/print?printview = pdf)

Adamson, F. (2008). Supervision as reflective inquiry. Retrieved September 3, 2008.

Online Article (http://www.sedl.org/pubs/change34)

Hord, S. (1997). *Professional learning communities: Communities of continuous inquiry and reflection.* Austin, TX: Southwest Educational Development Laboratory. Retrieved September 3, 2008.

School Change Toolkit (http://www.mcrel.org/toolkit/res/reflect.asp)

Mid-Continental Research for Education and Learning. (2008). *Asking the right questions: A school change toolkit.* (Sponsored by the U.S. Department of Education.) Retrieved September 3, 2008.

Writing Reflections (http://arccas.tripod.com/id32.html)

ARC CAS. (2008). Retrieved September 3, 2008.

FOR FURTHER READING

Campbell, V. M., Cignetti, P. B., Melenyzer, B. J., Nettles, D. H., & Wyman, R. M., Jr. (2004). *How to develop a professional portfolio: A manual for teachers* (3rd ed.). Boston: Allyn & Bacon.

Dietz, M. E. (2008). *Designing the school leader's portfolio* (2nd ed.). Thousand Oaks, Thousand Oaks, CA: Sage.

Rieman, P. (2000). *Teaching portfolios: Presenting your professional best.* Boston: McGraw-Hill.

Taggart, G. L., & Wilson, A. P. (2005). *Promoting reflective thinking in teachers: 50 action research strategies* (2nd ed.). Thousand Oaks, CA: Sage.

Tang, Y., & Joiner, C. (Eds.). (2006). *Synergic inquiry: A collaborative action methodology.* Thousand Oaks, CA: Sage.

For specific information related to this concept, see the Chapter 4 resources on the CD.

Additional rubrics for assessing and evaluating portfolios are provided on the CD.

PART II

A Guide for Developing Portfolios

Your Portfolio Journey

*Ten Steps for Organizing, Managing,
and Completing the Process*

*Developing a portfolio is a process that is personally challenging and, as a result, can lead
to enormous personal growth. The journey or process of putting together the portfolio is
just as important as the end product.*

—Hartnell-Young and Morriss (2007, p. 40)

CHAPTER OBJECTIVES

Readers will be able to

❑ outline 10 steps for implementing the
portfolio process,

❑ describe the major phases for organizing and
managing the portfolio process,

❑ set time lines and benchmarks in the
portfolio process,

❑ use standards and performance assessment
in portfolio evaluation and scoring, and

❑ explain potential pitfalls of the portfolio
process and how to address them

SCENARIO

It was easy to hear the frustration in Marga's voice as she shared her reflections on the portfolio process during her final presentation session as a teaching credential candidate at Sunshine University. She began, "In the end, I could see that the portfolio was a good thing, but it bothered me that I really could not see it as a good thing until the very end of our program, and . . . then it was too late!" Marga continued, "We heard only a few comments about needing a portfolio at the beginning of the program, during the Introduction to Teaching course, and then again at the very end, when we were supposed to turn it in. Most of our professors said nothing about it or about which assignments would make good artifacts. Had I known then what I know now, it would have been so much easier to build my portfolio because I would have saved more items from the courses and the program. At first, I did not understand how the assignments were related to the standards. I knew about the K–12 subject matter standards we were supposed to be teaching our elementary and secondary students, but little was said about the teaching standards and how the courses were helping us to meet them. It did not come together for me until the student teaching seminar, when we were given a full outline of the teaching standards and the recommended portfolio table of contents. It all finally started to make sense. It would have been nice to hear about the portfolio from each of our professors, and how their assignments addressed the various standards. Now I can see that the courses did address the standards, but that was not always made clear to us."

Several other students chimed in and nodded heads in agreement. "I threw away so much stuff once the class was over and I got the grade," commented Julio, another student. "Now that I look at the standards, I realize that it wasn't always the final grade in the class but the process I went through that was most important. The portfolio helps you identify and articulate that process. It's really hard to go back and collect or re-create those pieces at the end! I think it would have helped if our professors had talked to each other about the process and if each had mentioned the portfolio as it related to each course and the overall credential program. That would be a big support for the students!"

"You took the words right out of my mouth," declared Larry, another student. "What helped me prepare my portfolio was my master teacher sharing her portfolio from her credential program with me. She shared that each of her professors had discussed and used a portfolio development process throughout the program. I believe that our professors also need to talk to each other and agree on the guidelines for what artifacts to include and how they will be evaluated."

Dr. Young, the instructor for the Student Teaching Seminar and the final portfolio presentation session, shared these comments from students with the credential program chair and the education dean later that afternoon. As a result of the comments from Dr. Young and other education faculty at Sunshine University who had had similar experiences, portfolio guidelines were added to each course, along with suggestions for which assignments to include and how those assignments addressed specific teaching standards. Dialogues also began among all faculty members in the credential program regarding new strategies they could incorporate to support the students throughout the portfolio process.

OVERVIEW

As the scenario demonstrates, the portfolio is not simply a collection of artifacts to be turned in at the completion of a program, but rather a dynamic process of planning, reflecting, collecting, and evaluating that occurs throughout the entire program and, ideally, extends throughout one's career. The purpose of this chapter is to lay out 10 steps or phases for making the portfolio process meaningful, rewarding, and informative.

We use the term *phase* to indicate that there is overlap between the various steps, and many of the phases can take place simultaneously. Figure 5.1 lists each of the 10 phases, which will be described in more detail throughout the chapter. We begin with a brief description of the major phases and describe how they can be used as steps to guide the portfolio journey. We then explore potential pitfalls in the portfolio process and ways to avoid them. We continue with recommendations for setting up time lines and benchmarks to help with time management. Next, evaluation and scoring are discussed and practiced. We conclude the chapter with strategies for promoting continual renewal and evaluation through the use of portfolios.

THE MAJOR PHASES OF PORTFOLIO ORGANIZATION

Barrett (2001) identified five major phases of portfolio development. These include (1) collection of a wide variety of artifacts, (2) projection of a purpose for the portfolio, (3) selection of artifacts for a specific portfolio purpose, (4) reflection on the value and role of each artifact, and (5) presentation of the portfolio. These phases are explained in Table 5.1, where each phase leads to a new cycle of refining and modifying the portfolio.

Table 5.1 is a modification of Barrett's (2001) original table, with the inclusion of *projection* as a beginning phase in the process and inspection for self-assessment as a fifth phase. This reinforces the vital roles of having a vision, setting goals, planning, reflection, and assessment throughout the portfolio process. It also emphasizes the cyclical nature of portfolio development, in that each phase supports and helps to define the next. It is important to begin the process with projection and to keep projection as a major step that one returns to throughout the portfolio process as new goals and purposes are identified.

Step 1: Project a purpose and have a vision for the portfolio: Begin with the end in mind.

Before even starting to collect artifacts, it is imperative to begin with the end in mind (Covey, 1990). Having a clear purpose or goal helps to clarify the process. For the first step, students must project a *general purpose* for their portfolios and describe how they envision the portfolio process will serve them, recognizing the multiple purposes that portfolios can serve, as stated in Chapter 1. Having a vision for the portfolio encourages students to explore a broad range of ideas for sharing their knowledge, skills, and attitudes or beliefs. It also places them in the active role of laying out goals and objectives and making plans on how to accomplish their goals. In essence, having a vision motivates students to take action.

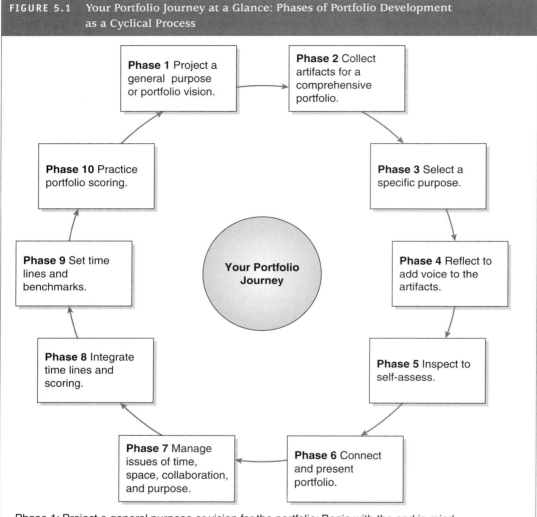

FIGURE 5.1   Your Portfolio Journey at a Glance: Phases of Portfolio Development as a Cyclical Process

Phase 1: Project a general purpose or vision for the portfolio: Begin with the end in mind.
Phase 2: Collect artifacts: Build a comprehensive portfolio.
Phase 3: Select a specific purpose for the portfolio and establish learning targets for artifacts.
Phase 4: Reflect: Add reflections to the artifacts to communicate their specific purposes.
Phase 5: Inspect to self-assess: Assess the value of each artifact and project future goals.
Phase 6: Connect and present portfolio: Collaborate with others for feedback and goal setting.
Phase 7: Manage issues of time, space, collaboration, and purpose.
Phase 8: Integrate time lines and scoring into the portfolio process.
Phase 9: Set time lines and benchmarks at regular intervals.
Phase 10: Practice scoring the portfolio: Become familiar with rubrics and scoring criteria.

For the second and subsequent times going through the cycle, refine your portfolio selections based on new portfolio goals and purposes resulting from assessment and evaluation of your earlier goals. Continue to add to your comprehensive portfolio as an ongoing process.

TABLE 5.1   Phases of the Portfolio Development Process

Projection	Students write a vision that describes their future goals and intentions. Students decide on the purposes for the portfolio (e.g., formative assessment, summative evaluation, or marketing). The desired focus for the portfolio is set. Preliminary planning begins for addressing time, space, and human issues.
Collection (General, for comprehensive portfolio or personal archive)	Students save artifacts that represent a wide variety of accomplishments, achievement of specific learning targets, and growth opportunities. This leads to numerous possibilities and choices for portfolio development.
Selection	Students review and evaluate the artifacts they have saved, and they identify those that best demonstrate achievement of specific standards or learning targets. The selection criteria should reflect the learning objectives of the portfolio.
Reflection	Students explain their thinking about each piece in their portfolios, evaluating their own growth over time and their achievement of the standards. It is recommended to include reflections on each piece, plus an overall reflection on the entire portfolio.
Inspection for self-assessment and projection	Students compare their reflections with the standards and performance indicators and set future learning goals. This phase transforms portfolio development into professional development.
Connection and presentation	Students share portfolios with the appropriate audience, including their peers and supervisors, and collaborate on the contents, process, and purpose of portfolios. The feedback at this stage can lead to public commitments of professional development and future goal setting.

Source: Adapted from Barrett (2001).

LET'S PRACTICE!

Activity 5.1   Forging a Vision for Your Portfolio

Take a few moments to brainstorm the many ways a portfolio could serve you. Look back at Chapter 1 and consider the many purposes that portfolios serve. Answer the following questions:

- What types of portfolios could help you in telling your story now and in the future?
- In what ways will you use the portfolio?
- What benefits would you like to experience as a result of having a portfolio?

At this point, we are casting a broad net for looking at possibilities for multiple portfolios, rather than limiting the portfolio to only one objective. Write down your ideas. What is your vision for your portfolio?

Step 2: Build a comprehensive portfolio or personal archive.

Closely aligned with setting a purpose, Step 2 involves building a comprehensive portfolio. The purpose of the comprehensive portfolio is to establish a personal archive for a variety of artifacts. The comprehensive portfolio is the initial building block for all subsequent portfolios. It is a reservoir of resources for presenting any number of stories to demonstrate your knowledge, skills, and beliefs. (We began this process in Chapter 2 with Activity 2.1, and an expanded description is in Chapter 10.) To facilitate this process, it is important to have a systematic way of organizing artifacts for easy access. Some general categories of artifacts include program documents, letters, candidate documents, field experiences, and assignments. (Additional ideas for organizing artifacts are presented in Chapter 6, and Table 6.11 presents some general categories for beginning to collect and organize artifacts for the comprehensive portfolio.) Such a system of preliminary organization will help in selecting artifacts for the later portfolios you develop. Figure 5.2 illustrates the role of the comprehensive portfolio in relation to the later categories of portfolios that can be developed, demonstrating how the comprehensive portfolio serves as the source for a variety of other portfolios, each with a specific purpose.

Step 3: Select a specific portfolio purpose with learning targets or standards and identify artifacts that match that purpose.

At this point, students select a specific purpose for their portfolios, and they become very selective in the artifacts they choose to fit that purpose. Since portfolios are used more and

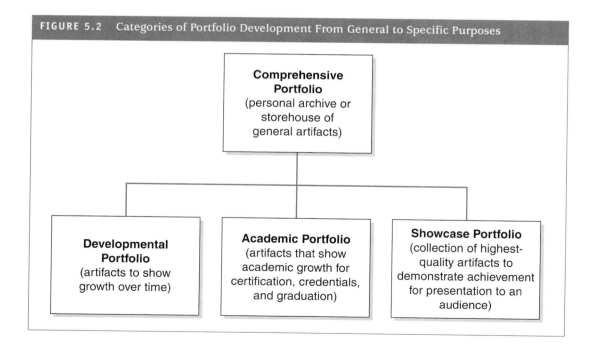

FIGURE 5.2   Categories of Portfolio Development From General to Specific Purposes

Comprehensive Portfolio
(personal archive or storehouse of general artifacts)

Developmental Portfolio
(artifacts to show growth over time)

Academic Portfolio
(artifacts that show academic growth for certification, credentials, and graduation)

Showcase Portfolio
(collection of highest-quality artifacts to demonstrate achievement for presentation to an audience)

more to make judgments or decisions (Hartnell-Young & Morriss, 2007; Mueller, 2008), it is important to clearly communicate the specific purpose at the very beginning of the portfolio as an introduction or executive summary. (Guidelines for writing portfolio introductions and executive summaries, along with samples, are included in Chapter 6 and on the CD.) For instance, if an achievement portfolio is desired for purposes of demonstrating completion of credential competencies, only artifacts would be selected that provide evidence of the credential standards or competencies. Likewise, if a showcase portfolio were desired for career advancement and job interviews, only artifacts would be selected that showcase the highest quality of performance aligned with the desired job requirements and qualifications. Students review and evaluate the artifacts they have saved and identify those that best demonstrate achievement of specific standards or learning targets. The selection criteria for artifacts should reflect the learning objectives of the specific portfolio. Remember, the same portfolio can be retooled to address a different purpose simply by changing the types of artifacts that are included and how these artifacts meet the learning targets.

For specific information related to this concept, see the Chapter 5 resources on the CD.

Step 4: Reflect on the value and role of each artifact and add reflections to communicate its purpose.

As emphasized in Chapter 4, reflections are the voice of the portfolio. Through reflections, students explain their thinking about each piece in their portfolio, evaluating their own growth over time and their achievement of the standards. According to Wolf and Dietz (1998) and Coghlan and Brannick (2004), reflections reveal episodes of learning and are essential companions to artifacts. Reflections go beyond simply describing the artifacts and their purpose, to examining the knowledge, skills, and attitudes of the portfolio designer, as well as his or her values and goals. We strongly recommend including reflections on each artifact or categories of artifacts, in addition to an overall reflection on the entire portfolio.

Step 5: Inspect artifacts to self-assess or ensure that they provide the strongest evidence of competencies and project future goals.

A natural follow-up to reflection is self-assessment, where one steps away from the portfolio process to analyze what is going well and why and what can still be improved upon in terms of artifacts and reflections (Montgomery & Wiley, 2008). Chapter 3 emphasized the importance of assessment and evaluation in the portfolio process. It also discussed using the portfolio as a tool to measure one's own growth and development. For Step 5, the artifacts are inspected to determine if they are serving the desired purpose in the portfolio. In this step, one conducts a self-assessment and modifies what is included in the portfolio to provide only the strongest evidence of the portfolio goals. One compares the reflections with the standards and performance indicators and sets future learning goals. This phase transforms portfolio development into professional development. Step 5 entails another level of projection or goal setting, where the earlier goals are reassessed and future goals are set. This phase of portfolio development fosters self-assessment skills through the cycle of inquiry into artifact selection and writing reflections on artifacts to document achievement of specific learning targets. It provides a mirror for viewing one's development in a variety of areas. Artifacts are also inspected to see that they provide a comprehensive and balanced profile of one's knowledge, skills, and attitudes. (In Chapter 6, we discuss more about the specific types of artifacts for each of the learning domains, including knowledge, skills, and dispositions or attitudes.)

Step 6: Connect with others to present the portfolio for assessment and evaluation.

For Step 6, students share portfolios with an appropriate audience, including their peers, instructors, and supervisors, and collaborate on the contents, process, and purpose of their portfolios. It is helpful to schedule several formative assessments of the portfolio while it is still in the developmental process, where students can receive feedback on how they may improve it. This goes back to Chapter 2, which described first-person, second-person, and third-person modes of action research that are designed for different audiences. To briefly review, in first-person mode, only the individual is the audience. In second-person mode, both the individual and a collaborative peer partner are involved. At the third-person mode, an entire community is involved. When portfolios are developed as a collaborative process, there may be many times for sharing the portfolio and receiving formative feedback and suggestions. This can be done in both the second-person and third-person modes. Many portfolio checkpoints can be set up along the way, where students become informed on the scoring and evaluation of the portfolio and are active participants in the process. When it is not collaborative, the portfolio may only be reviewed by instructors and supervisors, who also can provide vital feedback on what is going well in the portfolio development and how to improve it overall. The feedback at this stage can lead to public commitments of professional development and future goal setting. At other times, the portfolio may be shared only as a final product for informational or evaluation purposes. There are many scenarios for how and when a portfolio should be shared with different audiences (McNiff & Whitehead, 2006; Montgomery & Wiley, 2008; Mueller, 2008). These include opportunities to show growth, showcase excellence, celebrate a personal story, seek advice, document the steps in a long-term project, self-assess, plan new goals, and others. (More ideas are shared in Chapter 7 regarding ways to present the portfolio for different purposes and audiences and how to prepare for the **portfolio presentation**.)

Step 7: Manage issues of time, space, collaboration, and purpose.

One of the most challenging aspects for all participants involved in the portfolio process is managing the time and space it takes to develop a quality portfolio. Along with the previously mentioned steps, having a plan and a roadmap for the organization and management of time and space will make the journey easier. Forgette-Giroux and Simon (2000) suggest that the portfolio process involves four types of organizational issues, namely,

1. temporal or time issues,
2. spatial or issues of space,
3. human or collaborative issues, and
4. contextual or issues of purpose.

Temporal issues concern time spent on planning and scheduling portfolio assessment activities. *Spatial issues* deal with organizing the portfolio's format, design, and physical characteristics, including storage and access. *Human issues* include personal responsibilities, such as establishing and updating a table of contents, dating and sorting portfolio entries, writing reflections, and collaborating with others about the process. Last, *contextual aspects* have to do with specifying the purpose or objective of assessment and identifying the standards or appropriate learning targets.

Table 5.2 presents some questions to keep in mind at each phase of the portfolio process that address issues of time, space, collaboration, and purpose. These types of questions provide important guidance to students to maintain a comprehensive view of the portfolio and who needs to be involved; what should be done; and when, where, and how the process will take place.

Step 8: Address potential pitfalls by integrating time lines and scoring into the portfolio process.

Two potential pitfalls of the portfolio process are (1) time management, as previously mentioned, and (2) portfolio scoring. Both can be effectively addressed if they are integrated into the process as fundamental steps that are developed and communicated during the early planning stages. Portfolio time lines and scoring should also be revisited and modified at regular intervals throughout the process, based on feedback from instructors, supervisors, and students. The following section lays out specific recommendations for taking a proactive approach to time management and the scoring of portfolios. Table 5.3 presents additional portfolio management ideas. Table 5.4 introduces additional tips for keeping a portfolio.

Step 9: Set time lines and benchmarks at regular intervals.

Time management has been emphasized as one of the most critical elements in portfolio implementation (Barrett, 2001; Campbell et al., 2004; PATT, 2000). Establishing time lines with clearly defined **benchmarks** allows both students and instructors to schedule activities and pace themselves to complete the portfolio in a timely manner. The challenge is to identify relevant activities scheduled at appropriate intervals of time.

In specific programs, such as those leading to a teaching, administrative, or counseling credential, important times relevant to portfolio building come at the beginning, midway, and end of the program. There are also natural breaks, usually marked by semesters, quarters, or courses.

A sample time line is presented in Table 5.5, which identifies portfolio benchmarks that correspond to a candidate's time in a program. It has five suggested checkpoints that are appropriate for programs lasting a year or less. Note that these are only general indicators of the types of activities that facilitate pacing of the portfolio process. (Other sample time lines are available on the CD.)

There should be a continual process for verification of completion of competencies throughout the program. This documentation will be critical for summative evaluations. Each candidate will need to keep a record of the certification of competencies. Programs should develop a template or checklist for students to use. It is also recommended that students continue to reflect on their portfolios even after the completion of their programs

For specif
informati
related to
this
concept,
see the
Chapter 5
resources
on the CI

TABLE 5.2 Questions for Each Phase of Portfolio Development

Projection	*Contextual (Purpose)* • What purposes do I want the portfolio to serve? • What competencies do I want or need to demonstrate, and what criteria will I use to assess them? *Temporal (Time)* • What is a reasonable amount of time to allow for this process? *Spatial (Space)* • What form is best for storage and retrieval of artifacts? • What strategies can be used for managing and organizing artifacts and reflections? *Human (Collaborative)* • Who should be involved in the process, and how and when should they become involved?
Collection	*Contextual* • What artifacts represent achievement of specific standards and growth opportunities? • How do I reference each artifact (e.g., labels, reflections)? *Temporal* • When do I begin to collect, and for how long should I collect? *Spatial* • What form is best for storage and retrieval of artifacts? *Human* • Who should be involved in the collection of artifacts? • Who can support in the collection of artifacts and in what ways?
Selection	*Contextual* • What artifacts best represent achievement of specific standards and growth opportunities? *Temporal* • When do I begin to refine my selections, and for how long? *Spatial* • What form is best for ranking and separating artifacts during storage and retrieval (e.g., manila folders, color coding, file cabinet, sticky notes, reflections)? *Human* • Who should be involved in the selection and evaluation of artifacts? • Who can support in the selection and evaluation of artifacts and in what ways? • Who should be involved in establishing and reviewing criteria?
Reflection	*Contextual* • What types of reflections best articulate my thinking regarding each artifact and its role in evaluating growth over time and in achievement of the standards?

Source: Based on terms from Barrett (2001).

	Temporal • When is the best time to add reflections, and how do I schedule time for regularly adding and reviewing artifacts and reflections? *Spatial* • What form is best for storage and retrieval of reflections? • Where and how should I add reflections to the artifacts? *Human* • Who can provide support and give feedback on the artifacts and reflections? • What strategies can help with the storage and retrieval of reflections on a regular basis (e.g., sticky notes, index cards)?	
Inspection for self-assessment and projection	*Contextual* • When artifacts and reflections are compared with standards and performance indicators, what future learning goals can be set? *Temporal* • Is the time line appropriate for reaching the desired benchmarks, or should adjustments be made in future planning? • Have appropriate time lines and benchmarks been set for the program, and what adjustments should be made, if any, in looking toward the future? *Spatial* • Are the storage and retrieval systems adequate for demonstrating growth over time and achievement when compared with the standards and performance indicators, or should modifications be made for future enhancement? *Human* • Who can support in comparing artifacts and reflections with the standards and for setting future learning goals? • When can and should this type of collaboration be scheduled?	
Connection and presentation	*Contextual* • Is the overall purpose of the portfolio clear to my audience? *Temporal* • What is the best format for the presentation, given the time limitations? *Spatial* • What is the best format for the presentation, given the space limitations? *Human* • Who is the appropriate audience (e.g., peers, supervisors) for sharing the portfolio and collaborating on its contents, process, and purpose? • What is the best format for the portfolio presentation, given the specific purpose and the specific audience?	

TABLE 5.3 Portfolio Management Ideas

Source: Adapted from PATT (2000).

1. Set up a time line with due dates for installments in the portfolio.
   - Practice writing reflective statements for each potential portfolio entry.
   - Make sample reflection sheets for dry runs.

2. Review samples of completed portfolios with emphasis on the importance of appearance in the scoring (e.g., organization, table of contents, use of graphics).
   - Notice the incorporation of technology, such as electronic portfolios (see Chapter 8).

3. To ensure clarity of expectations, review the rubrics or scoring guides in advance.
   - Practice self- and peer scoring of projects and the portfolio itself, including oral and written comments to each other.

4. Make the portfolio process convenient!
   - Use materials that are readily available, such as manila folders, sticky notes, and storage boxes.
   - Store folders, alphabetically, in milk crates, cardboard boxes, or file cabinets.
   - Use binders equipped with a space for video- or audiocassettes.
   - Color code to distinguish among classes, or use different file drawers.
   - Establish regular portfolio review sessions (both in and outside the classroom, if possible).

TABLE 5.4 Tips for Keeping a Portfolio

Source: Adapted from PATT (2000).

1. Always place a table of contents with dates and page numbers at or near the front.

2. Keep work for each unit or course in a folder, and then select a certain number of pieces at the end of the quarter or semester.

3. Photocopy or keep electronic files (or both) of group work so that members can include the work in their portfolios.

4. Include the instructor prompt where possible with each work entered.

5. Photograph or scan work that is too cumbersome to fit into the folder.

6. Tape (audio or video) explanations of oral presentations.

7. Keep computer disks or printouts of relevant material.

8. Include photographs of pre-K–12 students carrying out their work (e.g., an experiment or a group activity).

9. Maintain electronic portfolios and hard copies in different location.

TABLE 5.5 Sample Portfolio Checkpoint Time Line (for programs one year or less)

Time Line or Time Interval	Benchmark or Activity	Sign-Off Date
Opening of Program: Checkpoint 1	• Review portfolio and scoring guide. • Review portfolio terminology and view sample portfolios, if possible. • Review portfolio rubric and standards.	
Checkpoint 2	• Draft a goal statement for portfolio. • Practice writing reflections as part of some assignments. • Revisit program goals and standards and project goals for next time interval. • Write an end-of-interval reflection. • Participate in informal portfolio exchanges and discussions, including sharing reflective statements, among candidates, peers, mentors, and program instructors. • If possible, have instructors sign off on portfolio competencies.	
Midway: Checkpoint 3	• You are now halfway through the program! • You should have addressed at least half of the program goals and standards with samples of artifacts and reflections for each. • Reflect on initial program goals and set goals for remainder of program. • Refine goal statements and ensure that each artifact has reflections, captions, and so on. • Share portfolios with peers and mentors for formative feedback and further goal setting. • Revisit vision and philosophy; rework if necessary. • Check for instructors' sign-offs on competencies.	
Checkpoint 4	• Continue to complete assignments focused on the remainder of the program standards and goals. • Revisit the portfolio rubric and contents guide, noting any gaps or missing data. • Continue to update selections and reflections on portfolio entries. • Participate in informal portfolio exchanges and discussions, including reflective statements, among candidates, peers, mentors, and program instructors. • Begin to differentiate artifacts, and start an initial showcase portfolio from the working portfolio. • Select specific artifacts and reflections for the showcase portfolio, including examples of growth and development toward the workshop or course goals and standards. • Revisit vision and philosophy; rework if necessary.	
End: Checkpoint 5	• Present completed showcase portfolio to workshop or course instructors and peers as summative evaluation of candidate and workshop or course. • Present completed showcase portfolio as evidence of desired competencies for targeted areas.	

For specific information related to this concept, see the Chapter 5 resources on the CD.

(Continued)

TABLE 5.5 (Continued)

Source: Adapted from PATT (2000).

Time Line or Time Interval	Benchmark or Activity	Sign-Off Date
	• You have completed a successful portfolio process. • Check for instructors' sign-offs on competencies.	
Ongoing Checkpoint	• Continue to update selections and reflections on portfolio entries. • Share portfolio with peers and mentors for formative feedback and further goal setting beyond the program. • Conduct informal portfolio exchanges and discussions among peers, mentors, and program instructors. • Begin retooling the portfolio. Project new goals and applications for professional development and growth (see Chapter 10: After the Credential Program, Now What? Keeping the Portfolio Alive)	

and use the portfolios to guide future areas for professional development or employment opportunities. This is described as an ongoing checkpoint that continues after the completion of the program, course, or workshop. (This process will be addressed more in Chapter 10, which discusses keeping the portfolio alive.) Portfolios can also be developed within a particular course or workshop as a way of helping students organize and systematically collect artifacts that document growth and progress toward course or workshop goals and objectives.

In some cases, as in mini courses leading to certification in a particular skill or competency, such as designing programs for special populations (e.g., Inquiry Approaches to Science and Social Studies for English Language Learners, Building a Comprehensive Partnership With Parents and Community, or Steps to Opening Your Own Charter School), developing and maintaining a portfolio can be a valuable resource once the course has ended. The time line and benchmarks are parallel, regardless of the type of program, although there may be fewer checkpoints for mini courses. Or a mini course portfolio may simply include evidence of assignments and reflections from a particular course, with an overall reflection at the end of the course regarding its value in the student's professional development and the student's self-evaluation of course performance.

If there is no formal portfolio process in place for an entire program, course and workshop portfolios are a good way to expose students to the portfolio process. Similar benefits will accrue in terms of inquiry, reflection, organization, and time management.

Table 5.6 provides sample checklists that can be used to document verification of introduction, development, and **mastery** of program competencies at various points of a teacher's preparation. Similar checkpoints are available on the CD for administrative and counseling credential programs. As portfolios are reviewed at certain checkpoints throughout the respective programs, reviewers might indicate when the portfolio was reviewed and the level of progress toward the standard or competencies emphasized in the program. Such a checklist can provide an overview of where and to what level specific competencies were

For specific information related to this concept, see the Chapter 5 resources on the CD.

addressed in individual courses. As we have mentioned, it is particularly helpful to have portfolio artifacts organized around specific standards. This is also true of assignments, such as writing lesson plans or developing organizational charts. More examples of aligning artifacts and assignments to standards are discussed in Chapters 6 to 8.

TABLE 5.6   Sample Portfolio Checklist for Teaching Credential Candidates

INTASC Principle	Introduced: Course, Date	Developing: Course, Date	Mastery: Course, Date
Principle 1: Knowledge of Subject Matter	EDUC 300, 9/7/09	EDUC 302, 1/6/10	EDUC 400, 6/15/10
Principle 2: Knowledge of Human Development and Learning	EDUC 300	EDUC 301	EDUC 400
Principle 3: Adapting Instruction for Individual Needs	EDUC 300	EDUC 304	EDUC 403
Principle 4: Multiple Instructional Strategies	EDUC 300	EDUC 302	EDUC 402
Principle 5: Classroom Motivation and Management	EDUC 300	EDUC 301	EDUC 402
Principle 6: Communication Skills	EDUC 300	EDUC 315	EDUC 400
Principle 7: Instructional Planning Skills	EDUC 300	EDUC 302	EDUC 405
Principle 8: Assessment of Student Learning	EDUC 300	EDUC 301	EDUC 415
Principle 9: Professional Commitment and Responsibility	EDUC 300	EDUC 305	EDUC 418
Principle 10: Partnerships	EDUC 300	EDUC 305	EDUC 449

For specific information related to this concept, see the Chapter 5 resources on the CD.

Step 10: Practice scoring the portfolio.

This final step in the portfolio journey addresses scoring the portfolio, as it is another potential pitfall in portfolio implementation. Students are encouraged to practice scoring their own and colleagues' portfolios to become more familiar with the criteria and levels of mastery on which they will be evaluated. To become more familiar with the scoring process, students should do mock scoring of assignments as part of their course activities.

These types of scoring activities are built into the portfolio time lines and checkpoints described in Tables 5.5. Scoring activities such as these further allow students to internalize the program standards and portfolio rubrics. They also allow for the portfolio scoring process to be broken down into predictable and manageable intervals.

Some of the concerns about scoring the portfolio involve the amount of time it takes to score, setting regular intervals for scoring, and establishing specific **scoring guidelines** and criteria to achieve agreement and consistency in assessing and evaluating the portfolio contents. In order for students to be more at ease with how portfolios are scored, it is important to get a clearer understanding of the common strategies that are used. Chapter 3 discussed the value of portfolios for both formative and summative evaluation and listed recommendations for helping portfolios become more reliable when used for certification purposes. Many of these recommendations centered around scoring.

Some other considerations for improving the portfolio-scoring process, suggested by PATT (2000), include the use of holistic scoring, which addresses the time issue, and collaborative scoring, which addresses setting criteria and fostering agreement and consistency in scoring, as part of portfolio professional development. Interval scoring is a third technique to break down the scoring process into manageable chunks and takes place at regular intervals or checkpoints throughout the portfolio process. Please see suggested checkpoints in Table 5.5.

Holistic scoring, according to PATT (2000), is getting a general impression of the entire portfolio. It is not a detailed review nor is it a checklist process or item-by-item search. Rather, an anchor assignment or examples of past portfolios, which have had each criterion or standard scored previously, are used for this scoring system. Because the portfolio is designed to be scored, it may become part of the program's or college's overall assessment and accountability system. Many universities are moving in this direction as commercial electronic portfolio programs, such as *TaskStream* and *FolioLive,* offer strong management tools to assist in scoring and documentation.

GENERAL PORTFOLIO SCORING PROCEDURE

One strategy recommended by PATT (2000) is a general portfolio scoring procedure designed to provide a simple feel for the portfolio and to minimize the time it takes to score. It involves three main steps:

1. *Start with a brief scan of the entire portfolio to get a general sense of its contents, organization, and purpose.* There is no detailed reading by the scorer at this point, only general impressions.

2. *Read the portfolio executive summary and review the artifact selected by the candidate as the best evidence of the standard or learning target under consideration.* Compare the item to the rubric or anchor piece to decide on a score. This should be done quickly to get a general view of the student's level of proficiency.

3. *Skim the remainder of the portfolio for further evidence beyond the initial score.* The scorer reviews other artifacts to support the standard and guide the scorer

in determining the actual level of proficiency if it seems to fluctuate between a higher or lower score.

Activity 5.2 allows you to practice portfolio scoring.

LET'S PRACTICE!

Activity 5.2   Exploring Sample Rubrics and Sample Scoring of Portfolios

The following activities will assist you in practicing the scoring of portfolios:

- Take some time to explore sample portfolios along with the rubrics or scoring criteria used to evaluate them. If possible, seek a variety of portfolio samples, each demonstrating a different level of proficiency, to allow you to review both strong and weak samples of evidence. Practice scoring each portfolio without looking at how it was evaluated. Did you agree with the scorer of the portfolio? Was there consistency in your scores compared to those of the evaluator? If there were differences, where did these occur?
- Collect as many program rubrics and scoring criteria from your current program as possible. Place them in your comprehensive portfolio for easy reference.
- As you and your peers complete various parts of your portfolios, do a portfolio exchange where you do mock scoring of a certain criterion in each others' portfolios. Use the program rubrics to evaluate each specified learning target. Use the holistic scoring technique as a strategy for scoring. Write out your evaluations of each others' portfolios and discuss the results with each other.
- Write down any questions or concerns you have about portfolio scoring and evaluation and share them in class.

The holistic scoring procedure is based on a process of estimating the proper score on the rubric. As an example, in the three-point portfolio rubric sample provided in Table 5.7 for teacher credential candidates, the line between *Credit* and *No Credit* is essentially the dividing line between proficient work and work that is not proficient. (Similar three-point sample portfolio rubrics for administrative credential candidates and counseling credential candidates are available on the CD). After looking at the primary evidence for the standard or criteria, the scorer should form an impression of whether or not the candidate demonstrates proficiency. This means that the scorer will always start on the Credit–No Credit line and determine if the candidate scores on the proficient or the not-proficient side. Once the scorer establishes proficiency, the rest of the artifacts in the portfolio are considered, to decide which of the two levels of proficiency is appropriate. For instance, if the scorer decides initially that the work seems proficient in the parameter for Content Knowledge in Planning and Instruction, he or she would then decide only between levels Credit and Exceeds Standard. If the work is not proficient, then the decision would be No Credit. This appears to be an easier approach for some people to use.

For specific information related to this concept, see the Chapter 5 resources on the CD.

TABLE 5.7 Sample Rubric for Teaching Credential Candidates

Directed Teaching, Demonstration of Competencies Evaluation Rubric		
INTASC Principle 1 Knowledge of Subject Matter		
No Credit	**Credit**	**Exceeds Standard**
Candidate provides little or no evidence of subject matter mastery, understanding of available classroom materials, and capacity to integrate appropriate subject matter into lesson plans.	Candidate provides sufficient evidence of subject matter mastery, understanding of available classroom materials, and capacity to integrate appropriate subject matter into lesson plans.	Candidate provides consistent and ample evidence of subject matter mastery, ability to adapt and augment available classroom materials to meet student needs, and capacity to integrate appropriate subject matter into lesson plans, based on student progress and interests.
INTASC Principle 5 Classroom Motivation and Management		
No Credit	**Credit**	**Exceeds Standard**
Candidate is unable to use instructional time effectively or efficiently. Candidate provides little or no evidence of the ability to develop and maintain expectations of appropriate student behavior. Candidate does not develop a productive learning climate or consider alternative classroom management routines to build one.	Candidate uses instructional time effectively and efficiently. Candidate provides evidence of the ability to create and maintain an environment for effective student learning along with expectations of appropriate student behavior. When classroom problems arise, candidate seeks solutions through alternative classroom management routines.	Candidate provides clear, consistent, and convincing evidence for the effective and efficient use of instructional time. Candidate consistently provides evidence of the ability to create and maintain an effective environment for student learning along with clear and consistent expectations of appropriate student behavior. When classrooms problems arise, candidate anticipates solutions by implementing alternative classroom management routines.

INTASC Principle 7 Instructional Planning

No Credit	Credit	Exceeds Standard
Candidate provides little or no evidence of planning for instruction. Plans do not reveal knowledge of state standards; integrate appropriate content; describe and align goals, materials, strategies, or assessment methods; use whole class and small groups; and connect to prior and future instruction.	Candidate provides sufficient evidence in planning for short- and long-range instruction. Plans show knowledge of state standards; describe and align goals, materials, strategies, and assessment methods; integrate appropriate content; use whole class and small groups; integrate available instructional technology; connect to prior and future instruction; and connect with students' lives, interests, and instructional needs.	Candidate provides consistent and ample evidence in planning for short- and long-range instruction. Plans show knowledge of state standards; describe and align goals, varied materials, strategies, and multiple assessment methods; integrate appropriate content; use whole class and small groups; employ effective technology; and clearly connect to prior and future instruction, students' cultures and interests, instructional needs, and other disciplines.

Source: Adapted from California State University (2004).

105

For specific information related to this concept, see the Chapter 5 resources on the CD.

Other scoring rubrics for portfolio presentations and portfolio documents are found in Chapter 7 and on the CD.

SUMMARY

We have provided 10 valuable steps for managing the portfolio journey in this chapter. Portfolios can be organized, goal-driven, living documents when implemented with careful planning and collaboration. Portfolios are also a valuable resource for providing concrete evidence of the knowledge, skills, and attitudes that have been mastered by the students. Through carefully following the 10 steps of the portfolio journey, a continual process is established for evaluating both students and programs. Inherent in portfolio development are projection, planning, reflection, inquiry, assessment, and collaboration.

Also, when the management of the portfolio becomes integrated into the portfolio process—for example, by establishing time lines and benchmarks or sharing strategies for scoring the portfolio—many of the common pitfalls can be avoided. In this way, the portfolio journey is easily approached and more consistently implemented. These 10 steps help in making portfolio development a transparent process whose value is understood by both students and instructors.

USEFUL RESOURCES

The following resources will be useful in developing your portfolio implementation plan.

INTASC (Interstate New Teacher Assessment and Support Consortium; http://www .ccsso.org/Projects/Interstate_New_Teacher_Assessment_and_Support_Consortium/)

The Web site a consortium of more than 30 states operating under the Council of Chief State School Officers (CCSSO), which has developed standards and an assessment process for initial teacher certification (Campbell et al., 2000).

Portfolio Development (http://www.sitesupport.org/module1/portfproc.htm)

Online professional development from Johns Hopkins and Morgan State Universities on the portfolio development process.

Portfolio Implementation Guide. (http://www.pde.state.pa.us/fam_consumer/lib/fam_ consumer/20/23/portig.pdf)

Pennsylvania Assessment Through Themes. (2000). Portfolio implementation guide. Retrieved August 25, 2005.

Practical Assessment, Research and Evaluation (http://PAREonline.net/ getvn.asp?v = 7&n = 4)

A peer-reviewed electronic journal.

Rubrics for Web Lessons (http://edweb.sdsu.edu/webquest/rubrics/weblessons.htm)

A site featuring a guide to creating rubrics and authentic assessments.

Student Reflection Samples (http://www.sitesupport.org/module1/INTASC_PRINCIPLE_1_1.htm)

A site featuring samples of student reflections based on INTASC Principles:

FOR FURTHER READING

Dietz, Mary E. (2008). *Designing the school leader's portfolio* (2nd ed.). Thousand Oaks, CA: Sage.

Hartnell-Young, E., & Morriss, M. (2007). *Digital portfolios: Powerful tools for promoting professional growth and reflection.* Thousand Oaks, CA: Corwin Press.

Hebert, E. A. (2001). *The power of portfolios: What children can teach us about learning and assessment.* San Francisco: Jossey-Bass.

Montgomery, K., & Wiley, D. (2008). *Building e-portfolios using PowerPoint: A guide for educators* (2nd ed.). Thousand Oaks, CA: Sage.

Rieman, P. (2000). *Teaching portfolios: Presenting your professional best.* Boston: McGraw-Hill.

Taggart, G. L., & Wilson, A. P. (2005). *Promoting reflective thinking in teachers: 50 action research strategies* (2nd ed.). Thousand Oaks, CA: Sage.

Contents of the Portfolio

The portfolio is most definitely an authentic assessment of candidates. The portfolio is not only a collection of the work completed, but it represents what we are capable of doing and what we have learned. The portfolio is, in a sense, a representation of us, the students, and the university as well as the professors who have influenced us, the students.

—Candidate reflection

CHAPTER OBJECTIVES

Readers will be able to

❑ develop a table of contents;

❑ develop an introduction, an executive summary, or both;

❑ develop a vision, an educational philosophy, or both;

❑ identify and develop personal documents for inclusion, such as an updated resume;

❑ develop reflective introductions to professional standards;

❑ describe how to identify, select, and organize artifacts to demonstrate competency in professional standards; and

❑ review the importance of summative reflections on the overall learning experience and quality of the program.

Jose was in the last semester of his teaching credential program. Denise, a colleague, also was completing requirements for her teaching credential. The completion of a portfolio that demonstrated their competencies in the standards designated by the state was a major requirement.

One day after a faculty meeting at their school, Jose and Denise were walking to their cars to attend their university class. Jose mentioned that he had been gathering a lot of stuff for the portfolio, but he was not sure whether he had the right documents or if he was missing information. Denise expressed the same concerns. She commented, "I have loads of stuff! What do we need besides our evidence for each teaching standard? Someone told me that I needed a resume. Someone else said I needed a vision or a philosophy. I am getting worried. I hope the professor will tell us what to include." Jose expressed the same sentiment. He also mentioned that it might be useful if he could look at some sample successful portfolios that had been done by other students.

A similar conversation was taking place among a group of administrative credential candidates who also had to assemble portfolios. John was commenting on the portfolio process to fellow colleagues: "When I first heard of the portfolio, I thought, 'No problem!' I'm a teacher and I've used portfolios in my school with my elementary students. I know how helpful they are for showing growth in my elementary students and helping them to evaluate themselves. Still, I did not really understand what I was in for as an administrative credential candidate. Portfolios are a lot of work! The process really helped me to think about what I was doing in each class and why and how that class or assignment would help me to grow as an administrator. The portfolio helped me to stay focused on the big picture of becoming a school principal. Having to keep and organize assignments into artifacts also helped me to think more deeply about each assignment and how it assisted me in developing skills and abilities as an administrator. I was constantly putting myself under a microscope to view and evaluate my progress. Completing an assignment was not enough until I figured out what that assignment or activity had to do with my overall profile as an administrator or educational leader. When I developed a workshop for paraprofessionals on legal issues surrounding their roles and responsibilities, I saw how this one activity addressed several administrative standards. The portfolio process helped me to clearly identify each standard and to cross-reference assignments, artifacts, and activities when appropriate."

OVERVIEW

The aspiring teacher and administrator candidates in the scenario are viewing the portfolio process through different experiential lenses. John has had some experience. He has used portfolios with his students. However, he is now experiencing the process as an adult learner. John also appears to have some familiarity with how to develop the portfolio, whereas Jose and Denise seem uncertain about what is expected. Even though students may be aware that they have to develop a portfolio, they are often unsure of what the most appropriate contents are and how to select them. Nearly all are clear that they must collect evidence linked to standards, goals, or objectives. Therefore, coursework and field artifacts usually are accumulated. However, many programs require that candidates in credential programs include other documents, such as a vision, a philosophy, previous credentials, professionally related certificates, a resume, and letters of recommendation.

In Chapter 5, we discussed the organization of the portfolio development process. Chapter 3 described how to systematically, over time, select, evaluate, and modify contents for inclusion. In this chapter, we discuss and highlight examples of typical portfolio contents. We begin with a discussion of the cover page and table of contents, which give an overview of the portfolio contents. Next, the introduction and summary statements are described, as well as how to develop the vision or philosophy and other documents to be included, such as a resume. Then a major section of the portfolio, which contains artifacts that provide evidence of levels of mastery in the standards, is addressed. The introduction to the professional standards and how to select and organize artifacts to demonstrate competencies is described. Also included is a table that can assist candidates in categorizing and cross-referencing artifacts to demonstrate levels of competency in two or more standards.

It is not our goal to show examples of all the possible ways that one might select contents for a portfolio, but rather to offer readers an idea of how they might develop, organize, and choose contents for their personal portfolios. Portfolio developers will need to tailor these suggestions to their personal circumstances. Most of the sample contents shown are for summative evaluation portfolios, because those portfolios are the most developed and comprehensive. To a lesser extent, some examples of contents used to satisfy the requirements of formative portfolios are provided.

PORTFOLIO COVER PAGE OR TITLE PAGE

For specific information related to this concept, see the Chapter 6 resources on the CD.

The *cover page* of the portfolio may be designed in the same way as a major paper, project, or book. Some programs may call for candidates to create a background design with specific information on the cover, and other programs may have guidelines for a preferred format. Sometimes a photo of the candidate might be included. Table.6.1 displays typical information that may be placed on the cover page. Other examples are on the CD.

TABLE 6.1   Sample Cover Page or Title Page

Portfolio Title
Name of the Candidate
Date of Submission (include semester or quarter, if appropriate)
Title of Program or Course
Instructor
Department or Division
University or Other Agency

PORTFOLIO TABLE OF CONTENTS

A well-organized portfolio provides a table of contents, which gives an overview of the contents and their location in the portfolio. A table of contents that is skillfully organized can facilitate a coherent presentation of the evidence contained in the portfolio. It allows the reader or presenter to locate specific artifacts quickly.

The contents are organized generally by major subheadings: Introduction or Executive Summary, Personal Information, Professional Standards and a listing of artifacts linked to the standards, and Reflections. Examples of standards include the following: for teaching, the INTASC (1992) standards. For leadership, the Interstate School Leaders Licensure Consortium's Educational Leadership Policy Standards (CCSSO, 2007). For counseling, examples of activities are presented that counselors may be expected to engage in that are related to the **National Standards for School Counseling Programs** (American School Counselor Association [ASCA], n.d.). The standards are included on the CD. Programs and candidates will most likely need to tailor their portfolio artifacts to regional or state standards.

For specific information related to this concept, see the Chapter 6 resources on the CD.

Table 6.2 shows what a table of contents for an end of single course portfolio might look like. Tables 6.3 shows sample sections for end-of-program portfolios. Tables 6.4, 6.5, 6.6, and 6.7 are sample end-of-program tables of contents for an aspiring elementary teacher, a secondary teacher, an administrator, and a school counselor, respectively The examples show how a table of contents might look for hard-copy portfolios. Note that Tables 6.5, 6.6, and 6.7 are for summative portfolios and show how artifacts may be used to demonstrate accomplishments in more than one standard. For hardcover portfolios, each major section and subsection of the table of contents should be arranged in a binder or similar container with section dividers, tabs, or other organizing features, which expedite quick location of contents. Additional sample tables are included in the CD. Table of contents designs for electronic portfolios are shown in Chapter 9 and follow the same basic guidelines presented here. The primary differences are the options for organizing the table of contents based on technology, such as **hyperlinks** and software programs.

TABLE 6.2   Sample End-of-Course Table of Contents

Name _____

Date _____

Portfolio Table of Contents

EDEL 405 Language Development in Elementary School

Journals and Reflections

   1. Journal Entries, Reflections (Treasures, etc.)

       (INTASC Principle 9, Professional Commitment and Responsibility)

(Continued)

TABLE 6.2 (Continued)

2. Technology (Intel® Copyright assignment, online journaling and discussions, Internet Explorations, etc.)

   (INTASC Principle 4, Multiple Instructional Strategies; ISTE NETS Technology Standards I, II, and III)

3. Video Reflections

   (INTASC Principle 4, Multiple Instructional Strategies; ISTE NETS Technology Standards I, II, and III)

English Language Development (ELD) Strategies and Assignments

4. Methods and Activities Presentation (TPR, Jazz Chants, etc.)

   (INTASC Principle 3, Adapting Instruction for Individual Needs)

5. Picture File Samples

   (INTASC Principle 4, Multiple Instructional Strategies; ISTE NETS Technology Standards I, II, and III)

6. Thematic ELD Unit

   (INTASC Principle 4, Multiple Instructional Strategies; ISTE NETS Technology Standards I, II, and III)

7. Multimedia PowerPoint Presentation of Unit

   (INTASC Principle 4, Multiple Instructional Strategies; ISTE NETS Technology Standards I, II, and III)

Fieldwork and Observations

8. Observation–Participation Report and Reflection

   (INTASC Principle 9, Professional Commitment and Responsibility)

9. LAS® Oral Language Assessment

   (INTASC Principle 8, Assessment of Student Learning)

Additional Assessments, Activities

10. Peer Evaluations

    (INTASC Principle 9, Professional Commitment and Responsibility)

11. Self-Evaluation

    (INTASC Principle 9, Professional Commitment and Responsibility)

12. Other (Bulletin boards, classroom pictures, letters to parents, student work, etc.)

TABLE 6.3   Sample Sections for End-of-Program Portfolio Contents

For specific information related to this concept, see the Chapter 6 resources on the CD.

Section	Contents
Introduction	Overview or executive summary of the portfolio
Personal and background information	Personal statement Vision Philosophy Resume Letters of reference Credentials and certificates Transcript from colleges, universities
Professional competencies	Professional standards with documentation (artifacts) of competencies
Reflections about the program	Both formative and summative reflections (there may be reflections in the section on standards, also)

TABLE 6.4   Sample Elementary Teacher Candidate Portfolio Table of Contents, With Examples of Three Standards

For specific information related to this concept, see the Chapter 6 resources on the CD.

Table of Contents Introduction	Yellow Tab
Personal Information	Orange Tab
Philosophy of Education	
Philosophy of Classroom Management	
Diversity Statement	
Resume	
Application to XYZ School District	
Transcripts	
Exams	
References/Letters of Recommendation	
Field Work and Directed Teaching, Including Learner's Products	Clear Tab
Principle 3: Adapting Instruction to Individual Needs	Red Tab
Weekly Objectives/Lesson Plans	
Suggestions for Modifying Lessons and Room Arrangement for Students (classroom maps)	

(Continued)

TABLE 6.4 (Continued)

Specific Examples of Different Types of Modifications (ELL, Inclusion)	
Principle 8: Assessment of Student Learning	Blue Tab
Language and Literacy Assessment	
• Reading Case Study	
• Alternate Ranking-Reading	
• High-Frequency Spanish Word List	
• Spanish Running Record and Comprehension Questions	
Spanish Reading Inventory Record	
General Content Area Assessment	
• Second Grade Content Standards—Science Center	
• Third Grade Content Standards—Thematic Unit	
Scoring Guides	
• Writing Rubric	
• Math Rubric	
Principle 9: Professional Commitment and Responsibility	Purple Tab
Back-to-School Night Information Documents and Video	
Critiques From Mentor	
Principal Observations and Evaluation	
Parent Links, Communications	
• Welcome and Homework Letter	
• Parent Call Log	
Workshops, Professional Development	
Conference Presentations	
Professional Memberships	
Service Learning and Community Service	
Reflections	
Growth Reflections	Green Tab
Program Reflection	
Reflections of the Portfolio Process	

TABLE 6.5 Sample Secondary Teacher Candidate Portfolio Table of Contents

Contents	Section
Personal Information • Philosophy of education • Diversity statement • Autobiography • Curriculum vitae • References and letters of recommendation • Transcripts	I
Teaching Standards (Example of Four Standards) Principle 1: Knowledge of Subject Matter • Written lesson plans (five best examples) • Course final research paper: Strategies for Promoting Literacy With Culturally Diverse Populations • Fieldwork and directed teaching logs and student work Principle 2: Knowledge of Human Learning and Development • Assessment records and plans for improvement of learning • Student reflection on learning with collaborative groups • Recordkeeping logs • Fieldwork, directed teaching logs, and student work Principle 4: Multiple Instructional Strategies • Video of student and teacher engagement during instruction • Written lesson plans (five best examples) • Course final research paper: Strategies for Promoting Literacy With Culturally Diverse Populations • Fieldwork, directed teaching logs, and student work Principle 5: Classroom Motivation and Management • Classroom management plan • Video of student and teacher engagement • Fieldwork, directed teaching logs, and student work	II
Reflections	III
Exams	IV

For specific information related to this concept, see the Chapter 6 resources on the CD.

INTRODUCTION OR EXECUTIVE SUMMARY FOR THE PORTFOLIO

The *introduction* or *executive summary* gives an overview of the purpose and major features of the portfolio. The introduction should set the tone in ways that engage the reader to antic- ipate a quality product that is reflective and one that provides substantive evidence of the candidate's performance in the required competencies. Figure 6.1 presents an example of a portfolio introduction.

For specific information related to this concept, see the Chapter 6 resources on the CD.

TABLE 6.6   Sample Administrator Candidate Portfolio Table of Contents, With Examples of Three Standards

Contents	Description	Artifacts and Evidence
Executive Summary	Overview of the portfolio	Executive Summary
Philosophy of Education	Program philosophy	Initial and end-of-program philosophy
Standard 1: Facilitating the Vision	A school administrator is an educational leader who promotes the success of all students by facilitating the development, articulation, implementation, and stewardship of a vision of learning that is shared and supported by the school community.	1. Vision 2. Single-school plan for student achievement (description and intent) 3. Memorandums about meetings for Social Studies Department vision development 4. Single-school plan for student achievement (division of work) 5. Examples of agendas and minutes for Social Studies Department meeting 6. Teacher evaluations of meetings 7. Example of agenda for first critical friends meeting 8. Memorandum about vision comments by Social Studies Department
Standard 2: School Culture and the Instructional Program	A school administrator is an educational leader who promotes the success of all students by advocating, nurturing, and sustaining a school culture and instructional program conducive to student learning and staff professional growth.	1. Professional development PowerPoint presentation 2. Equity report on test scores in U.S. history, regular and gifted classes, at Sunshine Middle School 3. Equity report on tracking at Sunshine Middle School 4. Critical analysis of special education in Sunshine Middle School 5. Critique on instructional program 6. Transformation plan for Sunshine Middle School
Standard 3: Managing the Organization	A school administrator is an educational leader who promotes the success of all students by ensuring management of the organization, operations, and resources for a safe, efficient, and effective learning environment.	1. Case study on Sunshine Middle School 2. Equity report on tracking at Sunshine Middle School 3. Transformation plan for Sunshine Middle School 4. Teacher's Handbook 5. Redesigned Social Studies Department curriculum 6. Professional development documents on standards implementation

TABLE 6.7   Sample School Counselor Portfolio Table of Contents

Statement of Purpose	
Section 1	Personal Background
1.1	Worldview
1.2	Professional experiences related to counseling
1.3	Academic background and current coursework
1.4	Professional association membership
1.5	Honors, awards, and grants
1.6	Publications
1.7	Certificates, credentials, and licenses (title and number)
1.8	Letters of recommendation and commendation
1.9	Specialized skills
1.10	Current resume
1.11	Community involvement and volunteer service
1.12	Mentor experiences
1.13	Political, legislative advocacy
Section 2	Standard A: Academic
2.1	Comprehensive guidance program
2.2	Plan for student results
2.3	Results data
2.4	Reflections and analysis of data
2.5	Other contributions
2.6	Personal reflections
Section 3	Standard B: Career
3.1	Guidance curriculum units
3.2	Guidance and Career Center plan
3.3	Classroom visitations
3.4	Student personal statements
3.5	Videos of career activities
3.6	Photographs of career libraries

For specifi
informatio
related to
this
concept,
see the
Chapter 6
resources
on the CD

(Continued)

TABLE 6.7 (Continued)

Statement of Purpose		
	3.7	Readings
	3.8	Technology applications
	3.9	Journal, learning logs
	3.10	Personal reflection and critique
Section 4		Standard C: Personal Social Development
	4.1	Guidance curriculum units
	4.2	Guidance and Career Center plan
	4.3	Presentations
	4.4	Videos of student activities
	4.5	Written contributions (newsletters, articles, publications)

For specific information related to this concept, see the Chapter 6 resources on the CD.

FIGURE 6.1   Sample Portfolio Introduction

Introduction

The contents of this portfolio cover the last two years of my work at Sunshine State University, as well as many activities that I did at Central High School as an English teacher in a large comprehensive high school. I am presenting a range of documentation that demonstrates my understanding of and competency in the principles. Many of these documents show my knowledge, skills, and dispositions for equity and my ability to work as a teacher in a culturally and linguistically diverse school.

I want to especially thank the many instructors and supervising teachers who have contributed to my growth in so many ways. They have given their time and expertise to provide support and guidance in the development of my vision and educational philosophy. Through our collective efforts, I have learned to look at the data of our school and see the inequities that we face daily. My work of the last two years has led me to look deeper at the meaning of what quality classes and schools should be like, to grow as a teacher, to gain skills in instructing students to attain a goal, and to understand the fundamental issues and strategies that are needed to be an effective teacher in an urban school.

Over the last two years, I have been working collaboratively with students, parents, administrators, staff, professors, and fellow candidates in my teacher credential program. I did individual projects and often worked collaboratively with a variety of individuals. Much of the work was done beyond the normal school day, often on weekends and late into the evening. The work in this portfolio demonstrates my completion of the goals and standards set by the School of Education at Sunshine University and by the state.

This is a living document and will go through many revisions as I continue to grow as a teaching professional. I plan to use this portfolio as an ongoing reflective document. I will add, delete, and revise its contents. I also plan to use it for future interviews.

THE VISION STATEMENT

Most programs require that candidates write a well-crafted vision statement that is developed over time. Research has established a relationship between vision and school effectiveness (Barth, 1990).

The development of a vision should be considered an important undertaking. It may be a short or a long discussion of what candidates view as a desired educational future. It may include what they expect to accomplish for students and themselves and how they expect to influence the setting in which they work. It should address their personal knowledge, skills, and dispositions. The vision usually reflects the personal beliefs and values of the writer. Barth (1990) gives some useful ways to think about and write a vision. He states that visions can emerge from such prompts as, "When I leave this school I would like to be remembered for . . ."; "The kind of school I would like my children to attend would . . ."; or "The kind of school I would like to teach in . . ." (p. 148). He describes a personal vision as

> one's overall conception of what the educator wants the organization to stand for; what its primary mission is; what its basic, core values are; a sense of how all the parts fit together; and, above all, how the vision maker fits into the grand plan. (p. 148)

School administrators are often expected to develop a shared vision with several stakeholders, which may include staff, students, parents, and community members. Hartnell-Young and Morriss (2007) suggest that developing a shared vision has the power to cause stakeholders to reflect on and clarify goals and values and what they expect to accomplish in the future.

Hartnell-Young and Morriss (2007) also state that "the artifacts selected for the portfolio should show how the vision is being realized" (p. 41). The vision should be reflected in practice. Many times students will ask, How long should it be? Visions can be a paragraph in length or longer. Programs usually have guidelines about the length they are seeking. We recommend that students fully develop well-thought-out reflective responses to the questions in Activity 6.1 and then tailor the length to specific situations. A sample vision is provided in Figure 6.2.

LET'S PRACTICE!

Activity 6.1   Activity for Developing a Personal Vision

First, reflect on and respond to the following questions.

- What are your values and belief about student learning?
- What are your personal commitments in helping all of your students to achieve learning goals?
- When you leave a school, how would you like to be remembered?
- What kind of school would you want your children to attend?
- In what kind of school would you like to teach, be a counselor, or be an administrator?

Next, draft your vision. This will not be a final product but one that will be continually reflected upon and revised as you develop professionally.

For specific information related to this concept, see the Chapter 6 resources on the CD.

FIGURE 6.2   Sample Teaching Vision

My Vision for Teaching

Becoming a teacher has been a lifelong dream. I have always wanted to be a positive influence in the lives of young people. When I was in grade school, my friend and I played school. I was always the teacher.

The teacher preparation program has helped me to gain a better understanding about the teaching profession. As a result of this program, I believe that I have the knowledge, skills, and dispositions to become an outstanding teacher. I have begun to develop a vision of what I would like to happen for children in my classroom. I know that I will constantly revise this vision over the course of my career.

I desire to teach in a school where there is a diverse population. I want to be the kind of teacher who cares about who my children are and one who is able to communicate a caring feeling to my students and their parents. I want all of my students to believe that they are able to achieve high academic standards and that they can be successful in their future schooling and careers. My students will love to come to school and will have respect for adults and their classmates. I want my students to be confident and have the skills to succeed. When students leave my classroom, I envision that I will stay in contact with them and that their experiences in my classroom will have a long-term, positive effect. I expect to hear that my students are doing well in the upper grades.

I know that some aspiring teachers do not have the same beliefs and expectations for all kids as I do. It is my vision that as I gain more knowledge, confidence, and success as a teacher, I would like to help my peers see the great potential of all children.

I have a passion for teaching and am excited about being able to fulfill my lifelong dream!

THE PHILOSOPHY STATEMENT

The philosophy statement presents the candidate's viewpoint about the educational enterprise. Like the vision, the philosophy usually reflects the candidate's attitude, beliefs, and values about education. The focus is on core beliefs and values. During the course of a program, candidates will formulate and revise their philosophy, hopefully reflecting growth and development. A sample philosophy statement is shown in Figure 6.3.

Montgomery (1997) highlights the need for prospective teachers to develop a classroom management philosophy. Administrators are interested in knowing how they would resolve issues of classroom management. She suggests that artifacts be included that show clear evidence of what the philosophy looks like in a classroom setting. A sample philosophy of classroom management is shown in Figure 6.4

FIGURE 6.3   Sample Philosophy Statement

Sunshine State University

Name: Future Teacher

Date:

Philosophy of Education Statement

I believe that one major factor in improving K–12 schools rests on valuing each and every child, regardless of his or her individual background and circumstances. Educators must strive to be responsive to every child and have an understanding of the knowledge, skills, and dispositions that they will need to be successful with their students. Great effort must be made to consider the factors that encompass each individual. I realize that this is a challenging goal, especially when there are so many students in a classroom; however, every interaction with a child must make a positive impact.

Another factor that needs to be addressed is improving parent involvement and school relations. If this is done effectively, I believe it would greatly improve student outcomes. Establishing a good relationship between teachers and parents should result in a greater understanding of how the child learns and how the learning can continue at home. Agreement among teachers and parents in learning and in discipline techniques is especially beneficial to students.

Improving the reading and writing skills of all children is essential. Students must be encouraged and supported to read and write in ways that result not only in academic competency but also in enjoyment of learning. Literacy development must be integrated with oral language to encourage students to be creative. Creativity leads to a revelation about the many possible ways one can express one's learning.

Educators must constantly be engaged in improving professional sources for learning and classroom working conditions if they are to be effective in teaching. I believe that teachers need to be patient and caring with all of their students. Classroom climates must be trusting and nurturing so students feel safe and secure. If a safe, secure climate exists, children will feel free to take risks and to ask questions. They will be more likely to explore, to be creative, and to be unafraid of failure. These are the kinds of classrooms that unlock the genius in children. This is what I hope for my children and my school.

CANDIDATE DOCUMENTS

Many programs view the portfolio as an ongoing *professional document* that offers the potential for continuous retooling or **revision.** Many candidates use their portfolios in preparation for job interviews and also bring them for presentations during interviews (this is discussed further in Chapter 10). Candidates are often encouraged or required to include documents that enhance their portfolios beyond solely providing evidence of meeting competency standards.

FIGURE 6.4   Sample Philosophy of Classroom Management

Philosophy of Classroom Management

The central theme of my classroom management philosophy is respect for oneself and others. The classroom is where students spend most of their time growing up and because students spend a majority of their time inside classrooms during their growing process, I believe the classroom needs to be a safe environment that promotes students' interest and affection for knowledge. Therefore, everyone inside the classroom needs to respect each other so that every individual will have the opportunity to pursue their interests.

I believe what lies at the heart of a well-managed class is empowering students to make successful decisions that is respectful of their surroundings. If it feels like the teacher holds total power over the students, then the students will likely lash out in order to feel like they have some control. Students are far more likely to resolve situations with solutions that they are guided to rather than given. This is because all humans are empowered by choice. Specifically, this helps create a higher level of self-efficacy in the students. Because the decision is theirs, they have to own their behavior and accept the consequences of them, enabling them to exert control over their situation.

A good way to create a positive classroom culture right from the beginning is to create classroom guidelines as a class, teacher included. If they decide as a group what is and is not appropriate, they are far more likely to understand why those guidelines are in place and choose to abide by them. This keeps every individual to be accountable to one another because it was a mutual agreement among the people of the classroom. In this way, respect for every individual can flourish by creating consistency and equality of treatment.

I believe the key to effective classroom management is to manage, not control. This is only possible in an environment where students make their own decisions, expectations are clear, and there is a spirit of cooperation and understanding present. To achieve this, the teacher must intervene early when there is a potential problem, teach positive character traits, have clear and understood classroom guidelines, and stress positive reinforcement rather than threaten punishment. Mutual respect needs to be established so that all levels of communication are clear and received without misunderstanding. This can help the teacher manage the classroom instead of controlling it.

Classroom management should resemble how a coach manages an athletics team. Every individual is a part of the team and each person has a role to play; therefore, every position is important, and no player is expendable. The teacher's role is to teach, guide, and encourage the students, the way a coach teaches the athletes how to play the game, guides them by calling out plays, and encourages the team to strive for improvement during and after every play. Understanding your own role in the classroom will force you to respect others because as a team, everyone should be on the same page, striving for the same goal.

Some of these personal background documents are an *updated resume, credentials, certificates, college or university transcripts,* and *letters of recommendation.* Candidates should take time prior to including these documents to obtain reviews from experienced and knowledgeable professionals. Instructors and site supervisors can provide suggestions for resume development and recommend how to secure letters of recommendation. After consultation with instructors, candidates may want to include other relevant documents that reflect their unique skills and talents. Candidates must be careful to protect any confidential information if the portfolio is left for review; only leave information with someone who is designated to handle confidential information.

Resume guidelines are useful tools. A resume will be needed as a marketing tool through out a professional career. The guidelines in Table 6.8 can assist in the development of a resume, and Figure 6.5 presents an example.

TABLE 6.8   Guidelines for Resume Development

Dos	Don'ts
1. Use high quality paper and Ariel or Times Roman fonts to make your resume stand out.	1. Don't use unusual fonts or colored papers.
2. Write a clearly stated objective.	2. Don't present an unfocused objective.
3. Length should be about two pages.	3. Don't include information that is not relevant.
4. Focus on positions held and accomplishments (e.g., "Developed, implemented and evaluated new learning strategies").	4. Don't include negative information.
5. Focus on qualifications that are a good fit for the position.	5. Don't use generalities.
6. Customize the resume to the job being sought.	6. Don't include experiences that detract from pertinent qualifications.
7. Use proper grammar. Ask two knowledgeable professionals to proofread the resume.	7. Don't rely totally on computer programs for checking spelling and grammar.
8. Place most recent information first. Pay attention to format (See sample resume and visit resume Web sites).	8. Don't have a cluttered format that is difficult to read.
9. Make sure that the e-mail address that you choose looks professional, such as "nicknichols@email.com" or "stephnichols@sunshineu.edu."	9. Don't use a "cutesy" e-mail address, such as "hotsy-totsy@email.com" or "joe6pack@email.com."
10. Use appropriate voice messages. While job hunting, tailor your voice message to your audience and eliminate music.	10. Don't have inappropriate voice messages or lengthy music intros.

Source: Adapted from Morsch (2009).

FIGURE 6.5 Sample Teacher Resume

Soon Tobe TEACHER

Street Address

City, State Zip

(999) 999–9999   *e-mail:* soontobeteacher@email.com

OBJECTIVE	To obtain a teaching position at the preschool or elementary level.
EDUCATION	Currently pursuing a BS in Elementary Education (Early Childhood PreK–3 emphasis) at Sunshine State University. Graduation date: May 15, 2009) Certification (following graduation): Early Childhood (PreK–3) and Elementary Education (1–6). *Overall GPA: 3.66; GPA in Education: 3.89*
	High School Diploma, High School High, May 2004. Salutatorian of graduating class.

TEACHING EXPERIENCE

Sunshine Tutoring Center—Teacher (August 2009–present)

Supervisor: Dr. Supervisor, EdD (999) 999–9999. Work with students, K–12 and all ability levels, to improve success in school through instruction in reading, writing, math, and study skills.

Student Teaching—Kindergarten (March 12–May 12, 2009)

Flatwood Elementary, Ms. Mentor Teacher

- Used centers for math, science, social studies, health, and writing to complement the child-based, hands-on curriculum.
- Implemented a positive discipline plan that promoted student responsibility, problem-solving skills, and student accountability.
- Worked with "reading and writing programs to encourage reading and writing at home, parent involvement, and listening, speaking, and writing skills.
- Implemented small groups. Reading instruction. Developed thematic unit on plants and gardening around major instructional goals.

Student Teaching—Fourth Grade (January 13–March 10, 2009)

Logan-Rogersville, Mrs. Very Good Teacher

- Created and implemented literature units on *Number the Stars* and *Mississippi Bridge*.
- Developed and taught writing unit on "why" stories.
- Developed supplemental materials to match the students' needs and to make material more interesting and meaningful. Adaptations were created for units for time, money, geometry, and weather.

Source: Adapted from Post (2009).

Practicums (2007—195 hours). Observed classroom *and* taught lessons one on one, to small groups, or to the whole class. Six classrooms total; two were multiage, Grades PreK–4.

- Developed and implemented thematic units on plants and seeds and insects.
- Completed lessons on various children's books, poems, and themes.
- Lessons involved cooperative learning, language experience approach, hands-on-minds-on experiences, and interdisciplinary teaching.

Volunteer Work (2008—70 hours). Volunteered as Teacher's Assistant, 6th Avenue Elementary; Preschool Teacher, Head Start; Mentor for K student, Literacy Center; and Elementary Science Fair Judge at Lincoln School.

Teacher's Assistant (2007—100 hours). Observed and interacted with individual students at SMSU Parenting Life Skills Center (adult parenting classes), University Child Care Center (4–5 year olds), and Fair Grove Elementary (2nd grade).

REFERENCES

On Request

LET'S PRACTICE!

Activity 6.2   Develop a Resume

Carefully review the resume guidelines and resume shown in Table 6.8 and Figure 6.5. Next, using the format shown in the example, develop a resume using the following categories:

1. Name; address; work, home, and cell phone numbers; e-mail address (be sure to keep this information current).

2. Career objective (e.g., teaching, school administrator, school counselor, curriculum specialist). Target the objective to the position being sought.

3. Education (most recent first).

4. Employment history (most recent first).

5. Related experience (most recent first; list only those that are related to the career objective, such as community work, parent involvement, etc.).

6. Specialized skills (highlight those that are relevant to the position you are seeking—e.g., bilingual, certification in visual impairment, mentor teacher).

7. Honors and awards (any accomplishments, honors, awards, or grants; e.g., dean's list, honor societies, National Science Foundation Science Through Literacy Grant, Bilingual Teaching Fellow).

8. Professional affiliations (any organizations that are related to the career objective).

9. Sources for references and letters of recommendation (professional references are preferred, such as employers or supervisors in related fields, former or current instructors, mentors).

For specific information related to this concept, see the Chapter 6 resources on the CD.

We have provided some sample links that include resume formats at the end of this chapter and on the CD with related Web links. We highly recommend that candidates visit their university career centers and human resources departments at their workplaces to obtain more information and assistance on resume development.

STANDARDS AND ARTIFACTS

If a portfolio is organized to demonstrate accomplishments in meeting standards, a *reflective introduction* to each standard is recommended. There is a full discussion about reflective statements in Chapter 4, and we suggest a review of that chapter. The introduction should reflect on the candidate's development and growth related to the standard. We urge that candidates provide rationales describing why each artifact presents solid evidence of competency in the standard or a particular aspect of the standard. Figures 6.6 and 6.7 show examples of introductory reflections to a standard for a teacher and an administrator candidate, respectively.

Portfolio artifacts provide tangible evidence to show a candidate's level of mastery or competency in a professional standard or goal. Care must be taken in selecting artifacts that best demonstrate competencies. Chapter 4 provides a comprehensive process to transform artifacts into evidence. To review, artifacts may represent current levels of mastery in the standards along three dimensions: (1) *knowledge*—what I have learned by attendance in classes and workshops and by reading relevant materials related to the standard, (2) *skills*—what skills I can effectively apply in the professional setting, and (3) *dispositions*—the beliefs, values, commitment, and desire to meet this standard. These three dimensions reflect three domains of learning: (1) the cognitive domain of knowledge (Bloom, 1956; Clark, 2007), (2) the psychomotor domain of physical or manual skills and abilities (Simpson, 1972), and (3) the affective domain of attitudes, dispositions, and beliefs (Krathwohl, Bloom, & Bertram, 1973; Zeichner, 1993, 2003). Table 6.9 gives examples of the three domains, along with suggestions for artifacts and the specific competencies they demonstrate.

Table 6.10 separates artifacts from different sources into specific categories. This type of information is useful in deciding where to locate artifacts for the portfolio as well as in cross-referencing artifacts that may appear in multiple locations.

Note: RICA Examination and Praxis II Subject Assessments information is available at http://www.rica.nesinc.com/ and http://www.ets.org/praxis, respectively.

FIGURE 6.6   Sample Introduction to a Standard for a Teacher Credential Candidate

Interstate New Teacher Assessment and Support Consortium Standards

Principle 1

Knowledge of Subject Matter

The teacher understands the central concepts, tools of inquiry, and structures of the discipline(s) he or she teaches and can create learning experiences that make these aspects of subject matter meaningful for students. (INTASC, 1992)

One of the first and most basic requirements of teachers is to know the subjects they teach. Knowledge of subject matter involves much more than simple facts or information about a specific content area, such as language arts, mathematics, social studies, science, art, music, or physical education. It also involves a strong understanding of the curriculum resources, instructional strategies, and classroom organizational structures to bring life to each content area. It further requires a clear understanding of the national, state, and district standards for each subject, along with the frameworks or curricular guidelines of what material to cover at each level. These are usually presented in the scope and sequence overviews for each subject and grade level.

Artifacts

In the Teacher Credential program, we were given numerous activities and assignments to familiarize us with the various content areas, such as where and how to locate **content standards** and curriculum frameworks so that we could align our lessons to the appropriate standards. I have included several standards-based lesson plans, which I developed and implemented during my internship. We were also required to conduct field observations in classrooms where the subjects were being taught, along with reviewing and evaluating curriculum resources to enhance understanding and teaching to a wide range of students.

I've included two of my midterm exams, in which we were asked to prescribe types of programs and materials that would be appropriate for teaching mathematics or science to English-language learners along with a theoretical foundation to support our recommendations. We were also asked to develop thematic units around several content areas that made practical, real-world connections for the student. I've included an inquiry-based thematic social studies unit on elections and the primary role they play in our government. This unit included field trips, learning centers, group projects, applications of technology, letters to parents, and samples of completed student assignments that were given as assessment, in accordance with the curriculum framework for social studies in the fifth grade.

Last, I've included my passing RICA (Reading Instruction Competency Assessment) Examination and Praxis II Subject Assessments (Professional Assessments for Beginning Teachers) scores as further evidence of subject matter mastery. I successfully passed both tests on my first attempt.

Interstate School Leaders Licensure Consortium (ISLLC): Standards for School Leaders

Standard 3

Managing the Organization

A school administrator is an educational leader who promotes the success of all students by ensuring management of the organization, operations, and resources for a safe, efficient, and effective learning environment. (CCSSO, 1996)

Being an administrator is a very difficult task. There are many behind-the-scenes activities that go on during the day, and one needs to be aware of everything for the school to function well. Although very chaotic at times, the routine activities are the same every day: The school opens at 7:00 a.m., the children eat breakfast, they line up, and the teachers pick up their classes and teach. Although the leader of the organization has to be aware of the daily routines and what needs to happen for the school to function, he or she also has to be diligent in making sure that all the adults in the school are working in ways that ensure that the educational needs of the students are being met.

Artifacts

The leadership program prepared us to meet this standard by requiring us to take a look at the school that we work with and to write a case study of our school in order to learn important information about the school. This offered me the opportunity to develop my knowledge and skills in finding, collecting, and analyzing data. I learned about a variety of achievement data and where to find it. I also learned how to look at and gain an understanding of the school's culture and the implications for leading change.

After analyzing the school case study, we were asked to create a plan to transform the school to make it a better learning environment. This required us to work in collegial learning groups to accomplish a common goal and to pool our knowledge and experiences. These artifacts provide complex information about how to manage change through gaining the knowledge and insights to understand organizational cultures, cultural contexts of organizations, and building teams for transformation to accomplish short- and long-term goals. We had to work together and collaborate on the plan.

I have also included a copy of my fieldwork log. During my fieldwork experience, I had the opportunity to act as the administrator designee for several days. It was then that I truly got a feel of what running a school is like. During one of my fieldwork days, I had to make sure that the school was up and running by the time the children arrived at the door. There were substitutes that needed to be called, classrooms to be covered for late-arriving teachers, even times I had to call the legal office for advice. I have included a memo from my mentor that documents my successful accomplishments of these tasks. She also included comments about this in my evaluation, which is included as an artifact. These artifacts also document skills and dispositions related to ISLLC Standard 3. The experience of being in charge of the school was intimidating; however, with the help of the people around me, I managed to get everything in order by the time the children were in the classroom.

TABLE 6.9 The Three Dimensions of Competence and Their Corresponding Learning Domains, With Sample Artifacts

Knowledge	Skills	Dispositions
Cognitive Learning Domain What I know or have learned by attendance in classes, workshops, and through course readings and related literature. Research and theoretical information or knowledge base.	*Psychomotor Learning Domain* Specific abilities and skills I have where I can apply my knowledge in authentic professional settings.	*Affective Learning Domain* Beliefs, attitudes, values, commitment, and desire I have to meet the standard.
Sample Artifacts	**Sample Artifacts**	**Sample Artifacts**
• Essays, written reports • Traditional exams • Certificate of completion • Literature reviews • Summaries or annotated reports • Research projects • Assessment reports • Case studies • Attendance at professional development locales • Memberships in professional organizations and subscriptions to professional journals • Theoretical introductions to assignments (case studies, thematic units, classroom management plans) • Course grades	• Essays, written reports • Research projects • Case studies • Action research • Literature reviews • Learning centers • Planning and implementing workshops • Thematic units • Pictures of bulletin boards, learning centers • Lesson plans • IEPs • Organizational charts • Drawings of floor plans • Videotapes of classroom management plans in action (authentic application of theories) • Examples of math and literacy assessments • Technology application plans (multimedia presentations) • Samples of student work and completed projects • Observations by literacy and mathematics instructors	• Philosophy of education statement • Reflections on assignments • Journal entries • Supervisor observation reports • Self- and peer evaluations • Documents on communication and collaboration in developing IEPs • Parent letters • Letters of commendation • End-of-course reflections • Summative reflections • Videotapes of classroom instruction that includes evidence of interactions with culturally and linguistically diverse students • Responses from students and parents • Student achievement • Evidence of expectations in assignments, rubrics, comments on students papers • Case study reflections

LET'S PRACTICE!

Activity 6.3   Selecting Artifacts

Select two artifacts that are going to be used as evidence toward mastery of a standard, goal, or objective. Ask the following questions about the selected artifacts in order to determine whether they are the best authentic examples of progress.

- What kind of content knowledge, skills, or dispositions are evident in these artifacts?
- Are the artifacts related to a competency in which you need to demonstrate development?
- How do these artifacts demonstrate the processes of action research and learning?
- What professional job-related skills are demonstrated?
- What beliefs, values, and expectations are evident in the artifacts? Are they consistent with your philosophy of education?
- Do you already have reflections written about these artifacts? If so, review the reflections to see if they need updating or modifying. If not, write a reflection for each of the two artifacts you selected that addresses the foregoing questions.

CATEGORIZING AND CROSS-REFERENCING ARTIFACTS

For specific information related to this concept, see the Chapter 6 resources on the CD.

Some type of graphic organizer or other tool should be used to help give an overview of how the collected artifacts are aligned to the standards. The Sample Artifacts Signoff and Ratings Organizer Using INTASC Standards (Table 6.11) illustrates a way to organize the artifacts for easy cross-referencing and to see quickly (1) if there is sufficient evidence for each standard (the organizer helps to answer the question, Is there a Swiss cheese effect: Are there holes where there is no evidence or minimal evidence?) and (2) which artifacts could serve as documentation for more than one standard.

Some artifacts can indeed provide evidence of competencies in more than one standard, particularly in fieldwork assignments with job-related responsibilities, such as case studies and unit plans. They can also demonstrate competencies in multiple domains. A **case study** is a comprehensive assignment and addresses several INTASC principles, such as Principle 1, (Knowledge of Subject Matter), Principle 2 (Knowledge of Human Development and Learning), and Principle 8 (Assessment of Student Learning). It also appears across all three learning domains described in Table 6.11. Please see the CD for an example of a case study. When cross-referencing artifacts, organize the table of contents and the portfolio sections in ways that accomplish this efficiently. Some candidates have expanded the organizer to record books and publications that they have read to assess whether there are voids in their literature or knowledge bases.

This organizer would be used over the course of the program. Table 5.5 in Chapter 5 outlines benchmark activities in portfolio development that include a column for signoff on competencies. Ideally, candidates' papers, field logs, and other artifacts can be rated and signed off in a timely manner by instructors, supervisors, and mentors on whether the documentation *minimally meets the standard, satisfactorily meets the standard,* or *exceeds*

TABLE 6.10   Suggested Artifacts

Personal	Academic	Field Assignment	Job Related
• Vision • Philosophy • Resume • References and other letters • Credentials • Transcripts • Letters and awards that are related to growth	• Course work • Reflections • Case studies, action research, research papers, and reports • Summaries and reflections on books, articles read • Class presentations • Use of Web sites • Knowledge and competencies in teaching diverse populations • Participation in conferences, in-service, workshops • Lesson study	• Journals • Learning logs • Fieldwork activities • Projects • Reports • Evidence of teamwork • Videos • Budget activities • Community involvement projects	• Personal assessments • Student assessments • IEPs • Lesson plans, unit plans • Student academic progress • Instructional assessments • Newsletters • Presentations to faculty, parents, community • Videos • Evidence of decision making, problem solving, use of data • Use of technology • Grant applications • Strategic planning documents

the standard as demonstrated in Table 6.11. The candidate could then indicate on the organizer the rating, the person who rated the artifact, and the date. Those rating the documents would use agreed-on scoring rubrics for consistency in ratings, using guidelines similar to those described in Chapter 5.

REFLECTIONS AND REFLECTIVE STATEMENTS

We want to stress that continual written reflections are an essential component of the portfolio process. These reflections record developmental and summative information about a candidate's growth. Chapter 4 highlighted the importance and the role of the reflective process in professional growth and provided some reflective prompts and sample reflections. A review of this information is useful to guide the writing of reflections for inclusion in the portfolio.

To review, portfolios many include several types of reflective statements. For example, *developmental* reflections might be for each section and subsection of the portfolio. These reflections are more specific to the task at hand. End-of-course or interim program reflections may also be included. The most comprehensive reflection, however, is *summative* and reflects on growth and development over the course of the program. It may reflect on the program in general, the portfolio process, and other information considered important to the candidate, the program, or both. See the sample case study in the CD for examples of a variety of reflections.

For specific information related to this concept, see the Chapter 6 resources on the CD.

TABLE 6.11 Sample Artifacts Signoff and Ratings Organizer Using INTASC Standards

Artifact	Principle 1: Knowledge of Subject Matter	Principle 2: Knowledge of Human Development and Learning	Principle 3: Adapting Instruction for Individual Learning	Principle 4: Multiple Instructional Strategies	Principle 5: Classroom Motivation and Management	Principle 6: Communication Skills	Principle 7: Instructional Planning Skills	Principle 8: Assessment of Student Learning	Principle 9: Professional Commitment and Responsibility	Principle 10: Partnerships
Case Studies										
Rating	Partially	Meets	Partially							
Instructor	Mims	Doyle	Johnson							
Date	3/09	6/09	6/09							
Lesson Plans										
Rating		Meets	Meets	Meets			Meets			
Instructor		Doyle	Nichols	Salcido			Johnson			
Date		6/10	6/10	6/10			9/11			
Instructional Assessments										
Rating	Meets	Exceeds	Meets					Exceeds		
Instructor	Bush	Salcido	Nichols					Bush		
Date	12/09	6/12	6/12					6/12		
Teaching Video										
Rating	Exceeds			Meets	Meets	Meets	Meets	Meets		
Instructor	Mims			Smith	Pulido	Doyle	Johnson	Bush		
Date	6/12			6/12	6/12	3/12	3/12	9/11		

LET'S PRACTICE!

Activity 6.4   Write a Summative Reflection on a Completed Project, Course, or Program

Respond to the following:

- What was the purpose of the course, project, or program?
- What knowledge, skills, and dispositions were learned as a result of the experiences?
- How did the experience add to your development as a teacher (counselor, administrator)?
- What areas need more growth? What would you improve?
- What were the strengths or needed improvements in the portfolio development process?

SUMMARY

This chapter discusses the major types of contents that are included in portfolios and provides some examples of portfolio contents. First, information and examples are given of tables of contents and the development of a vision and educational philosophy statements. Next, documents for inclusion, such as a resume, transcripts, and letters of reference, are presented. The section on standards provides information on developing reflective introductions and how to identify, select, and organize artifacts to demonstrate competency in professional standards.

Suggested ways to think about and organize artifacts are discussed, and then a description of the introduction to the professional standards and an explanation of how to select and organize artifacts to demonstrate competencies are presented. For each standard, we recommend that candidates provide a rationale to describe how each artifact presents evidence of competency in the standard or a particular aspect of the standard. We conclude the chapter with a discussion of the different types of reflections that may be included in the portfolio.

USEFUL RESOURCES

Samples of Candidate Reflections (http://www.sitesupport.org/module1/INTASC_PRIN CIPLE_1_1.htm) A site featuring samples of candidate reflections based on INTASC Principles.

Resume Web Links

Although most of these sites are teacher related, the information is useful for any educator.

Developing a Teaching Resume (http://www.mcpherson.edu/careers/resource_center/ Teaching%20Resume.doc)

This Web site provides rudimentary resume skills, a sample resume, and tips for student teachers and recent teacher education graduates.

Resume Development for Teachers. (http://www.stthomas.edu/lifeworkcenter/ documents/Teacher%20resume%20development.doc)

This is a detailed nine-page PDF file that focuses on developing a stellar resume.

Sample Teaching Resume (http://www.mnstate.edu/career/job_search/t-resume.pdf)

This Web site provides future educators with guidelines for creating a teaching resume. This site also provides a sample resume.

Teaching Resume Generator. (http://www.teachnology.com/web_tools/resume)

Making a resume just got simpler—type in your objective, education, work experience, and so on, and your resume will be created using a template, leaving you no need to worry about wasting time on computer applications and keyboarding skills.

FOR FURTHER READING

Barnes, P., Clark, P., & Thull, B. (2005). Web-based digital portfolios and counselor supervision. *Journal of Technology in Counseling, 3*(1). Retrieved May 2, 2005, from http://jtc.colstate.edu/V03–1/Barnes/Barnes.htm

Balch, B. V., Frampton, P. M., & Hirth, M. A. (2006). *Preparing a professional portfolio: A school administrator's guide.* Boston: Pearson.

Barth, R. S. (1990). *Improving schools from within: Teachers, parents, and principals can make the difference.* San Francisco: Jossey-Bass. Chapters 11 and 12 are very useful for vision development.

Boes, S. F., VanZile-Tamsen, C., & Jackson, C. M. (2001). Portfolio development for the 21st century school counselor. *Professional School Counseling, 4*(3), 229–231.

Campbell, C. A., & Dahir, C. A. (1997). *The national standards for school counseling programs.* Alexandria, VA: American School Counselor Association.

Clark, D. R. (2007). *Learning domains of Bloom's Taxonomy.* Retrieved March 16, 2009, from http://www.nwlink.com/ ~ Donclark/hrd/bloom.html

Hartnell-Young, E., & Morriss, M. (2007). *Digital portfolios: Powerful tools for promoting professional growth and reflection* (2nd ed.). Thousand Oaks, CA: Corwin Press.

Meadows, R. B., & Dyal, A. B. (1999, Winter). Implementing portfolio assessment in the development of school administrators: Improving preparation for educational leadership. *Education, 120*(2), 304–315.

Montgomery, K. (1997, Spring). Student teacher portfolios: A portrait of the beginning teacher. *The Teacher Educator, 32*, 216–225.

Salend, S. J. (2001). Creating your own professional portfolio. *Intervention in School and Clinic, 36*(4), 195–201.

7

Presenting and Sharing the Portfolio

You do not have to have a perfect portfolio that you would show from cover to cover. What you do want to have is a collection of items that you can strategically draw on to support claims you wish to make about yourself.

—Satterthwaite and D'Orsi (2003, p. 148)

CHAPTER OBJECTIVES

Readers will be able to

❏ describe how to prepare and retool a portfolio for a presentation;

❏ develop presentation strategies; and

❏ design ways to schedule, organize, and score portfolio presentations.

SCENARIO

There were 3 weeks before the end of the term, and the candidates in Instructor Brown's class were becoming anxious about their portfolio presentations. They had been told they would be given 20 to 30 minutes for presentations to an audience of colleagues, instructors, and school site supervisors. After the presentation, the audience would be given an opportunity to ask questions and make comments and recommendations.

The candidates had many questions, such as, What contents should we present? They had collected work representing 2 or more years of accomplishments. Should they present from each competency area? What artifacts should they present? What about their reflections, vision, resume, and other documents that they had included in the portfolio? Who was going to score their presentation and tell them whether they had passed?

Other concerns that came up about the presentations related to presenting a hard-copy versus an electronic portfolio. In this program, candidates had been given a choice of which format to use. Candidates who had chosen the electronic version wanted to know how they could share their portfolios. Would someone provide a projector? Should they bring their own computers? Those who had hard-copy portfolios were using binders and file boxes. They were concerned about how to handle and show their work.

These concerns made the instructor aware that the candidates needed more guidance in preparing for their portfolio presentations.

OVERVIEW

Presenting and sharing a portfolio provides another opportunity for students to engage in reflections, to self-evaluate, to showcase accomplishments, and to demonstrate evidence of professional development. Portfolio presentations may be (1) a component for a candidate's course or program evaluation, (2) an enhancement for a job interview, or (3) an ongoing professional-development document that is used for both self- and supervisor evaluation. In any case, those who are creating portfolio presentations need to develop skills in constructing and communicating a focused, compelling presentation that provides evidence of professional achievement in goals and national, state, or local professional standards (or some combination of these). Preparation for a presentation requires in-depth reflection (see Chapter 4) and organization of portfolio contents for ease of presentation to the target audience. Hartnell-Young and Morriss (2007) state, "portfolio presentation implies an audience and therefore is a communication between presenter and audience" (p. 64). Most portfolio presenters will benefit from some guidelines, opportunities to practice, critiques of their presentation, and suggestions on how they can self-evaluate their presentations prior to the scheduled presentation time.

The purpose and objectives of the presentation need to determine the timing, setting, configuration (room arrangement), and style (informal versus formal) of the presentation. Presentations are also guided by whether the presentation is for a preservice program credential or graduation, a job interview, or professional development. Another factor that influences the presentation style is whether the portfolio is formative or summative (see Chapter 3). This chapter mainly describes summative presentations, but many of the suggestions can be used for formative presentations as well. Many possibilities exist for presenting the portfolio, and we offer a few suggestions that we hope will assist candidates with the process. Future uses of the portfolio for academic and career advancement, along with additional ways to tailor the portfolio for these purposes, are presented in Chapter 10. The remainder of this chapter is about preparing, organizing, and presenting the portfolio and then evaluating the portfolio presentation.

TIPS FOR PREPARING YOUR PRESENTATION

Regardless of the format or venue (setting or location), some key questions should be asked and answered regarding the portfolio presentation. These are presented in Activity 7.1 and address the general *who, what, why, when, where,* and *how* of the presentation.

LET'S PRACTICE!

Activity 7.1   Key Questions for Preparing Portfolio Presentations

Answer the following questions in preparation for your portfolio presentation:

1. *Who* Questions:
   - Who is the audience?
   - Who will evaluate the presentation, the portfolio, or both?
   - Who will support and assist in preparing for the presentation?

2. *What* Questions:
   - What standards or goals am I addressing, and what artifacts need to be selected?
   - What is being assessed (e.g., personal information, standards, vision)?
   - What types of feedback will be provided?
   - What rubrics are being used to evaluate the presentation, and are they aligned to the purpose and goals?
   - What materials do I need for the presentation?
   - What is the appropriate attire?

3. *Why* Questions:
   - Why am I doing this presentation? (What are the purposes and goals for the presentation?)

4. *When* Questions:
   - When will the presentation take place (date and time)?
   - When will I start to prepare my presentation?
   - When will I rehearse my presentation?

5. *Where* Questions:
   - Where will the presentation take place?

6. *How* Questions:
   - How will I use portfolio rubrics as guides in preparing both the portfolio and the presentation?
   - How much does the presentation count toward a grade, certification, graduation, securing a position, on-the-job evaluation, and so forth?
   - How much time will I have for the presentation?
   - How much time do I need to prepare for the presentation?

Activity 7.2 summarizes other important information that should be considered in preparing for the presentation. The Portfolio Planner can serve as a quick reference. The presenter needs to carefully review each of the areas, which include

- purpose: personal, academic, or professional;
- timing: formative or summative;
- setting, location: classroom, conference room, office, or other;
- format or configuration: whole class, small group, or other;
- style: formal, informal, question and answer, or other;
- audience: colleagues, instructors, interviewers;
- format of portfolio: hard copy or electronic; and
- materials: handouts, projectors, and so on.

By combining Activities 7.1 and 7.2, a Portfolio Presentation Planning Worksheet has been developed, which can be used to address the key questions and to form a type of template to guide the planning for the portfolio presentation in the critical areas that need to be addressed. The Portfolio Presentation Planning Worksheet, presented in Activity 7.3, can also be used as an artifact after the presentation. We recommend that portfolio presenters complete this worksheet. Thoughtful, knowledgeable planning will usually ensure an effective presentation.

For a presentation, a well-developed portfolio needs only to be modified or adapted for a specific purpose. Only the best examples of high-quality evidence are presented, and those works should be keyed to the required national, state, and local goals and objectives or required national, state, or local professional standards. These artifacts should demonstrate knowledge, skills, or dispositions related to the standards.

As noted in Chapter 6, some artifacts may address more than one standard. The Artifacts Organizer by INTASC Standards (Table 6.11) or other professional standards, can be of great assistance in helping to select the artifacts. Those on which instructors, supervisors, and mentors have signed off and that *meet* or *exceed standards* should receive primary consideration for presentation. The rationales or reflections that were written to support the selection of particular artifacts are useful for scripting the presentation (see Chapter 4 and Figures 6.6 and 6.7 in Chapter 6.)

For specific information related to this concept, see the Chapter 7 resources on the CD.

Plan to organize the physical layout of a hard-copy portfolio so information is easy to find, attractively presented, and easy for the audience to view. Highlight sections of the documents that provide the best evidence of knowledge, skills, or dispositions related to the standards. The use of highlighters, underlining, color coding, or bold or enhanced type is suggested. Some candidates use sticky notes with notations or tabs on the document to point out and quickly locate pertinent information. The CD provides some visual examples of presentation layouts. Activity 7.4 can be a useful checklist for those making e-portfolio presentations.

Activity 7.2 Portfolio Presentation Planner

(Check or circle all that apply in each category)

Purpose	Timing	Setting/ Location	Format/ Configuration	Style	Audience	Type	Materials
Personal • Professional development • Reflection	**Formative Evaluation** (During course or program as a checkpoint)	Regular classroom Different classroom Office setting	Whole class Large group (15–20+) Small group (3–5)	Formal presentation Informal discussion Question and answer	Peers Supervisors Mentors Instructors	Hard-copy Electronic	Table Projector and screen Handouts/ summaries
Academic • Formative program evaluation • Summative program evaluation	**Summative Evaluation** (End of course or program)	Conference room Job location	Pair share (both partners share portfolios) Review panel Individual/ one-on-one Roundtable (everyone shares portfolio) Other	Interview Dialogue Other	Potential employers Program review panel Self Friends Other		Portfolio-at-a-Glance (Campbell et al., 2004) Evaluation/ feedback forms Presentation rubrics Other
Professional • Career advancement • Job interview **Other**							

139

Activity 7.3   Portfolio Presentation Planning Worksheet

Name: _____   **Date:** _____

Key Questions (Provide answers for each)

- Are the standards and goals for the presentation clearly stated?
- What is being assessed (e.g., personal information, standards, vision)?
- What rubrics are being used to evaluate the presentation, and are they aligned to the purpose and goals?
- What types of feedback will be provided?
- Who will be evaluating the presentation?
- How much does the presentation count toward a grade, certification, graduation, securing a position, on-the-job evaluation, and so forth?
- How much time will I have for the presentation?
- When will the presentation take place, and how much time do I have to prepare?
- Where will the presentation take place, and what additional materials will I need, if any?
- Have I used the portfolio rubrics as guides in preparing both the portfolio and the presentation?

Portfolio Presentation Checklist (Check or circle all that apply in each category)

Purpose	Timing	Setting/ Location	Format/ Configuration	Style	Audience	Type	Materials
Personal • Professional development • Reflection **Academic** • Formative program evaluation	**Formative Evaluation** (During course or program as a checkpoint)	Regular classroom Different classroom Office setting	Whole class Large group (15–20+) Small group (3–5)	Formal presentation Informal discussion Question and answer	Peers Supervisors Mentors Instructors Potential employers	Hard-copy Electronic	Table Projector and screen Handouts/ summaries

	Summative Evaluation (End of course or program)	Conference room	Pair share (both partners share portfolios)	Interview	Program review panel	Portfolio-at-a-Glance (Campbell et al., 2004)
• Summative program evaluation **Professional** • Career advancement • Job interview **Other**		Job location	Review panel Individual/one-on-one Roundtable (everyone shares portfolio) Other	Dialogue Other	Self Friends Other	Evaluation/feedback forms Presentation rubrics Other

The Specifics of My Portfolio Presentation on [Date: _____]

Who? (Audience)

What? (Standards, etc.)

Why? (Purpose)

When? (Date/duration)

Where? (Location/setting)

How? (Configuration)

Materials

Special Notes

Reflections on Presentation

LET'S PRACTICE!

Activity 7.4   Checklist for Developers and Audiences for a Digital Portfolio

Ask	Yes	No	N/A
Is the design clear?			
Is the text easy to read throughout the portfolio?			
Do the graphics load quickly?			
Are the graphics supported by text?			
Is navigation easy?			
Are the links obvious to the reader?			
Do the links lead to further information and lead back (no dead ends)?			
Is the use of color attractive?			
Is there a consistent style throughout?			
Are the sound and video files clear and informative?			
Are sound and video labeled and supported by text?			
Are there contact details for the developer?			
Is copyright acknowledged appropriately?			
Is there a clear indication of production dates for the portfolio?			
If the portfolio has been updated, is there information related to the updates?			

The audience and the type of setting for the presentation should determine the most appropriate container for the presentation. Hard-copy materials may be housed in a binder—a file that is transportable, expandable, and open at the top for easy access. Many office stores have milk-crate-type files that are open and lightweight. In programs in which portfolios have been developed over several years, one may need to scale down and re-sort documents for presentation. A thumbnail summary of all documentation for each of the standards and levels of proficiency can be distributed in a table-of-contents format, table format, or modified Artifacts Organizer format. Campbell et al. (2004) describe a process called "Portfolio at a Glance" (p. 95), which results in a brochure that highlights specific artifacts in ways that allow for a quick review of the portfolio. The process, which uses nine steps, is designed for teaching portfolios but could be adapted for administrator and counseling portfolios.

Writing the Brochure

1. *Reflect* on one standard at a time.

2. *Select* at least one artifact to feature within a standard.

3. *Focus* on the teaching behaviors that are evidenced in the one artifact.

4. *Reword* your teaching behaviors into concise, specific statements in the past tense.

5. *Clarify* your teaching behaviors by writing directly above the name of the artifact a short descriptor of the competency demonstrated.

6. *Continue* Steps 1–5 for each standard.

Assembling the Brochure

1. *Cut and paste* the list of information using a larger piece of paper or a computer.

2. *Edit* the contents of your draft brochure.

3. *Select* desktop design software that will assemble your text to catch the reader's eye. (pp. 95–96)

All of these processes provide an overview of documentation that is linked to each of the standards. The materials in the binder or file folders can be encased with plastic inserts. Binders with pockets are useful for insertion of a **USB flash drive** or a CD, which might contain media information for the presentation.

Electronic portfolios are becoming increasingly popular, and many programs are requiring electronic and Web folios. Chapters 8 and 9 are devoted to discussing how to design, organize, and develop electronic portfolios using Word, **PowerPoint**, and **Web-based** formats. The benefits of electronic portfolios are highlighted along with information on how to prepare for electronic presentations. A crucial factor that needs to be addressed regarding electronic portfolios is the setting for presentation. It is essential that the proper lighting and equipment be available and tested prior to the presentation. Candidates should have a hard-copy backup in case of equipment failure.

In order for instructors, interviewers, or others to access a presenter's Web folio prior to or after the presentation, a **Web address** can be included on the resume. However, it is essential to be cautious about the type of personal information that is placed on the Web and who might have access to the address. It is important to guard privacy and to remove any IDs or confidential information (Hartnell-Young & Morriss, 2007).

TIPS FOR SCHEDULING THE PRESENTATION

or specific
nformation
elated to
his
oncept,
ee the
hapter 7
esources
n the CD.

Plan the presentation for the required time block that is designed to meet the required goals and purposes (e.g., 20- to 30-minute time slots for each presentation). Timed presentations require rehearsing. If a high-stakes presentation is required, candidates should consider a rehearsal video that is staged for people who give useful critiques. Candidates might also want to use audiotapes. The CD presents examples of both hard-copy and electronic presentations.

Programs and instructors may use a variety of scheduling formats. When the contents of the portfolio previously have been rated for levels of proficiency in meeting standards, the presentation may be a culminating experience for candidates to share their accomplishments with one another. Another scenario might include instructors and field supervisors using the presentation as a component of a final evaluation on the demonstration of competencies. Yet another scenario might be candidates having the opportunity to simulate a portfolio presentation for a job interview.

If portfolio presentations are designed to include a variety of audiences, it is essential for students to strategically plan presentations for sharing. Some programs, particularly certification- and degree-granting ones, might require candidates to present portfolios to supervisors, mentors, or colleagues in areas in which the candidates aspire or are currently working.

Portfolios presentation should be prepared in a way that they can be presented at more than one location in order to accommodate school or district site field supervisors. It is desirable for a candidate to schedule a meeting with evaluators well in advance of the presentation. Some programs encourage candidates to leave their portfolios with their supervisors before or after the presentation. If the program implementation guidelines suggested in Chapter 5 are used, most supervisors and others who are involved in the candidates' development will be familiar with most aspects of their portfolios.

Candidates might want to reflect on what types of feedback they desire in addition to those required by their program. This will prove useful for their continued development. Candidates should follow up with letters of appreciation to anyone who assisted, supervised, or mentored them.

We suggest that candidates take time to select appropriate attire for the presentation. Presentations should be treated as a professional experience in which candidates are given an opportunity to demonstrate achievement and receive feedback for further development. It also can be a time for experiencing what may take place in a job interview. It is important to consider the audience and setting for presentation in selecting attire. Professional attire is suggested for summative presentations and those that include professionals from the field in the audience.

PRESENTATION FORMATS

There are a variety of presentation formats and schedules for portfolio presentations. Among the types of formats are

- presentations to a whole class or group of colleagues in one or two class sessions,

- end-of-course presentations during the program,
- presentations in small groups over several days, and
- portfolio conferencing.

Presentation agendas are designed based on goals, purposes, and a time frame. Presenters need to check for understanding regarding expectations for the presentation, and then a presentation outline should be prepared. Table 7.1 is a Sample Portfolio Presentation Outline. Please note that guidelines for the presentations vary. Guidelines for summative portfolios that are required for licensure or graduation will be given in advance. Candidates

TABLE 7.1 Sample Portfolio Presentation Outline

Name:		Portfolio:	Date:
Introduction and vision	5–10 min.	*Purpose of Portfolio Presentation: Overview* Gives a personal introduction (e.g., name, current position, level in program) Shares personal vision, philosophy, and educational platform States primary goals Describes specific objectives Addresses Standards A, B, and C	
Standard A	5 min.	*Selected Artifacts and Key Points: Highlights* Reflections on first artifact for Standard A Reflections on second artifact for Standard A	
Standard B	5 min.	*Selected Artifacts and Key Points: Highlights* Reflections on first artifact for Standard B Reflections on second artifact for Standard B	
Standard C	5 min.	*Selected Artifacts and Key Points: Highlights* Reflections on first artifact for Standard C Reflections on second artifact for Standard C	
Discussion; question and answer	10 min.	Invite dialogue and conversation; respond to audience questions	
Adjournment		Thank audience Determine how and when feedback will be provided (this may be done prior to presentation)	

for preservice, graduation, credential, and program completion should be thoroughly familiar with what is expected.

A presentation may also include a brief summary of growth in the professional standards by having candidates share their overall growth, reflections on the program, and the portfolio development experience (i.e., Artifacts Organizer, Portfolio at a Glance). Candidates should write letters or notes of appreciation to those who participated in the presentation.

There are a variety of sharing settings in which candidates might make their presentations. The *large-group setting* may use a rotation format. In this setting, candidates are divided into groups of four to six and they present portfolios to each other while the instructor or mentors circulate from group to group. Behavioral norms should be provided regarding how to facilitate a presentation. The *small-group setting* allows candidates to take turns in presenting individually. Every candidate gets an opportunity to present, and there is an instructor or mentor assigned to each group. In an *interview setting,* the candidate is usually directed about what to present. The potential employer may be very specific about what they want to see. Presenters in an *academic or professional development setting* will likely receive feedback on the presentation.

Portfolio conferences provide another format for sharing portfolios. Winsor and Ellefson (1998) have described the conferencing model as a valuable process for self-evaluation. They emphasize the potential of the portfolio as a lifelong tool for reflection and evaluation, a topic discussed more fully in Chapter 10. This conferencing process can be used in addition to or possibly as an alternative to traditional portfolio presentations. Winsor and Ellefson portray the portfolio as a lifelong tool for reflection and evaluation (a topic discussed more fully in Chapter 10), an alternative to traditional portfolio presentations, and the portfolio conference as an ongoing, dynamic formative model of assessment that engages the portfolio developer in the process of self-evaluation. Although they describe this process as mainly for student teachers, it has the potential to be adapted in a variety of settings and with other professionals, such as administrators and counselors.

The conferencing model uses student-led evaluation. In the conference, candidates share their perception of their development with supervisors. Supervisors then review *self-evaluations* and respond to the candidates. The responses of the supervisors are a significant component of the conferencing.

SCORING THE PRESENTATION

Because many presentation possibilities exist, rubrics are designed to address different purposes. Candidates usually receive scoring rubrics in advance of presentations to help them clarify expectations and terminology. This approach also gives candidates time to become familiar with the scoring indicators. More information on scoring portfolios can be found in Chapter 3 and 5. Sometimes in using scoring rubrics, candidates may score *below standard* in one category but score *meets standard* or *exceeds standard* in another category. An overall score will probably consider all of the indicators. Some indicators may have more importance than others. If so, indicators may be weighted in determining an overall score for the presentation.

Scoring rubrics are most likely based on

- specific expectations and grading criteria;
- the content of the presentation and the degree to which the standards, goals, or objectives are met; and
- how effectively the information is presented.

Tables 7.2 and 7.3 provide sample scoring rubrics. These are not for an evaluation of the total portfolio but for how the selected information from the portfolio is presented. These two tables can be used for summative or end-of-course presentations. Sample scoring rubrics for portfolios are also found in Chapters 3 and 5, and on the CD.

For specific information related to this concept, see the Chapter 7 resources on the CD.

TABLE 7.2   Sample Scoring Rubric for Portfolio Presentation

Partially Meets Standards	X	Meets Standards	X	Exceeds Standards	X
• Presents a limited picture of the candidate's philosophy and values		• Presents an adequate picture of the candidate's philosophy and values		• Presents an outstanding picture of the candidate's philosophy and values	
• Presents some evidence of competencies in standards		• Presents adequate evidence of competencies in standards		• Presents strong evidence of competencies in standards	
• Does not highlight strengths		• Highlights strengths		• Highlights strengths well	
• Little evidence of reflective engagement		• Adequate evidence of reflective engagement		• Substantial evidence of reflective engagement	
• Presentation is poorly communicated		• Presentation is clearly communicated		• Presentation is engaging and clearly communication	
• Takes more than allotted time for presentation		• Presents within the allotted time for presentation		• Presents adeptly within the allotted time for presentation	

TABLE 7.3 Sample Scoring Rubric for Portfolio Presentation

Methods and Activities Presentation Peer Evaluations					
Presentation of "The Very Hungry Caterpillar" using the natural approach. Percentage rankings, where 1 is Very High, and 5 is Needs Improvement.					
	1	2	3	4	5
Clarity of objectives	38	46	0	8	8
ELD1	67	23	0	5	5
ELD2	58	32	5	5	0
ELD3	71	24	0	5	0
ELD4	63	32	0	5	0
ELD5	67	23	5	5	0
Student involvement	82	9	9	0	0
General appeal	68	23	9	0	0
Used language-arts strategies	69	22	9	0	0

Presentation Strengths

Visuals such as real fruit and pictures of different types of caterpillars. Book (pictures), worksheet handout.

Got everyone involved.

Nice job of bringing closure to the lesson.

Visual aids.

Good incorporation of content with math, days of the week, vocabulary. Realia, days, charts, throwing fruit, good teamwork, nice review, yummy salad. Student involvement, worksheet for reinforcement.

YUM!

Great visuals, allowed for involvement.

Energy, organization.

Being able to see the actual fruit and writing the answers on the board really helped the ELD1 students.

Clever ways to determine participation.

Vocabulary.

Nicely articulated, good presentation of the book.

Very smooth and confident delivery. You both appeared to be trained, professional teachers.

Good presentation.

Good voice.

Student interaction, presentation.

Fruit salad given to students connected with lesson.

Range of activities, clear presentation, yummy fruit salad.

Loved how you connected real foods with the book.

Suggestions and Recommendations

Move at a slightly faster pace to accommodate all students.

Show more pictures of stages of butterfly.

Didn't help us understand healthy vs. unhealthy.

Repeat words in English, as well. Point to objects in picture. Have students repeat repetitious sections of book in unison, e.g., "But he was still hungry." Good, you did this!

You were beautiful! Don't change a thing!

Having some of the ELD4 and ELD5 students write the information on the chart. Explain terms, e.g., "real" vs. "imaginary"

Could be more fluently presented.

No recommendations. I thought it went very well.

How do you teach them "adding"?

Lesson was good, but maybe wait to give the fruit salad last.

More (bigger) pictures/visuals; anyhow, great job.

Some words are a bit too complicated for ELD1–2 students.

Additional Comments and Ideas

I liked the way you incorporated math into the activity.

Good job! Especially going at it first.

May be too easy for ELD5 students; they might lose interest in the topic. Overall, great presentation.

Good modeling with worksheet. Somewhat abstract for earlier levels, though the fruit helped.

Get it out, dramatize. Good pictures to reinforce stories.

What is healthy?

Great presentation. You incorporated science, literacy, and math.

Clever tying story to concrete fruit. Nice having class count together. Good gestures. Susan: nice gestures, voice, presentation of story.

Great lesson!

First part ran a little slow, but I'm sure with practice you'll be better. Thanks for the fruit.

Very well-prepared materially.

Overall, a great presentation.

Table 7.3 provides a sample of how a particular presentation was rated by a teacher credential candidate's peers. In the Strengths and Suggestions sections, each line represents the comments from a peer in a group evaluation.

SUMMARY

This chapter discusses how to prepare and develop the portfolio for presentation. Some presentation strategies and suggestions for scoring are offered.

The portfolio presentation should be focused and provide evidence of professional competencies in national, state, or local professional standards or learning targets. The portfolio contents must be organized for ease of presentation. Candidates need guidelines, opportunities to practice, and critiques of their presentation. Presentations should be guided by whether the portfolios are being presented at the preservice, job interview, or professional development levels and also by whether the portfolios are formative or summative. This chapter mainly focuses on program summative presentations but provides suggestions for formative presentations, such as portfolio conferencing.

Candidates need to retool their portfolios for presentation and check for understanding regarding the expectations for the presentation. The audience and the type of setting for the presentation should determine the most appropriate container for the presentation. Tips for scheduling presentations are discussed. There can be a variety of presentation formats and schedules, including presentations to a whole class or group of colleagues and presentations in small groups in one time period. Presentation formats vary, depending on goals, purposes, and the time frame.

FOR FURTHER READING

Hartnell-Young, E., & Morriss, M. (2007). *Digital portfolios: Powerful tools for promoting professional growth and reflection* (2nd ed.). Thousand Oaks, CA: Corwin Press.

Winsor, P., & Ellefson, B. (1998, Winter). Professional portfolios in teacher education: An exploration of their value and potential. *Teacher Education Quarterly, 68–81.*

CHAPTER 8

An Overview of Electronic Portfolios

Exploring the Options

> *It is not the strongest species that survive, nor the most intelligent, but the ones most responsive to change.*
>
> —Charles Darwin

CHAPTER OBJECTIVES

Readers will be able to

- ❑ become familiar with technology terms used in the chapter;
- ❑ articulate the benefits of electronic portfolios;
- ❑ determine when, where, and how to use electronic portfolios;
- ❑ explore options for creating electronic portfolios;
- ❑ explore options for presenting electronic portfolios;
- ❑ identify their personal preferences for designing their own electronic portfolios; and
- ❑ review strategies for maintaining privacy and security when creating electronic portfolios.

Greg is working on his elementary teaching credential and is faced with preparing his electronic portfolio. His friend Rachel is working on her single-subject secondary teaching credential and is also faced with preparing her electronic portfolio. Rachel is quite familiar with Microsoft PowerPoint and has decided to create hers using that tool. Greg is more familiar with Microsoft Word and opts to use that instead. Both are making their portfolios CD-based but also want to be able to eventually post them on the Web.

Greg voiced his concerns about the project to Rachel: "I know I'm going to make my portfolio in Word and present it on a CD, but I also want to eventually put it online. Will I be able to do that without having to make two portfolios?"

Rachel had seen online portfolios that used PowerPoint. "I know I can use PowerPoint to make a Web-based portfolio, but I'm not sure if I want to post it online. I would prefer to have mine on a CD that I can bring to an interview and give to the principal.

OVERVIEW

Both students in the scenario will be able to do what they want to do using their chosen tool. In addition to many others, both Microsoft Word and PowerPoint are good tools for creating an electronic portfolio, and both students can then convert their portfolios into Web-based portfolio if they so desire.

This chapter lists the benefits of electronic portfolios and suggests when and where to use them. Key technology terms are also defined for clarity. Next, the reader is guided through a variety of options for determining which tools and platforms best meet their preferences for both creating and presenting the portfolio. Last, a few words of caution are given to help maintain privacy and security in electronic portfolios.

FOUR OPTIONS FOR CREATING AN ELECTRONIC PORTFOLIO

1. The first method uses Word; it is CD-based and requires Word to view the portfolio. This method would be appropriate for students who are familiar with word processing and have entry-level file management skills.

2. The second method also uses Word; it is Web-based (however, this can also be CD-based) and is viewed using a Web browser (e.g., Internet Explorer, Firefox, Safari). This method would be appropriate for students who are familiar with word processing and have entry to middle-level file management skills.

3. The third method uses PowerPoint; it is CD-based, is viewed as a slide show, and requires PowerPoint to view the portfolio. This also applies to any artifact linked to the portfolio. For example, any artifacts that were created using Word requires Word to view these artifacts; any artifacts that were created using Excel requires

Excel to view these artifacts. This method would be appropriate for students who are familiar with PowerPoint and have entry-level file management skills.

4. The fourth method again uses PowerPoint; it is Web-based (and can also be CD-based) and is viewed using a Web browser. This method is appropriate for students who are familiar with PowerPoint and have entry-level to middle-level file management skills.

Remember that electronic portfolios created for the Web need not be uploaded onto a server to be viewed. They can be viewed from a CD using a Web browser.

TECHNOLOGY TERMS USED IN THE CHAPTER

CD-Based—When finished, an electronic portfolio is stored on a CD. It is viewed by accessing the CD in a computer. There is no need for an Internet connection to view the electronic portfolio.

USB Flash Drive—Also called **thumb drive**, stick drive, or **pen drive**, these small, portable storage devices are typically removable and rewritable. They have replaced the floppy disk for portable storage. Compared to floppy disks, they are much faster, hold much more data, have a more durable design, and operate more reliably due to their lack of moving parts.

HTML (HyperText Markup Language)—This is the most common markup language for Web pages.

Hyperlink—This is an electronic link to a specific document or artifact. A hyperlink is usually identified within the text by being bold and underlined or a different color.

Navigation Page—This is a page that has hyperlinks that are connected to specific documents or artifacts. An example would be the Table of Contents, with each entry hyperlinked to its corresponding document or artifact.

Ribbon—In Microsoft Office 2007, the menu and toolbars of earlier versions are replaced with the Ribbon. The Ribbon has groups of commands organized into various tabs.

Web-Based—When finished, an electronic portfolio is uploaded to a **server** that is online. The portfolio is then accessed from a Web site. An Internet connection is necessary to view the electronic portfolio.

WYSIWYG—"What You See Is What You Get." This acronym describes a common user interface where what is viewed on the screen is what will be on the final product.

BENEFITS OF ELECTRONIC PORTFOLIOS

Electronic portfolios do not limit the student to paper artifacts. By using an electronic portfolio, students can include multimedia artifacts, such as presentations that have audio or video included. Movie clips, audio files, narration, or an audio introduction to the portfolio can bring it to life. The combination of text, graphics, sound, and **digital video** can be very powerful. It allows different aspects of the students' work to be presented and reflected on (Hartnell-Young & Morriss, 2007). Instead of just having a lesson plan included in a portfolio, students can link to a video of them teaching the lesson. This video can also have audio comments from the student, pointing out aspects of the lesson that went very well, ideas or insights that the student got from the completed lesson, or things that would be changed the next time the lesson was taught. When using multimedia to demonstrate a lesson plan, reviewers can see the effects of the plan on the students (Montgomery & Wiley, 2008).

Storage of an electronic portfolio is a huge benefit. Portfolios traditionally have housed a myriad of artifacts, which are often stored in binders. A portfolio can become extremely cumbersome with the addition of more and more videos, pictures, audiotapes, CDs, and papers. As these artifacts are collected, the binders keep growing in both width and number. All this can be replaced by an electronic portfolio that can be stored on a CD, a **USB flash drive**, or online. Converting from a paper portfolio to an electronic one is not that difficult. Since the majority of written artifacts in a portfolio have been created digitally, the text is basically ready to format into an electronic portfolio. Any other artifacts to be included can also be digitized, either personally or professionally. Once digitized, these are ready to be organized into an electronic portfolio, too.

Portfolios can be stored on a computer hard drive, a **portable mass storage device** (USB flash drive, USB mini hard drive, MP3 player, smart phone, iPod), a CD, a DVD, a **commercial Web site,** an **educational Web site**, or any combination of these. The method of storage is determined by the intended method of presentation. A word of caution, however: No matter what media you decide on for electronic portfolio storage, always, always, always have another copy as a backup. For example, a CD left in a hot car can warp and become unusable. A Web-based server could crash, and although we hate to even think of it, a computer's hard drive could crash, too. A helpful thought to remember when creating electronic portfolios is, "Save early, save often—and save it in two places!"

Portfolios are often works in progress instead of finished products. This is especially true as candidates prepare their portfolios for credential or certification programs. New artifacts can be added as coursework is completed and standards are addressed without having to worry if the contents will fit their present binder. An electronic portfolio should therefore be thought of as a living document that chronicles ongoing work.

The creation and use of electronic portfolios also brings into practice the first three of five **National Educational Technology Standards** (NETS; International Society for Technology in Education [ISTE], 2008), which recognize that teachers use technology to enhance their productivity and professional practice. The first three NETS standards state that teachers should

1. facilitate and inspire student learning and creativity.

   Teachers use their knowledge of subject matter, teaching and learning, and technology to facilitate experiences that advance student learning, creativity, and innovation in both face-to-face and virtual environments.

2. design and develop digital-age learning experiences and assessments.

   Teachers design, develop, and evaluate authentic learning experiences and assessments incorporating contemporary tools and resources to maximize content learning in context and to develop the knowledge, skills, and attitudes identified in the *NETS for Students* (ISTE, 2007).

3. model digital-age work and learning.

Teachers exhibit knowledge, skills, and work processes representative of an innovative professional in a global and digital society. (ISTE, 2008, n.p.)

Many students are initially intimidated by the technologies used in creating electronic portfolios. But after completing their work, they usually see the usefulness, as well as the need to bring technology into their future classrooms (Wright, Stallworth, & Ray, 2002). The benefits of electronic portfolios seem to outweigh the disadvantages, especially through the process of feedback and reflection (Montgomery & Wiley, 2008). The form that an electronic portfolio takes is determined or limited by availability of appropriate software and hardware (Evans, Daniel, Mikovch, Metze, & Norman, 2006; Wetzel & Strudler 2006).

The most important feature of electronic portfolios is the ability to easily link artifacts to the standards that they address. These artifacts can include multimedia presentations as well as digital video clips. In addition, electronic portfolios give one the ability to link a single element that satisfies multiple standards to each of those standards without having to make multiple copies of the information. For example, if a teacher candidate creates a lesson that addresses three standards, electronic portfolios allow links to the same lesson from each of the three standards without having to create three copies of the lesson. Also, there can be links to each of the three standards that are covered from the single lesson. Electronic portfolios easily incorporate multidirectional links that solve complex navigational and organizational problems. The only disadvantage is the need to have a computer to view them.

WHEN, WHERE, AND HOW TO USE ELECTRONIC PORTFOLIOS

Portfolios in one form or another are being used in about 90% of schools, colleges, and departments of education as tools for making standards-based decisions regarding certification or licensure (Wilkerson & Lang, 2003). Other uses for portfolios have been described in Chapter 1 and expanded upon in Chapter 10.

OPTIONS FOR CREATING ELECTRONIC PORTFOLIOS: CD- OR WEB-BASED

As we have noted, one option for creating and storing electronic portfolios is Web-based. Some schools of education currently offer students space on school servers for Web-based portfolios. Other schools have contracts with commercial vendors that handle Web-based portfolios, such as TaskStream (www.taskstream.com) shown in Figure 8.1, Live Text (www.livetext.com), Chalk and Wire (www.chalkandwire.com), or FolioLive (www.foliolive.com). Students can store their portfolios on the school or commercial servers and give prospective

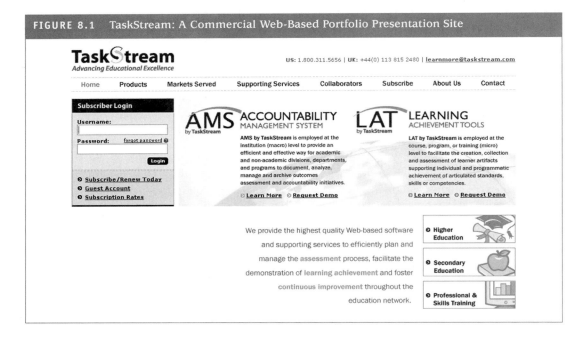

FIGURE 8.1 TaskStream: A Commercial Web-Based Portfolio Presentation Site

employers a Web address to view their portfolios at any time. These sites are **password pro-tected**. Guest IDs and passwords can be created or are provided to allow access to the portfolio for prospective employers. Students generally need some instruction or training in order to post a portfolio on a commercial site.

If school server and commercial-vendor online options are not available, the most common alternative is to make the electronic portfolio **CD-based.** A CD or DVD version is very versatile. Copies of the portfolio can be made for each prospective employer. There is also no need for an Internet connection to view a CD-based portfolio.

Various tools can be used to create electronic portfolios. Commercial portfolio sites have built-in Web tools. For students not using commercial portfolio sites, there are commercial products, such as Adobe's Dreamweaver (www.adobe.com) and Microsoft Word's PowerPoint and Publisher (www.microsoft.com). There are also open-source or free software products, such as Mozilla's SeaMonkey (www.seamonkey-project.org). These products use the **WYSIWYG** technology, which is similar to a word processor. Some tools require more technology experience than others. For the purpose of this book, we focus on using Microsoft Word 2007 and Microsoft PowerPoint 2007. In addition, we have provided the instructional activities for creating electronic portfolios using Microsoft Word 2003 and Microsoft PowerPoint 2003 on the CD.

When CDs or DVDs are used to store an electronic portfolio, there are options for its presentation. PowerPoint can be used to create an electronic portfolio, especially one with a number of videos, audio selections, and pictures. The PowerPoint-based portfolio can be presented using PowerPoint, or it can be converted to **HTML** (hypertext markup language) and be presented using a **Web browser** (see Figures 8.2 and 8.3). Both of these options work quite well with PowerPoint.

For specific information related to this concept, see the Chapter 8 resources on the CD.

FIGURE 8.2   Table of Contents Shown in PowerPoint. Sample of a table of contents from an electronic portfolio presented in PowerPoint.

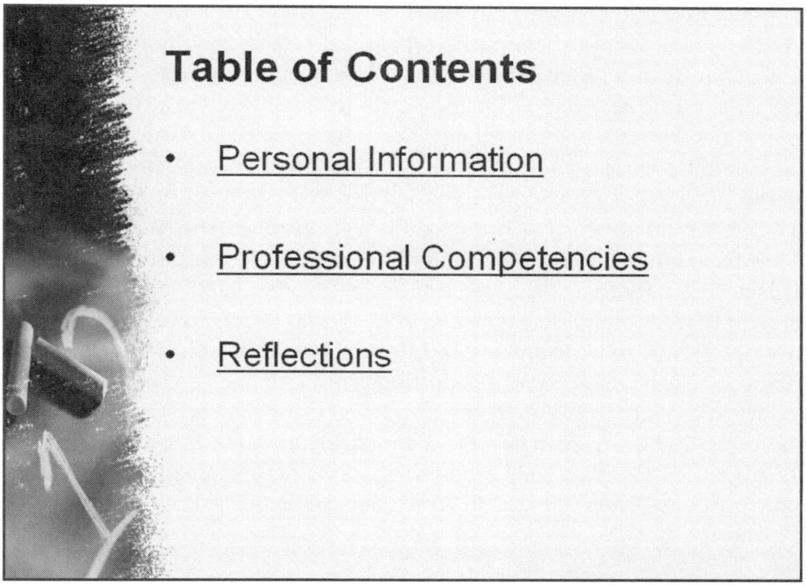

FIGURE 8.3   Table of Contents Shown in HTML. Sample of the same table of contents converted to HTML and presented in Mozilla Firefox.

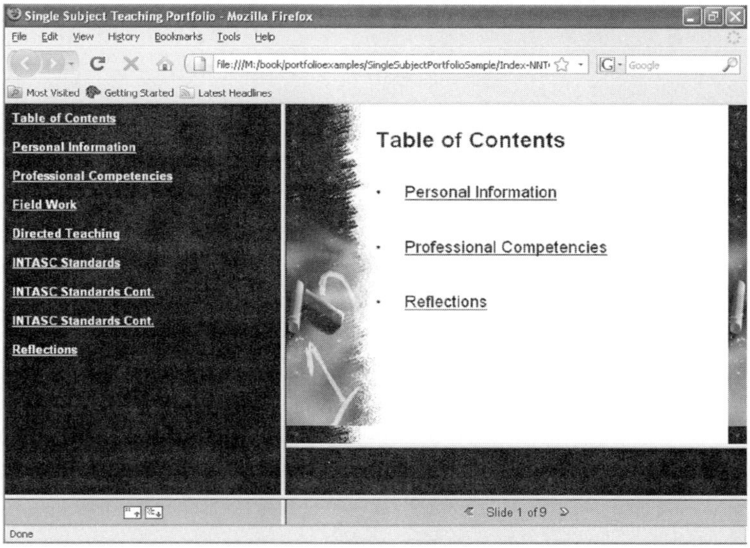

Other documents, such as certificates or credentials, can be scanned and easily included in an electronic portfolio using PowerPoint. The easiest and most universal format to scan these documents in would be the PDF, or portable document format. These documents can either be inserted into a PowerPoint slide or attached with a hyperlink. When a hyperlink is used, the viewer would click on the link and then the document would be shown using Adobe Acrobat Reader (www.adobe.com), a free program used to display PDF documents.

Whether to create a PowerPoint-based portfolio or convert it to a Web-based portfolio is usually determined by personal preference. Now, just because a portfolio is Web-based doesn't mean it has to be posted on the Web. After a portfolio is converted to HTML, it can either be **burned** onto a CD or it can be uploaded to a Web site for online viewing. If it is burned onto a CD, it would appear the same as if it were **live on the Web**. An advantage of having a Web-based portfolio on a CD is that the prospective employer, supervisor, or evaluator needs access only to a computer, not to the Internet itself.

Microsoft **Word** is often used as an electronic portfolio creation tool. Because many students already employ Word to word process, they feel comfortable using it. Like in the process of using PowerPoint, one can create electronic portfolios in Word that can be presented either in Word, or by converting Word to HTML, it can be viewed using a Web browser (Figures 8.4 and 8.5). Hyperlinks can also be made in Word to scanned documents. Just like in PowerPoint, these documents saved in PDF format will be viewed in Adobe Acrobat Reader. Also, like the PowerPoint electronic portfolios, those created in Word can also be burned onto a CD.

FIGURE 8.4 Table of Contents Shown in Word 2007. Sample of a table of contents from an electronic portfolio presented in Word.

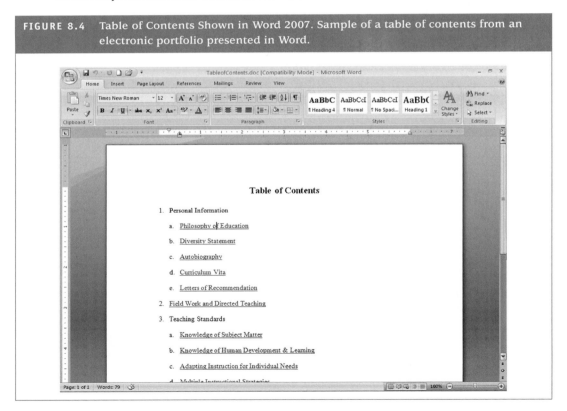

FIGURE 8.5   Table of Contents Shown in HTML. Sample of the same table of contents converted to HTML and presented in Mozilla Firefox.

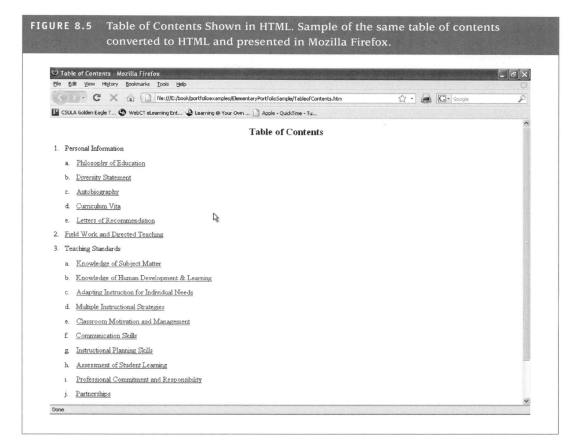

Posting an electronic portfolio on the Web or burning it onto a CD to be left with prospective employers allows employers to view students' work either with or without students present. Leaving a CD or a Web address is especially important if there is no time or equipment available during the interview to view the portfolio.

Let's take another look at the options for creating an electronic portfolio and the methods for presenting and storing them. Table 8.1 shows the various methods to be considered.

PRIVACY AND SECURITY: A WORD OF CAUTION . . .

In this age of identity theft, students need to pay special attention to a few parts of the Web-based portfolio. Before posting a portfolio live on the Web (unless it is password protected), you need to pay special attention to the way personal information is presented. For example, instead of showing an address and phone number, include an e-mail address. And instead of listing references, replace them with, "References available upon request." When student work is used, make sure to remove student identifiers unless

TABLE 8.1 Options for Creating and Presenting Electronic Portfolios

Program Used to Create Electronic Portfolio	Presentation and Viewing Options	
	Presentation Option	Program Used for Viewing
Microsoft Word	CD or DVD	Microsoft Word is needed for viewing. If any scanned PDF documents are linked, Adobe Acrobat Reader is also needed for viewing.
Microsoft Word converted to HTML	Online or CD or DVD	If posted online, an Internet connection is needed. A Web browser such as Firefox, Internet Explorer, or Safari is also needed.
Microsoft PowerPoint	CD or DVD	PowerPoint is needed for viewing. If any scanned PDF documents are linked, Adobe Acrobat Reader is also needed for viewing.
Microsoft PowerPoint converted to HTML	Online or CD or DVD	If posted online, an Internet connection is needed. A Web browser, such as Firefox, Internet Explorer, or Safari is also needed.

For specific information related to this concept, see the Chapter 8 resources on the CD.

written permission is given prior to inclusion. This would also include pictures of children, unless written permission is given prior to inclusion. See CD for a sample permission form. Make sure that the e-mail address you choose to list is appropriate. Prospective employers will have a completely different opinion of an applicant whose e-mail address is "hotsy-totsy@email.com" or "go-for-it@email.com" and one whose e-mail address is the person's name, like "nicknichols@email.com."

STORAGE OPTIONS

Although the most popular storage method is posting or uploading electronic portfolios to the Web, aside from CDs or DVDs, there are other storage options (Figure 8.6). To use the method of Web storage, a Web site must be available. Some schools offer this service, and some Web sites offer free storage space (but you usually have to put up with ad banners), or Web space can be purchased. Internet service providers also offer a limited amount of Web space along with a regular subscription. When deciding on a service for Web storage, make sure to pay attention to privacy issues discussed earlier.

As we've mentioned, an alternative to the Web-based method of electronic portfolio storage is the popular and inexpensive method of burning a portfolio onto a CD or DVD. CDs and DVDs are very inexpensive, and even if the equipment to create them is not available at home or work, many photocopying businesses offer CD or DVD burning services. A **CD** holds 700–800 **megabytes** of information. That is a lot of information unless digital video

FIGURE 8.6 Storage Devices. Clockwise from top left: (A) three types of USB flash drives, (B) USB flash drive bracelet, (C) portable hard drive, (D) CD-ROM (E) five types of flash memory cards, and (F) memory card reader.

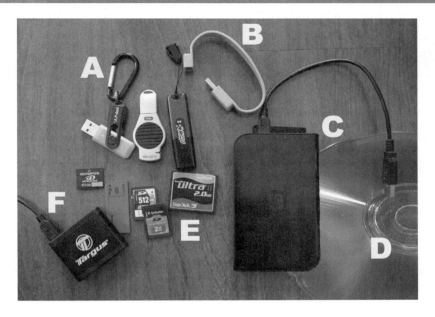

is included. Digital video eats up storage space extremely quickly. For example, 20 minutes of raw digital video can take up to 3 **gigabytes** of storage space. This digital video can be formatted using a variety of video programs so that the 20 minutes can fit on a CD and up to 2 hours can fit on a DVD. If quite a bit of digital video is included, a **DVD** is a good alternative storage media. A DVD holds 4.7 gigabytes. If a DVD is chosen for storage, make sure that a DVD-capable computer or player is available for the portfolio presentation. As an alternative, a second, CD-based version of the electronic portfolio should be considered. On this version, either omit the digital video or limit its size. This option is a good backup in case DVD capabilities cannot be met for the required viewing.

WHERE DO I STORE MY ELECTRONIC PORTFOLIO WHILE I AM WORKING ON IT?

USB flash drives are the storage method of choice while working on your electronic portfolio. USB flash drives come in a range of styles, including bracelets, and storage sizes from 64 megabytes to 32 gigabytes. There are also miniature hard drives, flash memory cards that are used in cell phones, cameras, and MP3 players. When using flash memory cards, if your computer doesn't have a card reader built into it, external card readers are readily available (Figure 8.6). Table 8.2 presents a storage device comparison chart.

TABLE 8.2 Storage Device Comparison Chart

Device	Capacity
CD-ROM	700–800 megabytes
DVD	4.7 gigabytes
Flash drive	64 megabytes up to 16+ gigabytes
Flash memory cards	64 megabytes up to 16+ gigabytes
MP3 player	256 megabytes up to 32+ gigabytes

The USB flash drives, MP3 players, card readers, and mini hard drives plug into the USB port on any Windows computer running Windows 98 second edition (SE) or later or on a Macintosh system 9 or later. Windows 98SE requires drivers to be installed, but the other operating systems need no additional software. These small, portable drives are fairly inexpensive and are very easy to carry. They fit right into a pocket or purse with no problem. Many also come with an attachable neck strap. The only problem with these devices is forgetting to disconnect them from the computer! Portable mass-storage devices allow students to keep a copy of their portfolios handy without lugging around a laptop. But beware! Always have a backup copy—it doesn't hurt to have two. If one gets lost or corrupted, starting from a backup is always easier than starting over.

LET'S PRACTICE!

Activity 8.1 Exploring Your Options and Preferences for Creating an Electronic Portfolio

Now that you have a clearer idea of the available options, it's important to decide which tools and presentation options best meet your needs.

- Consider the pros and cons for various tools and presentation options. Which do you prefer and why?
- Do you have access to commercially based sites? Yes___. No____. If yes, explore the site to determine if it will meet your needs and how you can gain access to the site.
- Are your files secured? Which files would require special privacy and security if made available electronically?

SUMMARY

In this chapter, we share some of the benefits and precautions in using electronic portfolios. A number of options for creating, maintaining, and presenting the portfolio are outlined to help students select which tools and options best fit their needs. A few words of caution are also given to ensure the privacy and security of electronic portfolios.

USEFUL RESOURCES

Adobe (www.adobe.com)

Acrobat PDF writer; DreamweaverWeb design software; Premiere digital video editing software; Photoshop graphics package.

CutePDF Writer (www.cutepdf.com)

A site that offers a free PDF writer program.

FolioLive Portfolios (www.foliolive.com)

An electronic portfolio Web site.

International Society of Technology in Education (ISTE) and National Educational Technology Standards (www.iste.org)

The International Society for Technology in Education (ISTE) is a source for professional development, knowledge generation, advocacy, and leadership for innovation in the Instructional Technology Field.

TaskStream Portfolios (www.taskstream.com)

An electronic portfolio Web site.

FOR FURTHER READING

Evans, S., Daniel, T., Mikovch, A., Metze, L., & Norman, A. (2006). The use of technology in portfolio assessment of teacher education candidates. *Journal of Technology and Teacher Education 14*(1), 5–27.

Hartnell-Young, E., & Morriss, M. (2007). *Digital portfolios.* Thousand Oaks, CA: Corwin Press.

Montgomery, K. & Wiley, D. (2008). *Building e-portfolios using PowerPoint: A guide for educators.* Thousand Oaks, CA: Sage.

Wetzel, K., & Strudler, N. (2006). Costs and benefits of electronic portfolios in teacher education: Student voices. *Journal of Computing in Teacher Education, 22*(3), 99–108.

CHAPTER 9

Creating Electronic Portfolios

I hear and I forget, I see and remember, I do and I understand.

—Confucius

CHAPTER OBJECTIVES

Readers will be able to

❑ organize artifacts into folders,

❑ name artifacts using naming conventions,

❑ determine which tool to use,

❑ create an electronic portfolio using Microsoft Word 2007,

❑ create a Web-based electronic portfolio using Microsoft Word 2007,

❑ create an electronic portfolio using Microsoft PowerPoint 2007, and

❑ create a Web-based electronic portfolio using Microsoft PowerPoint 2007.

SCENARIO

Esmeralda and Kim are two credential students who are reviewing the requirements in their EDIT 430, "Technology for Teachers," course. Kim is concerned when she reads that they must create an electronic portfolio as one of their assignments. Kim begins, "This technology stuff seems so unnecessary for the portfolio. I already have a hard copy of my portfolio, and my other professors have given me high marks on it. Why do I have to start all over again to create an electronic portfolio? This is such a waste of time!"

Esmeralda responds, "I thought that, too, at first. Then I realized how easy it was. You probably already have many of your portfolio files saved on your computer and saved by classes you are taking or standards you were working on. Organizing the files is half the battle. Once you organize the files, the trick is linking them together. Let me show you what I've done."

At that point, Esmeralda opens up her laptop computer and begins to share her electronic portfolio with Kim. She starts with the table of contents, and shows how the related files appear when she clicks on the appropriate links listed there. "You know," Esmeralda says, "the best part about these links is that as I complete my classes and need to add more to my portfolio, I just add more links to the table of contents! I can even make a copy and just include specific artifacts that I need."

"Wow," responds Kim, "How do you do that? Your table of contents looks just like mine, but it seems faster to get to the files your way. How can I begin to link my files? It seems so complicated. How do I get started??"

"Like this," Esmeralda says, "and don't forget, it's easy to update electronic portfolios for job interviews or graduate school!"

Esmeralda begins walking Kim through the process, using Esmeralda's electronic portfolio as a model.

OVERVIEW

As the students did in the scenario, we begin this chapter by having you look at how you have currently organized your portfolio files and making some important recommendations to facilitate the process of converting them into an electronic portfolio. We also look at the importance of correctly naming files and creating folders to keep your portfolio organized.

We then take you step-by-step through the creation of an electronic portfolio using four methods:

1. The first method uses Word; it is CD-based and requires Word to view the portfolio. This also applies to any artifact linked to the portfolio. For example, any artifacts that were created using Word require Word to view these artifacts; any artifacts that were created using Excel require Excel to view them; any artifacts that were created using Adobe Acrobat require Adobe Acrobat Reader to view them. This format is appropriate for students who are familiar with word processing and have entry-level file management skills.

2. The second method also uses Word; it is Web-based (and it can also be CD-based) and is viewed using a Web browser (e.g., Internet Explorer, Firefox, Safari). This format is appropriate for students who are familiar with word processing and have entry- to middle-level file management skills.

3. The third method uses PowerPoint; it is CD-based, viewed as a slide show, and requires PowerPoint to view the portfolio. This also applies to any artifact linked to the portfolio. For example, any artifacts that were created using Word require Word to view them; any artifacts that were created using Excel require Excel to view them; any artifacts that were created using Adobe Acrobat require Adobe Acrobat Reader to view them. This format would be appropriate for students who are familiar with PowerPoint and have entry-level file management skills.

4. The fourth method again uses PowerPoint; it is Web-based (this can also be CD-based) and is viewed using a Web browser. This format is appropriate for students who are familiar with PowerPoint and have entry- to middle-level file management skills.

Remember that electronic portfolios created for the Web need not be uploaded onto the Internet to be viewed. They can be viewed from a CD using a Web browser. Let's get started!

CREATING AN ELECTRONIC PORTFOLIO

There are some important steps to follow in creating an electronic portfolio. Gathering and preparing the files can be tedious, but doing this task carefully will avoid many problems. Pay special attention to file names and folder names. A little time and effort at the beginning stages will help you avoid many hours of troubleshooting and repairing links that do not work.

GETTING STARTED—NAMING FILES

Naming files and folders has always been easy to do on a Mac and is equally easy now with a Windows machine. Also, changing the name of a file or folder is not a difficult task. Just as important as collecting the evidence for a portfolio is making sure that some simple naming rules are followed.

Yes, it is acceptable and quite common to use multiword file names (e.g., Table of Contents.doc). However, this is not a good practice for portfolio files that *will* be used or even *might* be used in an electronic portfolio that will be posted on the Web. Mac and Windows servers don't seem to mind multiple-word file names, but Unix servers have a problem with them: Every time the server comes across a space, it inserts "%20." So if the file name is "Standard 1 lesson," it will be read as "Standard%201%201esson." And because the two phrases don't match, any link to that file won't work.

So instead of naming the file "Standard 1 lesson," name the file "Standard_1_lesson" or "Standard1Lesson." The use of the underscore (_) instead of a space is a safe alternative, as is just removing the spaces and running the words together. It doesn't seem to matter if the file names are long, as long as they are one word (Standard1Lesson), or use the underscore between words (Standard_1_Lesson). It does matter which special characters are used, however. The underscore (_) is fine, as is the dash (-), but the following are reserved characters and are not allowed: < > : ' " \ / | ? * . Keep the names simple and don't worry about punctuation. A misplaced apostrophe can make a file unusable! Instead of naming a file "nick's_resume.doc," name it "nicks_resume.doc" or "nicksresume.doc," and you will avoid many problems. Take the time to make sure that all file and folder names conform to this rule and rename text, audio, video, and graphic files as needed.

Use Windows Explorer or My Computer to look at file and folder names. If any of them use multiple words, rename them. The folders and file names in Figure 9.1 include multiword names. All of these folders and files must be renamed, making sure that all spaces are removed or replaced by an underscore. Figure 9.2 shows the file and folders as seen in Windows Explorer after being renamed. To rename a file or folder on a PC, right click on it and choose Rename. Then type the new name and press Enter. Make sure to check each file and folder as it is selected for use in the portfolio.

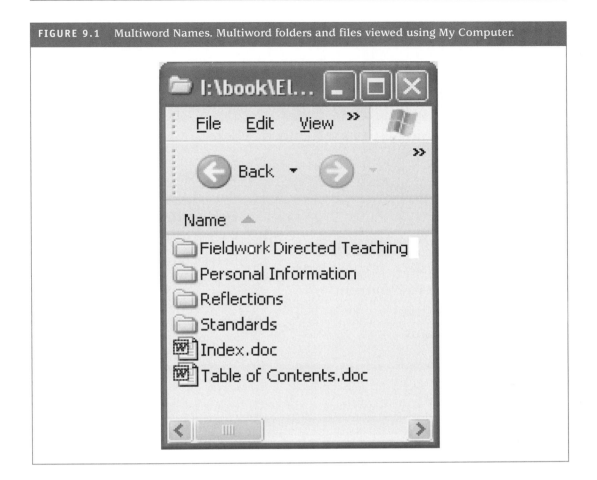

FIGURE 9.1 Multiword Names. Multiword folders and files viewed using My Computer.

LET'S PRACTICE!

Activity 9.1   Naming Files for Your Portfolio

Look at the files you have collected from previous activities.

- Look at the files in your Comprehensive Portfolio. Make sure that all the files and folders follow the file–folder naming rules.
- Look at the files in your Activity 3.2 Exploring Assessment and Categories Learning Targets. Make sure that all the files and folders follow the file–folder naming rules.
- Look at the files in your Activity 6.3 Selecting Artifacts. Make sure that all the files and folders follow the file–folder naming rules.

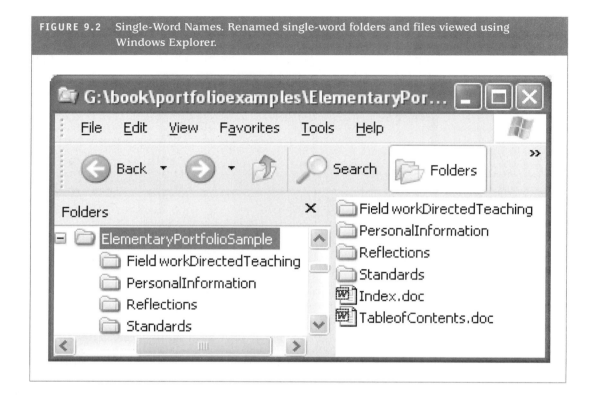

FIGURE 9.2   Single-Word Names. Renamed single-word folders and files viewed using Windows Explorer.

ORGANIZING FILES

Organization and presentation are two key elements in electronic portfolios. Before creating an electronic portfolio, organization is the crucial step. Portfolios are living documents, so the process of file collection and organization is a central step in achieving an error-free portfolio. Start by creating a folder for your portfolio and name it "Portfolio," or something similar—make sure that it's a one-word name. In Chapter 6, there are sample tables of contents.

The contents of the table of contents determine how many folders are needed and what they will be named. Subfolders can be created inside the Portfolio folder for each topic in your table of contents. To help organize the files, store all the artifacts for each topic in their corresponding folders. This will help in organizing the files. All folders and files used in the portfolio must be contained in the main Portfolio folder. In Figure 9.2, there is a listing of the folders created for an elementary teaching portfolio as seen in Windows Explorer. Notice that there are folders for each main category and that everything is located within the folder called "ElementaryPortfolioSample."

LET'S PRACTICE!

Activity 9.2   Organizing the Files for Your Portfolio

Look at what files you have collected for your Comprehensive Portfolio.

- Create a folder and name it "Portfolio."
- Create a draft table of contents using Word. After it is created, save this file inside the created Portfolio folder.
- For each item listed in the table of contents, create a folder inside the Portfolio folder. Make sure to follow the rules for naming these folders.

Once the folders have been created, add each piece of evidence in its appropriate folder (remember to check the file names and remove any spaces). The artifact files to be added inside the folders are the documents that have been created (lesson plans, student teaching logs, etc.) Don't be afraid to create folders within a folder to help you in the organization of these files.

All files, except for the file that starts the electronic portfolio and the table of contents, are kept within folders inside the main Portfolio folder. The starting file should be named "Index" and would contain the opening page. This organization makes it easy for the viewer, perhaps a potential employer, site supervisor, or reviewer, to access the portfolio without having to guess which of the 30 or so files should be opened first. Many people don't have the time to search for this information.

Look at the table of contents for an elementary credential portfolio in Table 9.1. Each main topic heading has a separate folder to house the artifacts for that topic. Table 9.2 shows one of the folders and some of the files that would be stored within it. Table 9.3 shows the table of contents for a single-subject credential portfolio.

Portfolios need to be kept up to date. Folders that correspond to the table of contents allow the student to add new evidence or find existing evidence for edits or other uses. Don't be afraid to add more subfolders to help keep artifacts organized. For instance, suppose there is a lesson plan on mammals that has five different files: the lesson plan, three worksheets, and a PowerPoint presentation. To keep all these files together, create a subfolder called "MammalsLessonPlan" inside the TeachingStandards folder. With all five files stored inside this subfolder, there is less risk of losing track of one of the files.

HANDLING NONDIGITAL ARTIFACTS

What if you ask this question: "I can't find the file for this great activity, but I do have a paper copy of it. Can I still use it for my electronic portfolio?"

TABLE 9.1 Elementary Credential Table of Contents and Corresponding Folder Structure

Elementary Credential Table of Contents	Corresponding Folder Structure

1. Personal Information
 	
  a. Philosophy of Education
  b. Philosophy of Classroom Management
  c. Diversity Statement
  d. Resume
  e. Application to XYZ School District
  f. Transcripts
  g. References and Letters of Recommendation
  h. Exams
	📁 PersonalInformation

2. Fieldwork and Directed Teaching	📁 FieldworkDirectedTeaching

3. Teaching Standards
 	
  a. Knowledge of Subject Matter
  b. Knowledge of Human Development and Learning
  c. Adapting Instruction for Individual Needs
  d. Multiple Instructional Strategies
  e. Classroom Motivation and Management
  f. Communication Skills
  g. Instructional Planning Skills
  h. Assessment of Student Learning
  i. Professional Commitment and Responsibility
  j. Partnerships
	📁 Standards

4. Reflections	📁 Reflections

TABLE 9.2 Elementary Credential Folder and Artifacts Within the Folder

Folder	Artifacts (files) Contained Within the Folder
📁 PersonalInformation	Application.doc Diversity_Statement.doc Exam-Scores.pdf Johnson_Letter_of_Rec.pdf Mims_Letter_of_Rec.pdf Nichols_Letter_of_Rec.pdf Philosophy_of_Classroom_Manangement.doc Philosophy_of_Education.doc Resume.doc Transcripts.pdf

TABLE 9.3   Single-Subject Credential Table of Contents and Corresponding Folder Structure

Single-Subject Credential Table of Contents	Corresponding Folder Structure

1. Personal Information
 	
  a. Philosophy of Education
  b. Diversity Statement
  c. Autobiography
  d. Curriculum Vitae
	PersonalInformation

2. Teaching Standards
 	
  a. Knowledge of Subject Matter
  b. Knowledge of Human Development and Learning
  c. Adapting Instruction for Individual Needs
  d. Multiple Instructional Strategies
  e. Classroom Motivation and Management
  f. Communication Skills
  g. Instructional Planning Skills
  h. Assessment of Student Learning
  i. Professional Commitment and Responsibility
  j. Partnerships
	TeachingStandards

3. Fieldwork and Directed Teaching	FieldworkDirectedTeaching
4. Reflections	Reflections
5. Exams	Exams

Yes! Access to a scanner and **Adobe Acrobat Writer** (www.adobe.com) or CutePDF (www.cutepdf.com) will allow you to scan the document and save it as a **PDF** file. Adobe Acrobat Writer is the standard for creating PDF files. PDF allows you to save your document so that anyone can open the file, regardless of what program it was created in. For example, if you have a mind map created in Inspiration software (www.inspiration.com), normally you would need Inspiration to open the file. But if you created a PDF file of the mind map, then anyone with Adobe Acrobat Reader would be able to view the file. Adobe offers a very reasonable discounted education price for educators. An alternative is CutePDF, which has a free version that can be downloaded. It doesn't have all the bells and whistles like Adobe Acrobat Writer does, but it works well. For instance, Adobe Acrobat Writer allows multiple pages to be scanned into a single PDF document, regardless of the scanning software being used. When using CutePDF, however, the scanning software must be able to scan multiple pages into a single file. Then the file is printed to CutePDF to convert it to a PDF file. PDF files can be viewed using **Adobe Acrobat Reader,** which is a free download at the Adobe Web site.

LET'S PRACTICE!

Activity 9.3   Making a PDF

Converting a document into a PDF file is as simple as printing the document:

(Please note: To complete this activity, CutePDF writer has to be downloaded and installed from www.cutepdf.com)

- Choose File.
- Then choose Print, and on the print menu, click the down arrow to the right of Printer Name.
- Next, choose CutePDF or Adobe Acrobat writer (Figure 9.3).
- Next, the Name File dialog box will appear.
- Name the file and save it in a folder.

The document has now been converted to a PDF file.

FIGURE 9.3   The Word Print Dialog Box. Click the down arrow to the right of Printer Name: and choose CutePDF instead of a printer. This will convert a Word document file into a PDF file.

Print

Printer

Name: CutePDF Writer   Properties

Status: CutePDF Writer   Find Printer...
Type:
Where: ☐ Print to file
Comment: Rip   ☐ Manual duplex

Page range   Send To OneNote 2007

⦿ All
○ Current
○ Pages:

Type page
ranges s
from the
section. For example, type 1, 3, 5–12
or p1s1, p1s2, p1s3–p8s3

Print what: Document   Zoom

Print: All pages in range   Pages per sheet: 1 page

                                      Scale to paper size: No Scaling

Options...   OK   Cancel

Other examples of nondigital media are letters of recommendation, certificates, creden-tials, and standardized test scores. All of these various documents need to be scanned to dig-itize them. However, converting scanned documents to graphics files (e.g., with the extensions .jpg, .jpeg, .tif, or .tiff) is not recommended. For instance, Greg in our scenario from Chapter 8 wants to include a copy of his credential. So he scans it and saves it as a JPG and includes it in the portfolio. But in order to fit it in his document, it needed to be sized down. Unfortunately, when he tries to view it, the credential is so small it is virtually unread-able. The answer to this dilemma is saving the scanned document as a PDF file. With a PDF file, if the document is too small, one can use the **zoom** feature to increase the size so that the document is legible (Figure 9.4). The PDF format is good for certificates, credentials, awards, letters of recommendation, test score documentation, seating charts, and so forth.

Nondigital photographs can be scanned using a scanner and a graphics program, such as Adobe Photoshop, Adobe Photoshop Elements, Microsoft Picture It! Photo, or Jasc Paint Shop Pro. Pictures should be saved in the **JPG** or **JPEG** format, which is the standard for photographs. When scanning images, some people save images in the TIFF format, which is great for archival files because it saves a lot of detail. This format is also very large. Unless the images are for

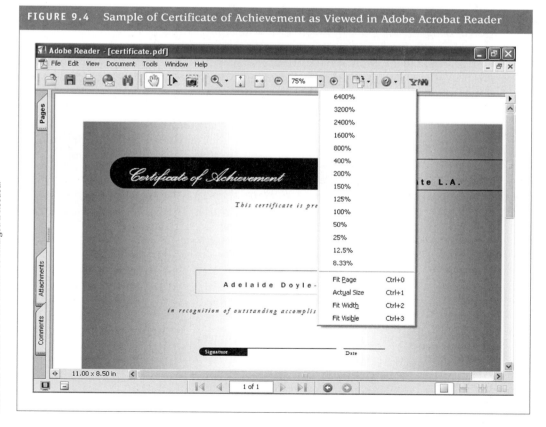

FIGURE 9.4   Sample of Certificate of Achievement as Viewed in Adobe Acrobat Reader

Note: This is viewed at 75% but can be enlarged if needed.

archival storage, JPG format works well for images. Once they are scanned, the images can be inserted into a Word document, PowerPoint slide show, or HTML page.

Many video cameras are digital and can be connected to a computer through a video capture card and a video editing program (e.g., Adobe Premiere, Adobe Premiere Elements, Pinnacle Studio, Microsoft MovieMaker). If your video is not digital, there are video capture cards that digitize the video as it is captured (www.pinnaclesys.com). Most photo stores and some warehouse stores will also digitize video. Once digitized and edited, this video can be inserted into PowerPoint. A number of online tutorials address this specific issue. Good places to start are www.lynda.com or www.atomiclearning.com, both of which are subscription sites but also have some free tutorials available.

By now, you should have chosen between using Word or PowerPoint for your electronic portfolio. If you will be using Word, just continue to the next section. If you will be using PowerPoint, jump ahead to the section called "Creating an Electronic Portfolio Using PowerPoint."

CREATING THE OPENING PAGE
AND TABLE OF CONTENTS IN WORD

In Chapter 8's scenario, Greg, the elementary credential candidate, preferred using Word to create his electronic portfolio. Here is how he would do that:

The opening page is like a first impression. Make it a good one! It shouldn't be too fancy; just clean and to the point. It should have your name, the date of the last revision, and maybe the logo of your school or some other supportive graphic. This page may be left white or have a background added. Figure 9.5 shows an example of an opening page without a background and Figure 9.6 shows an opening page with one. The opening page will have a link to the table of contents. Once the opening page is created, save it in the main Portfolio folder that you created. The opening file is called "Index.doc." Index.doc and the table of contents should be the only files not in a subfolder. Remember, don't use spaces in file or folder names.

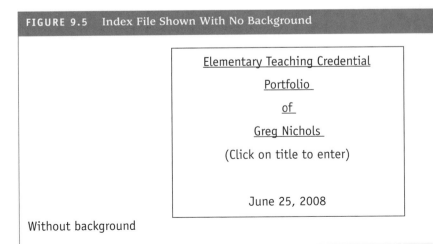

FIGURE 9.5 Index File Shown With No Background

Elementary Teaching Credential

Portfolio

of

Greg Nichols

(Click on title to enter)

June 25, 2008

Without background

FIGURE 9.6   Index File Shown With a Background

Elementary Teaching Credential

Portfolio

of

Greg Nichols

(Click on title to enter)

June 25, 2008

With background

Backgrounds can be very effective or very distracting, depending on how they are used. Make sure that the text is easy to read and that the background is pleasing to the eyes.

The Fill Effects dialog box shows options for the background, which include gradients (Figure 9.7), textures (Figure 9.8), patterns, and pictures. On the gradients tab, a single color, two colors, or preset colors can be used in a variety of shading styles. The direction of the gradient and the transparency can also be changed. These are simple and effective backgrounds. There is also a good choice of textures on the Texture tab. If Word doesn't have a texture or picture to meet your needs, pictures, photographs, or additional graphics can be imported. In Figure 9.6, a texture called "Stationary" was chosen. It is important, when using any type of background, to make sure that the text is clearly visible and not obscured by the background. A page with a plain white background is much better than a page with a great background that has unreadable text.

LET'S PRACTICE!

Activity 9.4   Inserting a Background

To insert a background in Word 2007, open the Table of Contents you previously created or any other word document.

- Click on the Page Layout tab on the Ribbon.
- On the Page Background group, click the down arrow.
- Then click on Fill Effects.
- Choose a color, gradient, texture, or even picture. Try different effects until you come across one you like.

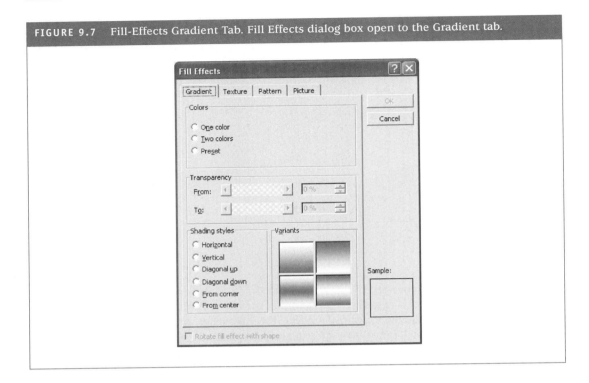

FIGURE 9.7 Fill-Effects Gradient Tab. Fill Effects dialog box open to the Gradient tab.

Earlier, we discussed creating the table of contents page (see Chapter 6). This page will act as the **navigation page** for the portfolio. It will look similar to a table of contents page in a book, except there will be no page numbers. Instead, each topic will be hyperlinked to the supporting documents. If you haven't done so already, create a table of contents page. It should have a similar style to the opening page and use the same color scheme. Name this file "TableofContents.doc" and save it in the main Portfolio folder.

WORD OR HTML—WHICH ONE IS RIGHT FOR ME?

The main difference between a Word document and a Word document converted to HTML is the way in which the file is viewed and what programs are necessary to view the digitized artifacts. A Word document is viewed in Word or is printed out on a printer. Any digitized artifacts saved as PDFs will also need Adobe Acrobat Reader to be viewed, and any other artifacts not created in Word will need the program they were created in to view them. For example, spreadsheets created in Excel need Excel in order for them to be viewed.

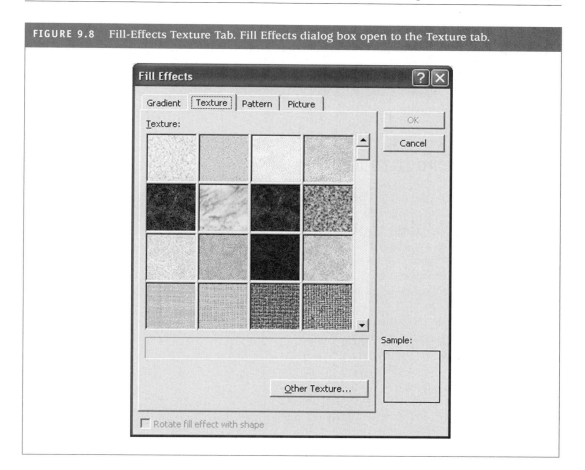

FIGURE 9.8   Fill-Effects Texture Tab. Fill Effects dialog box open to the Texture tab.

A Word document converted to HTML is viewed in a Web browser (e.g., Firefox, Internet Explorer, Safari). Any PDF files would also be viewed in a Web browser, and Excel files can also be converted to HTML. Other file formats that cannot be converted to Web format *can* be converted to PDF format (see Activity 9.3). A Web browser is used whether the files are uploaded to the Web or saved on a CD, a hard drive, or any other large-capacity storage device. An HTML file does not have to be uploaded to the Web but can be if there is Web space is available.

When viewing a portfolio in Word, to follow a link, the user must hold down the Control (Ctrl) key as the link is clicked and a new Word document is opened. So if the user clicks on 14 different links but does not close each document after viewing it, there could be 14 different documents open at the same time. In HTML, the user clicks on the link (without having to hold the Ctrl key) and it opens the next page in the same window, not a new one. So if the user clicks on 14 different links, there will still be only one browser window open.

The user is also able to review previously viewed pages by clicking on the Back button on the browser. Both formats are acceptable, although the Web-based portfolio is more portable and easier to view.

If the portfolio is going to be Web-based (uploaded to the Web or not), continue with this section. If your portfolio is going to be Word-based, skip the next section and go to the section on creating links.

CONVERTING WORD FILES TO HTML

To preserve the original electronic portfolio, a copy should be made. It is strongly suggested that the copy, rather than the original, be converted to HTML. All Word files need to be converted to HTML, but the PDF files do not.

Consider who will be looking at your file. What kind of computer will they have and what browser will they use—Firefox, Explorer, or something else? Don't narrow the viewing audience (or job prospects) by thinking that everyone uses Internet Explorer. Yes, Word converted to HTML does work *best* in Explorer, but that's because they are both Microsoft products.

Make sure to click the down arrow on the right of "Save as type" and select Web Page. The page title is "Elementary Teaching Credential." This can be changed by clicking on the

LET'S PRACTICE!

Activity 9.5   Setting Word 2007 Options

By making a minor setting adjustment, your presentation will be available to more than just Internet Explorer users. It will also be available to be viewed in other Web browsers, such as Firefox and Safari. So before converting your Word 2007 documents to HTML, follow these steps:

- Click on the Office Button, located where the word File used to be, and a dialog box will open.
- Then on the bottom right of the menu, click on Word Options, and an options dialog box will open. Click Advanced and scroll all the way to the bottom.
- Click on Web Options as shown in Figure 9.9. Click on the Browsers tab. Make sure that the option for "People who view this Web page will be using:" is set to "Microsoft Internet Explorer 4, or Netscape Navigator 4, or later." This will enable more people to view your portfolio.

FIGURE 9.9   Setting Browser Compatibilities

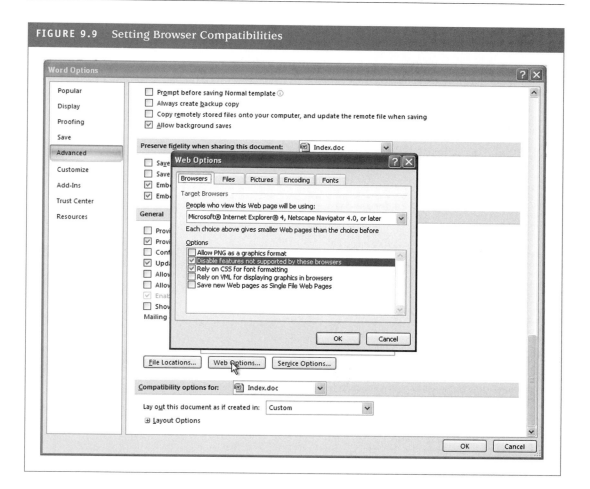

LET'S PRACTICE!

Activity 9.6   Converting a Word 2007 File to HTML

After the adjustments made in Activity 9.5, you are ready to convert a Word file to HTML; follow these steps:

1. Click on the Office Button , located where the word File used to be, and a dialog box will open.
2. Click on Save As, then on Other Formats.

3. A Save As dialog box will open (Figure 9.10). Make sure to click the down arrow next to Save As Type and choose Web Page.

4. Each file should have a very short descriptive title—this is *not* the file name. The title is what is shown on the very top of the Web browser as each page is viewed. Click on the Change Title button to add a title (Figure 9.10). For instance, the opening page title would most likely be "Elementary Teaching Credential Portfolio" or "[Your Name]'s Portfolio."

5. After giving the page a title, click OK.

6. Before the file is saved (i.e., converted), make sure that the file will be saved in the correct folder.

7. Check the "Save in:" folder and make sure it is your main Portfolio folder (Figure 9.10).

8. Then click Save.

FIGURE 9.10   The Save As HTML Dialog Box in Word

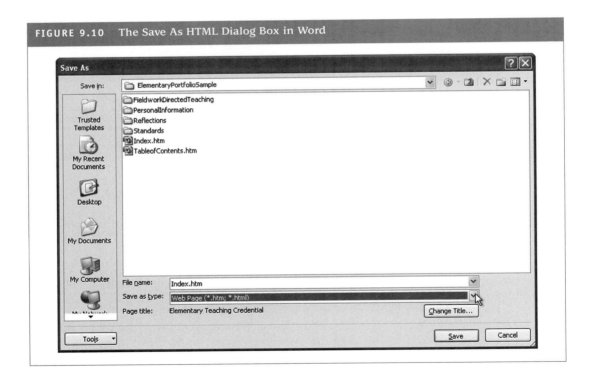

Change Title button. This file will be saved in the ElementaryPortfolioSample folder. This location can be changed by clicking the down arrow to the right of "Save in:" and then navigating to the correct folder.

Word creates an HTML file, as well as a folder with all the necessary files, to have this page viewed online. Not all files require Word to create folders. If there are any backgrounds or images, Word puts a copy of these files in a folder. These files must be available for the documents to be viewed correctly using a Web browser. Don't erase them, or it will not work! Just be aware that there will be a new folder for some of the Word files that were converted to HTML. Save each of the files in their original folders. For instance, if there is an artifact called "Organized1.doc" saved in the TeachingStandards folder, then when it is saved as HTML, it should again be saved in the TeachingStandards folder. Thus, a new file named "Organized1.htm" (and if needed, a new folder called "Organized1_files") will be created by Word and saved in the TeachingStandards folder.

This same sequence needs to be completed for all of the Word documents in the portfolio. (For converting PowerPoint files, see the section on PowerPoint, which follows.) Just be sure to check the folder that is listed next to "Save in:" to make sure that it is correct.

Once all the files have been converted to HTML, the files are ready to be linked. If the links are created before the files are converted, problems will occur. Instead of linking to another Web page, it will be linked to a Word document. That is, instead of viewing the linked page in a Web browser, the link will open in Word or the user will be prompted to save the file instead of being able to view it. If this does occur, the error can be fixed by making sure that file is converted to HTML and editing the link to the file.

CREATING LINKS IN WORD

Creating links allows a viewer to navigate through an electronic portfolio. Links are the equivalent of turning a page or using tabs on a paper portfolio. Linking pages together is the same in a Word document and a Word HTML document. Remember, a Word HTML document is a document created in Word and then converted to HTML. Even though it is viewed using a Web browser, it is still edited using Word. It is important to note the following, however: If the file is double clicked on to edit, it will not open Word, but it will open a Web browser. So to edit Word HTML documents, first open Word, then click on File and Open and navigate to the file to be edited. Another alternative is to right click on the file and choose Open With, then choose Word.

An important note to remember: Link Word files to Word files and link Word HTML files to Word HTML files. A Word file will end in ".doc"; a Word HTML file will end in ".htm." The following are instructions to link files regardless of whether they are Word (.doc) or Word HTML (.htm).

Similar steps will be taken to link the artifacts back to the table of contents. It is extremely important that all of the folders and files for the portfolio are located within the

LET'S PRACTICE!

Activity 9.7 Linking Word 2007 and Word HTML Files

If you haven't done so already, create an opening page for your academic or growth portfolios. Make sure to name it Index. To create a link from the opening page (Index file) to the Table of Contents file, follow these steps:

- Highlight the text (Figure 9.11) that will be linked. Make sure that the file has been saved in the main portfolio folder before creating a link.
- From the Ribbon menu, click on the Insert tab.
- Then in the Links section, choose Hyperlink (Figure 9.12).
- The Insert Hyperlink dialog box will open (Figure 9.13).
- In the "Link to:" column, the Existing File or Web Page should be selected.
- In the "Look in:" column, the Current Folder should be selected.
- Then click on the table of contents file. (Remember, .doc files link to .doc files and .htm files link to .htm files.)
- Then click OK.

FIGURE 9.11 Selecting Text

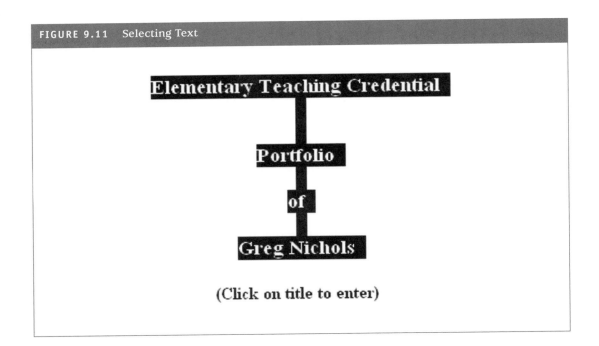

FIGURE 9.12   Inserting Hyperlink

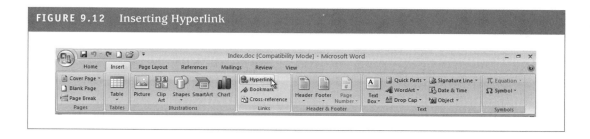

FIGURE 9.13   Insert Hyperlink Dialog Box Connecting Word Documents

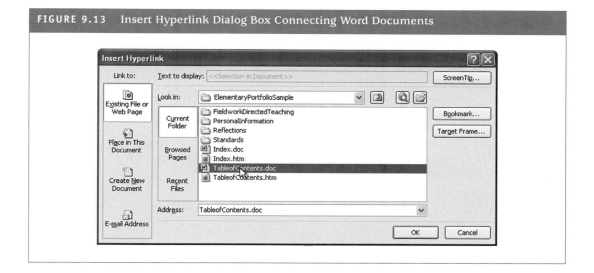

main portfolio folder. If they are not, then when the main folder is burned onto a CD or copied to another storage device, folders and files will not be copied.

As mentioned before, the procedure is virtually the same for creating a link in a Word HTML document. The only difference is that instead of selecting Index.doc as for the Word document link, you would choose Index.htm for the Word HTML document.

Figure 9.14 shows the Insert Hyperlink dialog box for the HTML documents. Notice that the only difference is the addition of HTM files and a few new folders.

So, to repeat, the steps in creating a hyperlink in Word 2007 are as follows:

1. Open the document in Word.

2. Highlight the words that will be the "clickable" text.

3. From the Ribbon menu, click on the Insert tab.

4. Then in the Links section, choose Hyperlink.

FIGURE 9.14 Insert Hyperlink Dialog Box Connecting HTML Documents

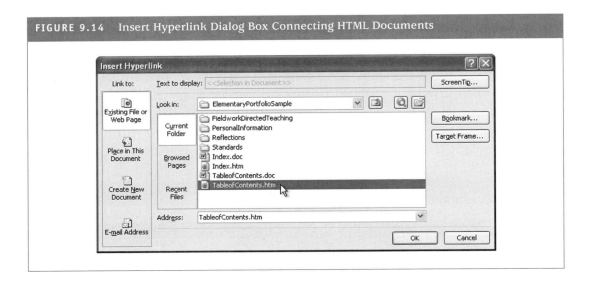

5. From the Insert Hyperlink dialog box, select the file to be linked. Remember, link Word (.doc or .docx) to Word documents and link Word HTML (.htm) to Word HTML files.

6. Then click OK.

LINKING WITH THE TABLE OF CONTENTS

Now that the opening page is linked to the table of contents, it is time to link all the topics from the table of contents page to the supporting materials. This time, open the TableofContents file (Word file or Word HTML file). Follow the same steps described previously for each file. The same procedure for linking is followed, no matter what kind of file is being linked. If the file to be linked to is not in the folder that is currently open, either double click on the folder to open it (if it is visible in the dialog box) or click the down arrow to the right of "Look in:" and navigate to the correct folder (Figures 9.13 and 9.14).

After all of the links are made from the table of contents page, half the work is done. At this point, users can travel from the table of contents to the linked pages but not back again. So by making minor modifications to each file, a link back to the table of contents can be added. At the top of the page (Figure 9.15), the bottom of the page, or both top and bottom, add a line of text that reads, "Back to Table of Contents." Once this is added, then save the file. This added text will be used to create a link back to the TableofContents page.

FIGURE 9.15   Sample Philosophy of Education Page With "Back to Table of Contents" Link Added

Back to Table of Contents

PHILOSOPHY OF EDUCATION STATEMENT
(Sample)

I believe that one major factor in improving K-12 schools rests on valuing each

and every child regardless of his or her individual background and circumstances.

Educators must strive to be responsive to every child and have an understanding of the

LET'S PRACTICE!

Activity 9.8   Linking Back to the Table of Contents in Word 2007

Open the file that will link back to the table of contents:

- Highlight the text that will be linked: "Back to Table of Contents."
- From the Ribbon menu, click on the Insert tab.
- Then in the Links section, choose Hyperlink (Figure 9.12). The Insert Hyperlink dialog box will open (Figure 9.13 or 9.14). The Insert Hyperlink box opens to the folder where the file being worked on is saved. In most cases, this will not be the same folder as the table of contents file.
- To navigate back to that file, click on the down arrow to the right of "Look in:" and choose the main portfolio folder. In this case, the folder would be ElementaryPortfolioSample. In this folder, the file TableofContents is found.
- Click on the file TableofContents.
- Then click OK.

Without these links back, the user will have difficulty returning to the table of contents and will need to restart the portfolio each time in order to open any of the other artifacts. In some cases, along with the link to the table of contents, a second link may point to further supporting materials. This would be the case for the lesson plan on mammals we mentioned before. On the lesson plan, links would be added to each of the three worksheets and to the PowerPoint presentation. Remember, if this is a Web-based portfolio, all of these files would be previously converted to .htm files.

SAVE YOUR CHANGES

As modifications are completed (or are in progress), be sure to save the changes and save often. The modifications that need to be made are the creation of all the links on the table of contents page to the supporting documents and then a link back to the table of contents page on each of the supporting documents. In some cases, as in the mammals lesson plan, there may be an additional link to more supporting materials.

"Save early, save often" cannot be said often enough. Then, at the end of your work session, make a copy of the entire portfolio folder. This copy should include some type of date indicator. For instance, if the original folder is named "elementaryportfolio," the backup could be named "elementaryportfolio_6–22." This would indicate that the version was saved on June 22. This aids in identifying the most recently revised version.

TEST THE LINKS

It is a good idea to test each link as it is created. Word allows a link to be followed by holding down the Control key (Ctrl) and then clicking on it. Word HTML files should also be tested by using a Web browser. Notice that if there is no returning link on the other page, navigation is awkward. Once all of the links have been created, test the entire portfolio. It is easy to miss a link that returns to the table of contents or links to the wrong file. Should a link navigate to a wrong file, editing the link is simple:

1. Highlight the hyperlinked text.

2. Right click the highlighted text.

3. Select Hyperlink. The Insert Hyperlink dialog box will open, as in Figures 9.13 and 9.14.

4. Select the correct file.

5. Click OK.

Once all the links are working, make sure all the files are saved, and then make a copy of the Portfolio folder. This copy should be burned onto a CD or copied to a large-capacity storage drive.

CREATING AN ELECTRONIC PORTFOLIO USING POWERPOINT

What are the differences between creating the electronic portfolio using Word and creating it using PowerPoint? The main difference is found in the opening file and the table of contents. These two files will be created in PowerPoint instead of Word. Just like in the electronic portfolio in Word, the artifacts have already been created. These artifacts are saved as various types of files (e.g., Word, PowerPoint, PDF, JPG). PowerPoint is used to connect all the files together for easy access.

PowerPoint is used for creating not only teacher education portfolios but also professional portfolios used in educational administration, educational counseling, and master's degrees.

In Chapter 8's scenario, Rachel, a secondary teaching credential candidate, was more familiar with PowerPoint and wanted to create her electronic portfolio with it. Here is how she would do it:

Organizing the files and folders is exactly the same as stated earlier in "Getting Started—Naming Files." Remember to use only one-word names or names that use an underscore (_) between the words instead of spaces. Start out by creating a main Portfolio folder. In this case, it will be called "SingleSubjectPortfolioSample." Inside this folder will be subfolders that correspond to the categories in the table of contents. Inside each of the subfolders will be all of the files that contain the artifacts (see Table 9.3). In Figures 9.16 and 9.17, the topics from the single-subject table of contents are used to create corresponding subfolders. The artifacts supporting these topics will be contained inside these subfolders. The only files outside of the subfolders are the PowerPoint version of the opening file (Index.ppt) and the PowerPoint HTML version of the opening file (Index.htm).

FIGURE 9.16   Listing of Folders for Single-Subject Credential

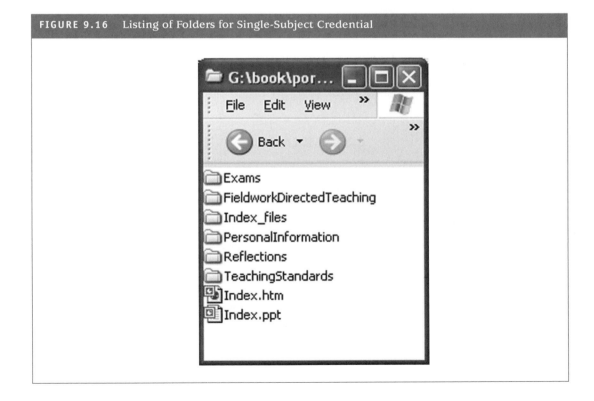

FIGURE 9.17   Listing of the Word Documents and Converted Word HTML Documents Contained in the PersonalInformation Subfolder

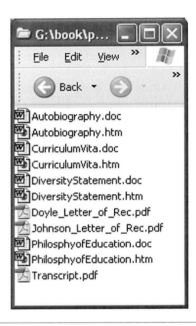

LET'S PRACTICE!

Activity 9.9   Creating the Opening Page and Table of Contents in PowerPoint

PowerPoint offers a wide variety of backgrounds for designing an opening slide for your portfolio.

- Remember to choose a background that allows the text to be seen clearly and read easily.
- Change the font color so it will stand out for easy reading.
- Choose a "Title slide" layout for the opening slide. This slide should contain your name, the purpose of the portfolio, and an appropriate graphic (Figure 9.18).

PowerPoint doesn't provide as much height as Word does, so don't try to put too much information on one slide.

- Click the New Slide icon or click on Insert, New Slide.
- The next two slides will be the table of contents.

FIGURE 9.18 Portfolio Opening Page in PowerPoint

Because there isn't a lot of room on each slide, the table of contents lists only the main categories. Each category will link to another slide that will list the subcategories, and these subcategories will be linked to the supporting artifacts. The first two slides for the table of contents are shown in Figures 9.19 and 9.20. Once the table of contents is set, then it will be linked to its supporting artifacts. It would be a good idea to include one more slide after the table of contents. On this slide, you can thank the viewers for taking their time to consider your qualifications. It would be a nice way to let the viewer know the portfolio presentation is completed. Save the PowerPoint file, name the file "Index.ppt," and save it in the SingleSubjectPortfolioSample folder. This should be the only file in that folder along with the subfolders that contain all the other files. In Word, the opening page and the table of contents are in two separate files. In PowerPoint, they are on different slides but in the same file.

Remember, if the portfolio is going to be HTML-based, don't create the links until all the artifacts have been converted to HTML (all except the PDFs and JPGs). This includes all of the artifacts created using Word or any other program.

Again one might ask, "PowerPoint or HTML, which one is right?" PowerPoint is a presentation tool, so viewing an electronic portfolio works well. Like Word, PowerPoint can be converted to HTML. The main thing is to decide how the portfolio is to be viewed *before* linking all the files. If you decide to go with the HTML conversion, it is strongly suggested that you convert all Word and PowerPoint files to HTML instead of converting just the PowerPoint

FIGURE 9.19　The First Slide From the Table of Contents in PowerPoint

Table of Contents

- Personal Information

- Professional Competencies

- Reflections

FIGURE 9.20　The Second Slide From the Table of Contents in PowerPoint

Personal Information

- *Philosophy of Education*
- *Diversity Statement*
- *Autobiography*
- *Curriculum Vita*
- *Letters of Recommendation*
- *Transcripts*

files. Another consideration is whether the person viewing the HTML version of the portfolio is using Firefox, Safari, or Internet Explorer. There is one extra feature available in Explorer, which is a full-screen, Web-based slide show. If Word documents are not converted to HTML, when a Word document is accessed, Word opens and the documents are viewed in Word, not in a Web browser.

As in the previous discussion about Word or HTML, it all depends on how you would like to present the portfolio. Is the intent to keep it on CD or post it to the Web? Will the person viewing the portfolio need PowerPoint and Word on their computer or just a Web browser? Don't forget, just because the portfolio is converted to HTML doesn't mean that it has to be posted on the Web. It can still be distributed on CD, and it is easier to view in HTML.

If the portfolio is going to be Web-based (uploaded to the Web or not), continue with this section. If the portfolio is going to be PowerPoint-based, skip this section and go to the section on creating links.

CONVERTING POWERPOINT TO HTML

Just like in Word, consider who will be looking at your PowerPoint file. What kind of computer will they have and what browser will they use—Firefox, Safari, Explorer, or something else? Don't narrow the viewing audience (or job prospects) by thinking that everyone uses Internet Explorer. Yes, PowerPoint converted to HTML does work *best* in Explorer, but that's because they are both Microsoft products. By making a minor setting adjustment, your presentation will be available to more than just Internet Explorer users. It will also be available to be viewed in other Web browsers, such as Firefox and Safari.

LET'S PRACTICE!

Activity 9.10   Setting PowerPoint 2007 Options

In PowerPoint, follow these steps:

- Click on the Office Button, located where the word File used to be, and a dialog box will open.
- Then on the bottom right of the menu, click on PowerPoint Options, and an options dialog box will open. Click Advanced and scroll all the way to the bottom.
- Click on Web Options, as shown in Figure 9.21. Click on the Browsers tab. Make sure that the option for "People who view this Web page will be using:" is changed to "Microsoft Internet Explorer 4, or Netscape Navigator 4, or later." This will enable more people to view your portfolio.

FIGURE 9.21 PowerPoint Web Options Dialog Box

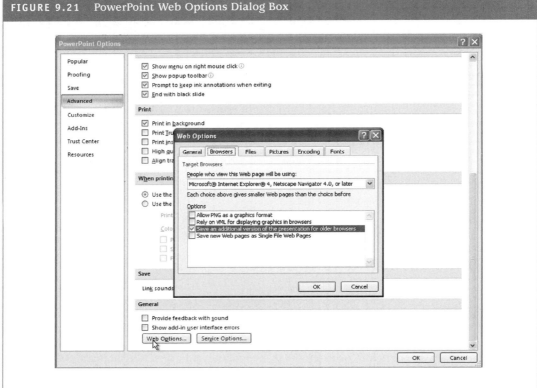

LET'S PRACTICE!

Activity 9.11 Converting PowerPoint 2007 Slides to HTML

After the options covered in Activity 9.10 have been set, follow these steps:

- Click on the Office Button ⎙ , located where the word File used to be, and a dialog box will open.
- Click on Save As, then on Other Formats.
- A Save As dialog box will open (Figure 9.22). Make sure to click the down arrow next to "Save As Type" and choose Web Page.
- As with Word, click on the Change Title button and add a short but descriptive title for the page. Remember, this is not the file name, just the name that appears at the top of the Web browser window. Make sure that the file will be saved in your main Portfolio folder (in this case, it is called SingleSubjectPortfolioSample).
- Then click Save.

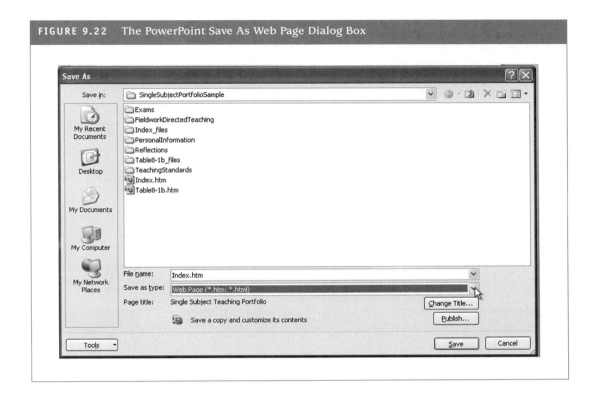

FIGURE 9.22 The PowerPoint Save As Web Page Dialog Box

PowerPoint will create an HTML file and a folder with all of the needed files. Don't erase this folder, or the presentation will not work! Follow these same steps and convert any other PowerPoint files included in the portfolio, making sure to save them in their original folders. When finished, convert all of the Word documents to HTML also. That way, when the portfolio is viewed, all the artifacts are viewed in the Web browser and Word doesn't need to be opened. Refer to these steps, which were covered earlier in this chapter.

CREATING LINKS IN POWERPOINT

Creating links in PowerPoint is similar to Word. In PowerPoint, two types of links will be created. The first type of link connects within the PowerPoint file. The second type of link connects to other files (just like what was done previously in Word). This first example is linking within a PowerPoint file. With the opening file opened in PowerPoint, move to the first slide for the table of contents. Unlike in Word, the opening page and table of contents are already linked by the slide show.

LET'S PRACTICE!

Activity 9.12   Creating a Link in PowerPoint 2007

To create a link that connects within a PowerPoint file, do the following:

- Highlight the first point (Figure 9.23).
- Then on the Ribbon, click on Insert.
- Then click Hyperlink in the links section, and the Insert Hyperlink dialog box will open just like it did in Word (Figure 9.24).
- In the "Link to:" column, choose Place in This Document.
- In the Select a Place in This Document column, choose the slide that corresponds to the highlighted text.
- Click OK, and the link is complete.

FIGURE 9.23   Highlighted Item to Be Linked

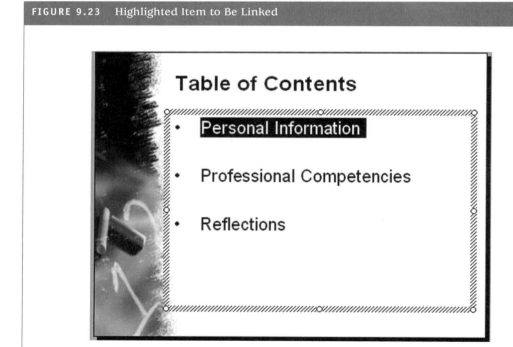

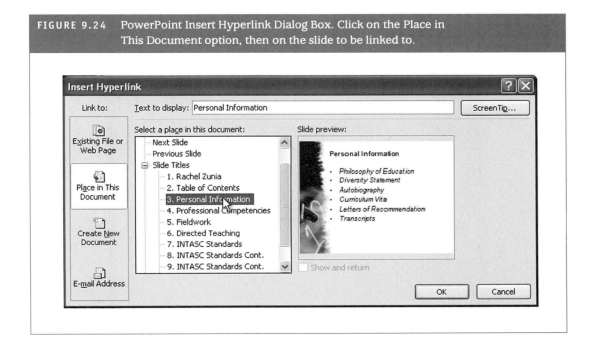

FIGURE 9.24   PowerPoint Insert Hyperlink Dialog Box. Click on the Place in This Document option, then on the slide to be linked to.

Now we will create the second type of link. This link connects to another file. This would be used to link to artifacts such as lesson plans, observation reports, or video clips.

LET'S PRACTICE!

Activity 9.13   Creating a Second Link in PowerPoint 2007

To create a link to another file in PowerPoint, follow these steps:

- Highlight the first point (Figure 9.25).
- Then on the Ribbon, click on Insert.
- Then in the Links section, click Hyperlink, and the Insert Hyperlink dialog box will open just like it did in Word (Figure 9.26).
- In the "Link to:" column, choose Existing File of Web Page.
- In the "Look In:" column, double click on the PersonalInformation folder, which is where the Philosophy of Education file can be found.
- Then click on the file PhilosophyofEducation.htm or PhilosphyofEducation.doc if it is not Web-based.
- Click OK and the link is complete.

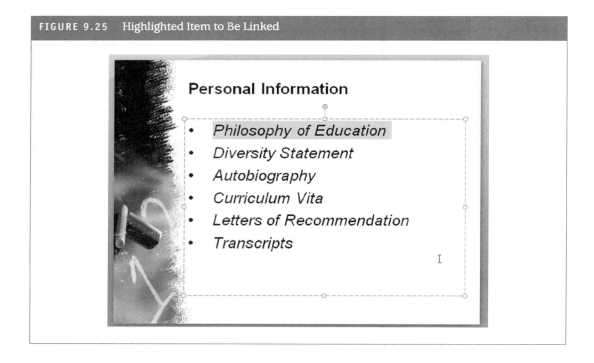

FIGURE 9.25 Highlighted Item to Be Linked

Personal Information
Philosophy of Education
Diversity Statement
Autobiography
Curriculum Vita
Letters of Recommendation
Transcripts

FIGURE 9.26 PowerPoint Insert Hyperlink Dialog Box. Click on the Existing File or Web Page option, then double click on the folder that houses the artifact to be linked to. Then click the file to be linked.

Insert Hyperlink
Link to:
Text to display: Philosophy of Education
ScreenTip...
Existing File or Web Page
Look in: PersonalInformation
Current Folder
Autobiography.doc
Autobiography.htm
CurriculumVita.doc
CurriculumVita.htm
DiversityStatement.doc
DiversityStatement.htm
Doyle_Letter_of_Rec.pdf
Johnson_Letter_of_Rec.pdf
PhilosphyofEducation.doc
PhilosphyofEducation.htm
Bookmark...
Place in This Document
Browsed Pages
Create New Document
Recent Files
Address: PersonalInformation\PhilosphyofEducation.doc
E-mail Address
OK
Cancel

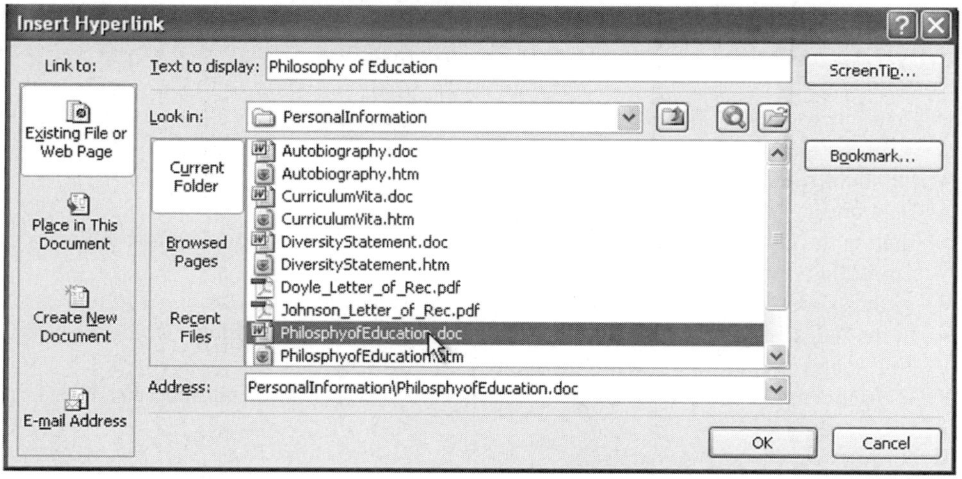

If the folder that the supporting material is in is not visible, click on the down arrow to the right of "Look in:" and navigate to the folder where it is located. It is extremely important that all of the folders for the portfolio are located within the main Portfolio folder. If they are not, when the main folder is burned onto a CD or copied to another storage device, all of the folders will not be copied. These same steps will be repeated to link all of the artifacts to the table of contents.

As mentioned before, save the files and save them often. After all your links are created, test them. Additional links may be needed to link multiple file examples together, as mentioned previously with the mammals lesson plan. Unlike Word, PowerPoint automatically opens a new window for each link, so links back to the table of contents are not needed. To return to the table of contents, just close the window. After all the links are working, save the portfolio and create a backup of the entire project. It can now be burned to a CD or uploaded to a Web site.

If any additional materials need to be added later, add new folders, files, and links as necessary. Save the changes, test the links, and the portfolio is ready to be distributed again.

SUMMARY

Whether the portfolio is created in Word or PowerPoint, the real work is in collecting and organizing the files. All files must be contained within a portfolio folder and then organized inside this portfolio folder using subfolders. The Comprehensive Portfolio Folder would be the portfolio folder. With the organization of the subfolders, it is easy to create a portfolio for a specific purpose, such as the showcase or presentation portfolio. This is done by just selecting subfolders that have the necessary artifacts to match the purpose of the portfolio and linking them to the table of contents. A number of portfolios can be created this way. The contents of each portfolio are determined by the specific purpose. With this file structure in place, updating or editing the portfolio is fairly easy. In addition, by keeping all the files inside the portfolio folder, it is easy to create multiple copies of the portfolio.

Electronic portfolios are versatile, living documents. As students progress in their careers, artifacts can easily be added. This progression may even result in a change in focus for the portfolio, reflected by updating the opening page and table of contents to fit the new focus.

USEFUL RESOURCES

Adobe (www.adobe.com)

Acrobat PDF writer; Dreamweaver Web design software; Premiere digital video editing software; Photoshop graphics package)

CutePDF Writer (www.cutepdf.com)

A free PDF writer progam.

FolioLive Portfolios (www.foliolive.com)

An electronic portfolio Web site.

International Society of Technology in Education (ISTE) and National Education Technology Standards (www.iste.org)

The International Society for Technology in Education (ISTE) is a source for professional development, knowledge generation, advocacy, and leadership for innovation in the Instructional Technology Field.

Online Tutorial (www.atomiclearning.com)

An electronic portfolio Web site.

Online Tutorials (www.lynda.com)

Web-based tutorials on a variety of computer programs.

Open Source Web Design (www.oswd.org)

A resource for developing Web pages using open source software.

Pinnacle Software (www.pinnaclesys.com)

A Web site with digital video software and hardware.

Scanning Tips (www.scantips.com)

A useful resource on how to scan documents.

TaskStream Portfolios (www.taskstream.com)

An electronic portfolio Web site.

FOR FURTHER READING

Evans, S., Daniel, T., Mikovch, A., Metze, L., & Norman, A. (2006). The use of technology in portfolio assessment of teacher education candidates. *Journal of Technology and Teacher Education, 14*(1), 5–27.

Hartnell-Young, E., & Morriss, M. (2007). *Digital portfolios.* Thousand Oaks, CA: Corwin Press.

Montgomery, K., & Wiley, D. (2008). *Building e-portfolios using PowerPoint: A guide for educators.* Thousand Oaks, CA: Sage.

Wetzel, K., & Strudler, N. (2006). Costs and benefits of electronic portfolios in teacher education: Student voices. *Journal of Computing in Teacher Education, 22*(3), 99–108.

PART III

The Future of Your Portfolio

10

After the Credential Program, Now What?

Keeping the Portfolio Alive

Portfolios should not be seen as an end in themselves but as an ongoing tool in a practice that includes routine opportunities for thoughtful reflective dialogue throughout the school community.

—Zeichner and Wray (2001, p. 614)

CHAPTER OBJECTIVES

Readers will be able to

❑ describe ways to use the portfolio as an ongoing reflective companion,

❑ retool the portfolio for ongoing assessments and reflective inquiry,

❑ retool the portfolio for academic and career advancement,

❑ describe patterns of strengths or gaps that exist in knowledge and experiences,

❑ use strategies for selecting contents for the different portfolio purposes, and

❑ use the portfolio for presentation in career and educational advancement.

Linda and Glenn had successfully completed their degree and credential programs. Glenn decided that he wanted to start teaching as soon as he could find a position. He wanted to teach in the neighborhood where he grew up. Linda was thinking about substituting while she decided whether she really wanted a teaching career. Although she had passed all of her courses, her student teaching experience was rated only as "meets standards." She also was thinking about applying to graduate school. She thought she might need a master's degree to deepen her knowledge about teaching, particularly teaching reading to children whose primary language is not English.

Glenn told Linda that he had talked with some friends who had been teaching for a while and they had shared information about applying for jobs. One friend, Miguel, had updated and used his portfolio in several interviews. He mentioned that reviewing his artifacts and presenting some information from his portfolio gave him a sense of security and confidence. The more he used it, the more at ease he became with the process. He had to do some minor revisions after the first interview. He received many positive responses about his portfolio documents. Miguel had several job offers. He wasn't sure if the portfolio had been the pivotal factor in securing a job, but he felt that it gave him confidence in presenting himself.

Another friend, Rick, told Glenn that he also had used his portfolio in an interview, but it turned out to be a disaster. He brought his 3-inch hardcover binder to the interview. This was the same one he had from his teacher preparation program. When he opened the binder to find some information, his notebook fell off the table and the papers scattered all over the floor. He was so flustered and embarrassed that he was barely able to answer subsequent questions. Rick eventually found a job, but it was not the top job that he was seeking. He wondered if better preparation and use of the portfolio could have helped him secure the job he really desired.

The following week, Linda and Glenn talked at graduation rehearsal. Glenn told Linda that he had several interviews coming up. He had visited the career office, and they had given him some ideas about how to prepare for interviews. However, he was feeling insecure about the interviews and was curious about how his portfolio might help in an interview setting. Linda suggested that he ask his friend Miguel to give him some tips and to help him with a mock interview. Linda volunteered to participate in the mock interview. She wondered if the portfolio would be useful in making her competitive for a master's program. As they continued to talk, they concluded that learning how to use their portfolios in interviews and other career advancement experiences may be a significant and valuable enhancement to their teacher preparation program.

OVERVIEW

In reflecting on experiences and research about portfolio development, we feel strongly that the reflection and engagement in the self-evaluation phase while assembling and organizing a portfolio has value for lifelong learning. Development of portfolios should not be terminated at program or degree completion. Portfolios have the potential to become meaningful enhancements for job searches and interviews, job evaluations, and most important, as dynamic documents for self-evaluation and accomplishments in one's career. Examining one's portfolio can be a source of pride in what has been achieved and an inspiration for further accomplishments. In this chapter, we offer some suggestions on how to continue the portfolio experience throughout teaching or other professional careers, including some ways to retool the portfolio for specific purposes and presentations.

THE PORTFOLIO AS A REFLECTIVE COMPANION FOR ONGOING ASSESSMENT

As candidates transition from preparation programs to the next phase of professional development, their portfolios can become interactive, reflective companions for documenting growth and development. The reflection, inquiry, and evaluation skills that were acquired during preparation programs serve as resources and support for future professional growth. These areas were discussed in Chapters 2, 3, and 4. Preservice professionals who have become experienced in presenting their portfolios now have some valuable skills on how to articulate, highlight, and document their very best achievements. These skills are a significant professional asset.

You might ask, What might be some future uses for a portfolio during a professional career? There are several academic and professional areas in which the portfolio has constant utility. Up-to-date, well-developed portfolios have many potential benefits. Table 10.1 describes how to use the portfolio for academic and professional development and career advancement. It also suggests other arenas for future portfolio use.

Study Table 10.1, and then, using the table in Activity 10.1 as a guide, list the possible ways you can retool your current portfolio for future professional growth.

LET'S PRACTICE!

Activity 10.1   Selecting Types of Portfolio Development for Future Use

Areas	How the Portfolio Would Be Used	Time line for Preparing the Portfolio

For specific information related to this concept, see the Chapter 10 resources on the CD.

TABLE 10.1 Academic and Career-Advancement Uses of Portfolios

Academic	Use
Graduate school or credential programs	Interview preparation: Provides a readily available review of professional achievements, strengths, and weaknesses prior to the interview; can be used for mock interviews.
	In the interview: Demonstrates the ability to document and provide evidence of achievements in a professional arena; provides readily available past academic records and selected graded course papers that are related to the sought after academic area.

Professional Areas	Use
1. Assessment and reflective inquiry	Provides a powerful internal source for pride and joy in accomplishments, as well as information on areas where growth is needed. Provides a prompt and a focus to self-assess progress, what is working, and what needs to change in knowledge, skills, or dispositions, which can lead to seeking out critical friends to further the process. Portfolio Artifacts Organizer provides quick overviews regarding professional levels and focus. Has potential to inform and influence supervisor evaluation.
2. Future employment, job interviews	Assessment: Assists in assessing whether knowledge, skills, and dispositions are aligned with employment opportunities.
	Interview preparation: Provides a readily available review of professional achievements, strengths, and weaknesses prior to the interview; can be used for mock interviews.
	In the interview: Has the potential to provide focused evidence of accomplishments in areas related to school or district goals; demonstrates ability to document and provide evidence of achievements in professional arenas and, if needed, academic achievements.
3. Promotional or lateral advanced position or certification opportunities	Gives a competitive edge, if able to show quality artifacts in the relevant areas. If up-to-date, facilitates the gathering of materials needed, such as for National Board certification.
4. Supervisor evaluation	Provides documentation for what has been accomplished and demonstrates levels of accomplishment; provides evidence of program and project implementation; can provide nontraditional types of information, such as parent, student, and colleague letters and electronic information.
5. Professional resource bank	Demonstrates professional efficacy and is a ready source of guidelines for future projects. Holds a rich source of literature and documentation of successful achievements or examples of how challenges need to be addressed. Provides a resource for sharing information with colleagues.
6. Professional development	Identifies the areas where professional development needs to begin, deepen, or be revisited from another perspective. Helps patterns of strengths and where improvement is needed become visible.

ONGOING ASSESSMENTS AND REFLECTIVE INQUIRY

One of the most exciting and potentially beneficial ways to use the portfolio is to enhance professional practice (Mosely, 2004–2005; Yancy, 2001). The focus is not only on career advancement but also on improving current professional practice. Klecka, Donovan, and Fisher (2007) conducted a study with 14 teacher educators in the development of electronic portfolios. One of the findings that they characterize as remarkable was the effect the process had on how teachers viewed their practice. They state, "Nearly all members shared the sentiment of one participant: 'The process has made me analyze my practice in ways I had not expected to," (p. 34). From these analyses, the teachers reflected on how to revise their teaching, increase advocacy, and reframe their teaching practice by utilizing the students' perspective. Theel (2001) comments that, "Perhaps one of the most valuable benefits of the portfolio process lies in the development of a new norm for the profession, placing discussion and debate about what constitutes '*good teaching*' into a public forum" (p. 2).

Hartnell-Young and Morriss (2007) suggest that new principals use portfolios to show evidence in their annual performance goals. Dietz (2008) points out that for educational leaders, portfolios are often viewed as busywork, but she emphasizes the need for leaders to take the time for their own learning. She states, "Leaders must be learners" (p. 13). The portfolio process for school and district leaders can be as powerful for them as it is for teachers. Dietz further states that

The portfolio process

- Builds a professional learning community,
- Creates the space for reflections and collaboration, and
- Accomplishes this in the context of goal setting and achievement toward meeting professional, site, and districtwide goals. (p. 13)

Engaging in ongoing action research leads to a high level of professional growth by assessing progress and then reflecting on what to celebrate and what to improve. Opportunities to collaborate with colleagues enhance the process. Mueller (2008) describes a *growth portfolio* as one which shows growth or change over time; helps develop process skills, such as self-evaluation and goal setting; identifies strengths and weakness; and tracks the development of one or more products or performances. When a portfolio is retooled as a growth portfolio, it is not be limited to merely showcasing the best work, but can contain any relevant artifacts related to particular standards, goals, or objectives. (An end-of-program growth portfolio with a growth plan is on the CD.)

It is important to use agreed-upon rubrics to evaluate progress toward professional standards, goals, and objectives. This requires clarity in defining roles and expectations. Reflective activities that involve practitioners in designing how to improve practice can provide specific real-world examples on strategies for improvement. Quality time and supports are needed in order for these types of professional developments to be effective, and these activities need to be integrated into an ongoing school and district culture that values high levels of professional development (Dietz, 2008; Klecka et al., 2007).

For specific information related to this concept, see the Chapter 10 resources on the CD.

ACADEMIC AND CAREER ADVANCEMENT

Academic and career advancement require that your portfolio be tailored for specific uses, and a *comprehensive portfolio* or working portfolio (see Chapter 1) can be a rich resource. It can be developed and kept in a file drawer, box, or binder or in an electronic format. Your comprehensive portfolio is an up-to-date storehouse from which artifacts and other materials can be selected for a variety of professional purposes. The contents are concrete evidence of professional accomplishments that are collected over time and are similar to those described in Chapter 6. As you develop and improve professional competencies, new and improved documentation that reflects new experiences should replace earlier items. Your comprehensive portfolio will have more information than is needed for any one type of purpose described in Table 10.1. The major areas include personal information and documentation of achievement in professional standards. The resume, references, and professional evaluations begin to play a more prominent role in academic and career advancement and in promotions and lateral position changes. Accomplishments, talents, and personal characteristics as viewed by others will be noted by those seeking to hire or grant admission to you . This comprehensive portfolio storage system still needs to have a current table of contents and some type of artifacts organizer, for ease in locating and analyzing artifacts as they relate to goals, areas, and standards.

In retooling the portfolio for academic advancement, areas related to your goals should be researched. Before applying to a college or university, consider research programs, types of degrees, professors' research and publications foci, the vision and philosophy, and the institution's mission. Is also wise to inquire about job placement records and support for career and academic advancement. Web sites provide valuable, current information about enrollment, **demographics**, achievement, goals, organization, and so on. Site visits can provide copies of newsletters and other information about institutional climate, setting, and conditions.

When retooling for a particular job setting, this background research is essential. This information helps in the selection of artifacts that make a connection with the employment setting. Employers like to feel that a prospective candidate has a special desire to work for them and has some familiarity with their institution. For school or district employment searches, tour the area of prospective employment to become familiar with students' neighborhoods. This will give information not only about neighborhoods but also about business, community, recreational, and religious sites in the area. Lack of background knowledge may give the impression that a candidate is not focused on a specific job or goal nor has any particular interest in the school or district. When schools or districts are selective about whom to employ, those who do not research current employment opportunities may end up at the bottom of the list.

Also seek out background information about desired career advancement opportunities. For lateral or promotional opportunities, become familiar with the job requirements, time demands, role expectations, salary ranges, education requirements, and other unique aspects of the position. Talking with others who hold similar positions may be useful, but a note of caution is in order: Personal experiences and perspectives vary and have the potential to inaccurately sway your view of a prospective job opportunity.

For teachers and counselors, opportunities exist for career advancement through National Board certification. Teachers and counselors who successfully complete the rigorous process are recognized and certified as highly accomplished educators. Some districts and states provide financial incentives. Quoting from the NBPTS (2009) Web site, in order to apply, teachers and counselors must meet the following requirements:

- Hold a bachelor's degree
- Have completed three full years of teaching/counseling experience
- Possess a valid state teaching/counseling license for that period of time, or, if teaching where a license is not required, have taught in schools recognized and approved to operate by the state (p. 1)

On the Portfolio page branching from its For Candidates page, NBPTS goes on to say,

Teachers and counselors are required to submit a portfolio to document their teaching practice. The portfolio will consist of four entries:

- One classroom-based entry with accompanying student work
- Two classroom-based entries that require video recordings of interactions between you and your students
- One documented accomplishments entry that provides evidence of your accomplishments outside of the classroom and how that work impacts student learning (p. 1)

As you can see, the National Board requires direct evidence of teaching or counseling and comments that describe, analyze, and reflect on the evidence. We urge that teachers and counselors become familiar with National Board Certification. Figure 10.1 is a print screen that shows a menu tabs and a screen page of the portfolio menu.

SELF-ASSESSMENT AND REFLECTION: WHAT PATTERNS OF STRENGTHS OR GAPS EXIST?

A comprehensive portfolio serves as a marvelous tool for reflection of personal growth and future planning. Also, since it provides a broad collection of artifacts that demonstrate the full range of your knowledge, skills, and dispositions, a review of the contents can indicate patterns of strengths or possible gaps that exist.

The Artifacts Organizer and Table of Contents (see Chapter 6) can assist with analyzing how much documentation is available in the areas of focus for a job or for seeking higher-education admission. After the initial review of artifacts, you may note patterns and gaps in experiences or knowledge or both. Analyze these two documents for areas that appear to be strengths, those needing development, and those in which there is minimal or no experience. Many interviewers ask candidates to identify their strengths and weaknesses and to describe how they plan to improve in weak areas. If there are major knowledge or

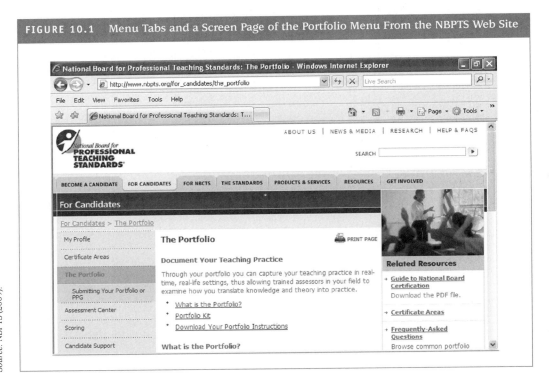

FIGURE 10.1 Menu Tabs and a Screen Page of the Portfolio Menu From the NBPTS Web Site

Source: NBPTS (2009).

For specific information related to this concept, see the Chapter 10 resources on the CD.

experience gaps, candidates may need to reconsider seeking advancement opportunities until those gaps are addressed.

Table 10.2 gives an example of a way to document areas of strength and those that need development. The table is an organizational tool that helps to facilitate the analysis and can be used to prepare for advancement opportunities and for self- and supervisor evaluation. Consider this table as a tool that should be updated at least on an annual basis. This provides an excellent opportunity for ongoing self-evaluation. A template is provided on the CD.

LET'S PRACTICE!

Activity 10.2 Gap Analysis

Carefully review Table 10.2 and then do a gap analysis. Write a reflective statement about strengths and weaknesses. Celebrate the strengths and then develop a plan to work on the areas that need improvement. Share with colleagues.

TABLE 10.2   Gap Analysis Tool: Profile of Strengths and Areas for Development

Date: _____ Current Position: _____

Focus Area (goal, standard, etc.)	Areas of Strength	Areas That Need Development	Strategies to Improve
Example: INTASC Principle 1, Knowledge of Subject Matter	Knowledge: 3.8 GPA, all As in my major (mathematics); current in my subject matter; member of National Council of Teacher of Mathematics (NCTM); attended several mathematics conferences; currently enrolled in a master's degree program.	Skills: Still learning to differentiate instruction; not much documentation to demonstrate success in this area. Dispositions: Not sure that I have high enough expectations for kids that are not achieving; not sure I believe they can achieve in my Algebra 1 classes or at higher math levels.	Skills: Currently working with a mathematics coach; I am observing her teach, and she is observing my classes and critiquing my lessons and then coming in for a follow-up; this will continue. Dispositions: I need to find out about places where kids are succeeding in math and see what those teachers do; I need to believe that it can happen; I plan to seek help in this area by observing others and learning to use their strategies; I am reading some research, discussing my problem with my instructors at the college, and looking at Web sites for information.
(Continue with other focus, goal, or standards areas)			

SELECTING CONTENTS FOR DIFFERENT PORTFOLIO PURPOSES

After you have done your research and analyzed patterns of strengths, weaknesses, and gaps, it is time to assemble a *focused portfolio*. Earlier in the book, Table 1.1, 1.2, and 1.3 show some examples of several different types of portfolios and their possible uses. To recap, the major areas include personal information and documentation of achievement in professional standards.

Review Chapter 4 and Table 4.4 on how to transform artifacts into evidence. This information proves valuable in the evaluation and selection of artifacts for inclusion in a focus portfolio. It might begin with three major components: current personal information, achievement in professional standards, and letters of reference. As previously mentioned, we recommend that you update material on an annual basis at a minimum and place update reminders on a calendar. Resumes and other pertinent information should be kept current and updated electronically.

These focus portfolios are prepared for a specific purpose and with a goal in mind, such as employment or promotion. They differ from a comprehensive portfolio in size, function, and portability. Table 10.3 gives an example of how to organize artifacts to prepare concurrently for various focused portfolios. This requires a retooling of the Artifacts Organizer presented in Chapter 6. The organizer in Table 10.3 can be used as an indicator system for briefly noting *yes, no,* or *maybe* about the inclusion of an artifact, or it can be expanded to include descriptive and reflective notations. The notations will probably prove more valuable, but they require a time commitment. Opportunities sometimes become available unexpectedly, and an updated information resource provides an up-to-the-minute labor-saving tool.

TABLE 10.3　Artifacts Organizer for Academic and Career Advancement

Focused Portfolios (Sample) Review or Include in Focus Portfolio: Yes, No, Maybe				
Artifact	Professional Standard, Goal, Academic Area	Focus: Master's Degree Program	Focus: Curriculum Coach	Focus: National Board Certification
Case studies Dates: 1/05; 6/05	INTASC Principle 1: Knowledge of Subject Matter; Principle 2: Knowledge of Human Development and Learning; and Principle 3: Adapting Instruction for Individual Learning	Yes: Able to apply knowledge to classroom teaching; demonstrates academic writing and beginning skills as a researcher.	Yes: Demonstrates curriculum knowledge, collaboration with peers, leadership in my department, ability to self-evaluate and critique my teaching.	Yes: Case study links to NBPTS for Mathematics: Adolescence and Young Adulthood Certificate. Good example of description, analysis, and reflection (still needs work).

Artifact	Professional Standard, Goal, Academic Area	Focus: Master's Degree Program	Focus: Curriculum Coach	Focus: National Board Certification
Agendas and students' work and achievement data from lesson study. Groups dates: September 2003–June 2005, approximately every 3 weeks	INTASC Principle 1: Knowledge of Subject Matter; Principle 3: Adapting Instruction for Individual Learning; Principle 4: Multiple Instructional Strategies; Principle 8: Assessment of Student Learning	Yes: Recent comments from my colleagues indicate that my plans, student work, and assessments demonstrate outstanding knowledge of assessment in the area of content standards, and my achievement data indicate effective teaching.	Yes: Recently (see agendas), I have facilitated lesson sessions; my facilitation, leadership, and communication skills with colleagues are becoming very effective; we have professional dialogues about improvement; we challenge assumptions about what is possible and leave with improvement strategies; a sense of efficacy pervades our group.	Yes: Most recent artifacts are aligned with all five core propositions: (1) Teachers are committed to students and their learning, (2) teachers know the subjects they teach and how to teach those subjects to students, (3) teachers are responsible for managing and monitoring student learning, (4) teachers think systematically about their practice and learn from experience, and (5) teachers are members of learning communities.
Teaching Video Date: October 2008; January 2009; May 2009	INTASC Principles 1–8	Maybe	Maybe	Yes

The sample artifacts in Table 10.3 have notations and indications of whether they should be considered for review or for inclusion in a focus portfolio or both. There are examples of indicators for inclusion (*yes, maybe, no*) and some examples of notations. This organizer is designed as an initial system only for selecting artifacts for use in focus areas. Requirements for some portfolios, such as national board certification and other specific areas, involve more extensive preparation. A template for Table 10.3 is included in the CD.

For specific information related to this concept, see the Chapter 10 resources on the CD.

Once the documents for the focused portfolio have been finalized, create a table of contents for each focus area. This serves as a preparation tool and as a document that can be shared with others. Campbell et al. (2001) show a way to display contents using an organizational tool titled "Portfolio at a Glance." This tool gives a thumbnail overview by naming the artifacts under each category that are included in the portfolio (see the Further Reading section at the end of this chapter). A modified table of contents could serve a similar purpose.

PREPARING HIRING OR INTERVIEW PORTFOLIOS

There have been many studies and articles that have focused on the use of teacher-developed portfolios in applying and interviewing for jobs. Many of them have centered around the use of electronic portfolios (Bartell et al., 1998a, 1998b; Snyder, McKelvey, & Edwards, 1998; Strawhecker et al., 2007–2008). Others have been focused on the types of evidence that hiring officials like to see in a portfolio (Montgomery, 1998; Mosely, 2004–2005; Polansky & Semmel, 2006; Snyder et al., 1998; Strawhecker et al., 2007–2008; Theel, 2001). These studies and articles provide useful information about what hiring officials are looking for in teacher portfolios and some of their concerns about portfolio use.

It is possible to get some clues about what employers value. Strawhecker et al. (2007–2008) conducted a study on the hiring practices of K–12 teachers in a Midwestern state. Survey data was used to assess the types of content and the pros and cons of portfolio use during the hiring practice. Employers commented that the benefits were that they were able to view real artifacts, they were able to get a comprehensive picture, and they got a sense of the candidate's organizational skills. They also stated the convenience of using an electronic portfolio. The drawbacks of using an electronic portfolio in the hiring process include the time it takes for the presentation, that the interview might not be the optimal time to present it, that it was too hard to judge the quality of the work, and the concern that applicants would only show their best work.

Table 10.4 describes what 37 principals said they would like to see in a teacher portfolio. The percentages are from high to low. Personal documents, such as the resume, references letters of recommendation, and college transcripts, received the highest percentages. More than 50% of the principals desired to see evidence of lesson plans, reflections on teaching experience, teaching philosophy, previous work experience, and student teacher evaluations. Examples of work in college methods classes received the lowest rankings. Although this information cannot be generalized to all administrators and districts, it appears to be a reasonable guide of what hiring officials might expect. More information on this topic can be found in the Further Reading section at the end of this chapter.

In structured interviews with K–12 principals and four key district officials, Theel (2001) found that lesson plans; photographs of projects, activities, and teacher–student interaction; and supporting examples of classroom practice should be included in addition to an educational philosophy, credential, letters of reference, and transcripts. This is similar to the responses of the principals surveyed by Strawhecker et al. (2007–2008) and Snyder et al. (1998). Snyder and colleagues recommend the inclusion of a 3–5-minute video highlighting

TABLE 10.4 Principals' Desired Portfolio Artifacts by Percentage ($n = 37$)

Desired Portfolio Artifact	Percentage of Participants Choosing This Response
Candidate's resume	94.6
References	94.6
Letters of recommendation	89.2
College transcript	83.8
Student teacher evaluations	78.4
Candidate's previous work experience	78.4
Candidate's teaching philosophy statement	64.9
Video clip of candidate interacting with students in a classroom setting	64.9
Evidence of reflection on teaching experiences	56.8
Sample lesson plans	54.1
Sample tests, other assessment instruments	35.1
Artifacts to document experience with ethnic and cultural diversity	24.3
Artifacts that document community service learning activities	21.6
Examples of candidate's work in college methods classes	18.9

Source: Strawhecker et al. (2007–2008).

an area such as teaching strategies and that candidates be prepared for the following three major situations:

Situation #1—An administrator may require your portfolio as evidence of your abilities.

Situation #2—An administrator may look at it and process the information only if you offer it.

Situation #3—You may offer the portfolio, but it may not be examined, or the portfolio may not be asked to be examined at all. (p. 9)

PORTFOLIO PRESENTATION FOR CAREER AND EDUCATIONAL ADVANCEMENT

Many of our former students who have used their portfolios for employment interviews shared their sense of confidence about the abilities it describes. They also found themselves able to articulate their accomplishments prior to and during the interview. Possessing real-world, concrete evidence to demonstrate achievements helps in responding to interview questions. They also shared that some potential employers are favorably impressed with the assembled body of information about their achievements. However, there can be challenges in using portfolios in an interview. Remember Rick's experience described in the opening scenario. His portfolio fell off the table and scattered all over. Moreover, he also had not retooled his portfolio.

To prepare to use the portfolio in an interview setting for career or academic advancements, we offer the following suggestions:

1. *Select contents carefully*. In prior sections, we discuss retooling, analyzing strengths and weakness, and organizing artifacts by focus areas. Now it is time to select the *key contents for the focused portfolio*. These are the best of the best. We recommend including about two artifacts for each goal, standard, or job area. The resume should be added, and so should other pertinent personal information documents, if critical to the interview. Snyder et al. (1998) report results from a study of 72 school administrators that indicate that "it is critically important that portfolio be well organized, focused on educational issues, and be easy to read" (p. 7). They also emphasize that portfolio presenters be aware of time factors, cogent in their remarks, and thoroughly familiar with their portfolios.

2. *Select a container*. Select and prepare the container for the portfolio contents. Review Chapter 6 for detailed suggestions on highlighting information, for example. A container should have a professional appearance and allow ease in accessing the documents so that no attention will be diverted from the interviewee. For hard-cover portfolios, a binder with a zipper gives a professional appearance. For organizing the contents, tabs, sticky notes, and other tools can be used for quick location of documents. A soft-cover binder that can be inserted in a briefcase can also be used. If disks, CDs, or other electronic information is included, be sure to store them in pockets with three-hole plastic inserts or in the pocket of the notebook cover. Use three-hole plastic sheet protectors for ease of access and to protect documents. Another container that might be considered is a light plastic organizer with several pockets that can be labeled. These allow for folders to be inserted. Folders can be color coded and labeled. These organizers look attractive and professional. Attractive containers are constantly becoming available. Check with one of the many office supplies stores. All documents should be printed and photocopied on high-quality paper. Remember to bring only copies, not original documents, to leave with prospective employers. Electronic portfolios should be considered only if interviewers deem them appropriate. If so, candidates should check to see if the setting is appropriate and bring their own hardware. It is advisable to have hard-cover backups, or candidates can simply share a table of contents and provide a CD or Web site address—before, during, or after the interview. Strawhecker et al. (2007–2008) reported that administrators ranked having the Web site address to view the portfolio in a computer at 51.4% for a delivery method; the CD received a 22.9% rating, and the DVD delivery method received a 25.7% rating (see Table 10.5).

TABLE 10.5   Principals' Desired Delivery System for Portfolio (n = 37)

Desired Delivery System for Portfolio	Percentage of Respondents
Web site address	51.4
CD	22.9
DVD	25.7

Source: Strawhecker et al. (2007–2008).

3. *Find one or more reviewers.* Seek out someone who is a knowledgeable professional in the focus area to review and give honest critiques about the authenticity, quality, and suitability of the contents, the organization for ease of presentation, and the appearance of the portfolio. Any documents that are not adequate need to be deleted unless they can be authentically retooled. Documents may need to be reformatted or have more substantive reflections. Another document from the comprehensive portfolio might be better suited, or you may need to eliminate evidence in that area at this point; this may be an area for growth. Documents should not be redone or added to in ways that present inflated information. Only what is authentic should be included. Be sure to demonstrate appreciation of the review of your portfolio with a thank-you note or other gesture.

4. *Conduct mock interviews.* Now it is time to rehearse using the portfolio in an interview. Be sure to do the research about the focus area discussed earlier. Develop interview questions from the information gathered from the research. Mock interviews give you a chance to find out how well the container or electronic format and organization of the portfolio work. Finding, taking out, pointing to, and presenting evidence for sharing in an interview requires lots of practice. In video and audiotape rehearsals, be sure to rehearse potential interview questions with colleagues and friends. To get an honest assessment, give them a rating sheet. Always show appreciation with a thank-you note or other gesture. These suggestions may sound time-consuming, but consider the time spent as an investment in your growth in becoming an outstanding reflective practitioner, able to self-evaluate your professional growth and its potential value for career advancement.

5. *Share the portfolio.* It is advisable to inquire about the best time to share the portfolio: prior to, during, or after the interview. If the portfolio is left, leave only a copy. Purchase an inexpensive but attractive soft-cover binder or something similar. Be sure it is labeled. Do not leave any confidential information, such as documents that may have a Social Security number or other personal or student confidential information. Remember that the portfolio used during the interview is a supplement. Its purpose is to enhance, not to draw attention away from your

comments or responses to questions. When the opportunity arises to refer to documentation in your portfolio, prepare the interviewers for the presentation of evidence from the portfolio with a statement such as, "I have had experience in this area, and I have a document in my portfolio that provides a good illustration of what I have accomplished." Quickly identify the document, hold on to it, and point to pertinent highlighted information as you answer the question. Do not pass the document around, because the interviewers may focus on the document and not fully listen to your answer. Share with them that you will leave this or any other appropriate information for their review. Snyder et al. (1998) suggest that if pictures are being presented that there be an explanation, location, and date below each picture.

There will be many opportunities during your career to present portfolio documents for sharing. They will be valuable during evaluation conferences, with colleagues who are problem solving about a particular educational issue, during professional-development sessions, and in other professional and academic arenas. As the portfolio gets used and valued as a professional growth companion, it promises to become an essential professional-development tool for reflective educators.

SUMMARY

In this chapter, we discussed the portfolio as a continual companion for professional development and its use in several areas of career and academic advancement. Maintaining a *comprehensive portfolio,* which is a storehouse covering a broad range of documents, provides evidence of professional accomplishments. This storehouse becomes the source for developing *focused portfolios* assembled for specific academic or career-advancement purposes. Suggestions and templates are provided to assist in retooling and presenting the portfolio for specific goals, such as employment, professional advancement, and evaluation. Information is provided on how to use the portfolio to present evidence of professional growth and achievement for evaluations, interviews, and other career development settings.

Research on professional practices indicates the increasing use of portfolios in colleges and schools of education and in organizations such as the NBPTS that require submissions of portfolios for documenting professional achievements.

USEFUL RESOURCES

Visit career development offices, libraries, and Web sites that have useful information on preparing resumes and job-seeking-skill development.

Developing Job-Seeking Skills (http://www.udel.edu/CSC/jobskills.html)

A Web site that provides an abundant supply of information on different career options and developing job seeking skills. Provided by the career services center at the University of Delaware.

Developing a Teaching Resume and Cover Letter (http://www.atozteacherstuff.com/pages/1876.shtml)

Guidelines for creating a teaching resume and cover letter, with samples.

Developing Your Resume (http://www.managementhelp.org/career/resumes.htm)

A workshop series from Purdue University writing lab.

Job-Seeking Exercise Workbook (http://www.nwtc.edu/Services/SES/Stu_skills.htm)

A job seeking skills exercise workbook. Provide a step-by-step process to improve your job seeking skills.

NBPTS Web Site (http://www.nbpts.org)

National Board for Professional Teaching Standards official Web site.

Pongo Resume Online Tool (http://www.pongoresume.com)

A Web site that provides resume templates that can be customized.

FOR FURTHER READING

Abernathy, T. V., Forsyth, A., & Mitchell, J. (2001). The bridge from student to teacher: What principals, teacher education faculty, and students value in a teaching applicant. *Teacher Education Quarterly, 28*(4), 109–119.

Brown, G., & Irby, B. J. (2000). *The career advancement portfolio* (2nd ed.). Thousand Oaks, CA: Corwin Press.

Campbell, D. M., Cignetti, P. B., Melenyzer, B. J., Nettles, D. H., & Wyman, R. M. W., Jr. (2001). *How to develop a professional portfolio: A manual for teachers* (2nd ed.). Boston: Allyn & Bacon.

Dietz, M. E. (2008). *Designing the school leader's portfolio* (2nd ed.). Thousand Oaks, CA: Corwin Press.

Liu, E. (2003, April). *New teachers' experiences of hiring: Preliminary findings from a four-state study.* Paper presented at the meeting of American Educational Research Association (AERA), Chicago, IL.

Liu, E., & Johnson, S. M. (2006). New teachers' experiences of hiring: Late, rushed, and information-poor. *Educational Administration Quarterly, 42*(3), 324–360.

Montgomery, K. (1997, Spring). Student teacher portfolios: A portrait of the beginning teacher. *Teacher Educator, 32,* 216–25

Mosely, C. (2004–2005). The value of professional teaching portfolios to prospective employers: School administrators' views. *The Professional Educator, 27,* 58–72.

Rieman, P. (2000). *Teaching portfolios: Presenting your professional best.* Boston: McGraw-Hill.

Snyder, J., McKelvey, T., & Edwards, D. (1998). *Constructing your portfolio for the teacher interview.* Slippery Rock, PA: Slippery Rock University, Office of Career Services.

Satterthwaite, F., & D'Orsi, G. (2003). *The career portfolio workbook: Using the newest tool in your job-hunting arsenal to impress employers and land a great job.* New York: McGraw-Hill.

Strawhecker, J., Messersmith, K., & Balcom, A. (2007–2008, Winter). The role of electronic portfolios in the hiring of K–12 teachers. *Journal of Computing in Teacher Education, 24,* 65–71.

Glossary

action research: in the most general sense, researching one's actions by simply asking questions about one's actions for the purpose of learning from them in order to improve upon them and grow; defined as a systematic approach used to improve one's own practice (McNiff, 2003; Mertler, 2009; Reason & Bradbury, 2004; Sagor, 2003)

Adobe Acrobat Reader: free software created by Adobe Systems (www.adobe.com) that allows one to read and print portable document format (PDF) files

Adobe Acrobat Writer: software created by Adobe Systems (www.adobe.com) that converts files into to portable document format (PDF)

application: demonstrates understanding of the subject by using knowledge in situations; can be either expressive or inventive in nature (PATT, 2000)

artifacts: concrete examples of work that are collected to demonstrate a particular knowledge, skill, or disposition (Brown & Irby, 2001)

assessment: the act or process of gathering data to better understand the strengths and weaknesses of student learning, as by observation, testing, interviews, and so on (PATT, 2000); an ongoing, developmental process to measure growth and change over time

authentic: genuine, real-world, meaningful applications or examples; the use of actual products that are related to whatever is being observed or measured

authentic assessment: any performance assessment that is a real-world and valid indicator of what is being measured; for example, real-world evidence of instructional practice may include requiring a candidate to write and implement a lesson in an actual classroom

benchmark: the level of performance that is to be achieved at certain points; description of student performance at various developmental levels that contribute to the achievement of performance standards (PATT, 2000)

burn: the act of recording information onto a CD or DVD

case study: a description and examination of a student, school, or district; the subject of the study is usually kept anonymous.

CD: compact disc; an optical media that stores up to 700 megabytes per disc, used mainly for music or file storage

CD-Based: meaning when finished, an electronic portfolio is stored on a CD and viewed by accessing the CD in a computer

classroom management plan: an assignment in which teacher credential candidates begin developing a management system, usually including a philosophical statement or theoretical foundation; a description of classroom rules, expectations, and boundaries; a description of instructional and assessment strategies, and a process for motivating students to do their best (Charles, 2005)

commercial Web site: a Web site that is owned and operated by a person or business and is primarily used for commerce, generally for a fee

competencies: abilities or proficiencies, what one is capable of doing; having requisite or adequate ability or qualities; having the capacity to function or develop in a particular way (Merriam-Webster, 2009)

content standard: articulates what students should understand and be able to do within specific content areas (e.g., identifies and uses appropriate strategies for various problem types)

criteria: guidelines, rules, characteristics, or dimensions that are used to judge the quality of student performance, indicating what is valued in student responses, products, or performances; they may be holistic, analytic, general, or specific (PATT, 2000)

culturally responsive: a practice and pedagogy that expects high student and educator achievement; one that is aligned and consistent with the cultural traditions and knowledge of students and draws upon, affirms, and validates prior experiences, language, frames of reference, and performance styles of bicultural peoples (Johnson & Bush, 2005); sometimes referred to as *culturally relevant, congruent,* and *synchronized teaching* (Gay, 2000)

demographics: a statistical description of the composition of populations using indicators such as race, ethnicity, gender, language, and socioeconomic status

digital video: full-motion video stored in the form of 0s and 1s, using the binary system; either recorded on a digital camera or converted from analog video using a digital camera or computer with an analog-to-digital video capture card

dispositions: attitudes, beliefs, or values; often viewed as the beliefs or affective and philosophical aspects of an individual

DVD: digital video disc; an optical media that stores up to 4.7 gigabytes per disc, used mainly for video storage but can also hold files

educational Web site: a Web site that is used primarily for education; free or fee-based

electronic portfolio: a collection of artifacts housed digitally that are then organized and used for a variety of purposes, such as assessment, evaluation, and academic and professional advancement; can be housed online or on a storage device

evaluation: a final or summative process of determining overall progress, usually considered the culmination of a program or course of study

final grade: the summative grade a person receives at the end of a course

formative: a developmental process that takes place over a period of time, each part of the process building on earlier stages; in formative evaluation, evidence is gathered at different times in a program or course to measure progress and to indicate areas of strength and those that need improvement and used to form judgments on how to proceed; usually gathered at the beginning and midpoints of or at intervals during a program

gigabyte: about 1 billion bytes or 1,000 megabytes; approximately equivalent to 500,000 pages of text with 2,000 characters per page; abbreviated as GB

high-stakes assessments or tests: tests that are used for accountability purposes to judge the relative goodness or weakness of institutions, with high visibility and results for schools and districts usually published in newspapers and on state and district Web sites; for instance, tests such as the SAT, and GRE are often used as part of the information to decide admission into programs, colleges, and so forth, and high school exit exams may determine whether an individual graduates from high school regardless of grades received

HTML: hyper text markup language; the most common markup language for Web pages

hyperlink: an electronic link to a specific artifact, usually identified within the text by being bold and underlined

inquiry: a question or questions posed for investigation about practice; for portfolio purposes, inquiries involve a process of collecting, sorting, selecting, describing, analyzing, and evaluating evidence to answer questions on how well the evidence represents the candidate's accomplishment of a goal, standard, or objective

INTASC Standards: the Interstate New Teacher Assessment and Support Consortium (INTASC), a consortium of more than 30 states operating under the Council of Chief State School Officers (CCSSO), which has developed standards and an assessment process for initial teacher certification (Campbell et al., 2000)

Interstate School Leaders Licensure Consortium (ISLLC):   National leadership and policy standards that have been developed through the Council of Chief State School Officers. The standards were released in 1996 by the Interstate School Leaders Licensure Consortium (ISLLC) which is a consortium of states and associations that developed the model for standards and assessments for school leaders. Over the years, the standards have become known as the ISLLC standards.

JPG or **JPEG:**   the Joint Photographic Experts Group is a compression format for color bit-mapped images (photographs) and is named after the committee that set the compression standard. Files stored in this format have the .jpeg extension or .jpg extension

link: *see* hyperlink

live on the Web: information posted live and accessible to anyone via the internet

marketing portfolio: portfolio used for employment interviews and other professional activities related to advancement

mastery: the highest level of competency or proficiency in knowledge or skills

media: tools used to store and deliver information or data

megabyte: also called meg or MB, is about 1 million bytes, equivalent to about 500 pages of text with 2,000 characters per page

National Board for Professional Teaching Standards (NBPTS) Certification: facilitates access to opportunities for career advancement for teachers and counselors, recognized thereby as highly accomplished educators; quoting from their Web page, "Like board-certified doctors and accountants, teachers who achieve National Board Certification have met rigorous standards through intensive study, expert evaluation, self-assessment and peer review. NBPTS offers 25 certificates that cover a variety of subject areas and student developmental levels"; for additional information, go to http://www.nbpts.org

navigation page: a page that has hyperlinks that are connected to specific artifacts, such as a table of contents with each entry hyperlinked to its corresponding artifact

National Educational Technology Standards (NETS) for Teachers, Administrators, Students and Technology Facilitators and Leaders: standards developed by the International Society for Technology in Education (ITSE) for students, teachers, and administrators that assist in developing ways to measure proficiency and set future goals for the knowledge, skills, and attitudes needed to succeed in the 21st century electronic age; for further information, see http://www.iste.org/AM/Template .cfm? Section = NETS

National Standards for School Counseling Programs: ASCA's Ethical Standards for School Counselors adopted by the ASCA Delegate Assembly, March 19, 1984, revised March 27, 1992, June 25, 1998 and June 26, 2004; see http://www.school counselor.org/content.asp?pl = 127&sl =173&content id =173

password protected: for security, access to the protected information available only with the correct password

PDF: portable document format; allows documents to be copied or e-mailed, no matter what program was used originally to create it, viewed using Adobe Acrobat Reader (www.adobe .com), which is free software

pen drives: *see* USB flash drive

performance assessment: tasks that ask students to perform, create, or do something as a demonstration of what they know and can do; such tasks preferably require analytical thinking and problem-solving skills and often require trained human judgment for scoring (Hill, 1999 as cited in PATT, 2000)

portable mass storage device: allows storage of large files (e.g., USB flash drive, mini-USB hard drive)

portfolio: electronic or hard-copy collections of artifacts that have been selected over time to provide evidence of a learner's competency, providing evidence of knowledge, skills, and dispositions related to achieving a standard, goal, or objective

portfolio presentation: the presentation of a portfolio to an audience as evidence of progress toward or completion of a particular goal, either during a program as a formative assessment, at the end of a program as a summative evaluation, or during an interview

posting: the act of copying files to a Web site and loading them onto the server, enabling a portfolio to be viewed on the Web

PowerPoint: Microsoft's presentation software program; for more information, see www.microsoft.com

practicing educator: one who is currently serves in a position such as a teacher, counselor, or administrator

reflection: the act of considering one's actions critically, analyzing them, and determining their success in meeting desired outcomes and what steps can be taken to improve that success, most effectively captured in writing; captions or small statements and explanations used to give voice to the various artifacts collected in the portfolio (Barrett, 2001; Burke, 1997; Wolf & Dietz, 1998)

reflective inquiry: a process of tracking or examining one's actions by constantly asking questions about the reasons for doing the actions or activities in order to learn from them

revision: a modification of work that takes place through a process or review, editing and changing for the purpose of improvement

Ribbon: groups of commands organized into various tabs in Microsoft Office 2007, which replace the menu and toolbars of earlier versions

rubric: a tool used in authentic assessment to assess or establish criteria that are complex and subjective (also called a *scoring guide*), designed to simulate real-life activity and show levels of performance on a standard or skill over a continuum, ranging from high or expert level of performance to low or ineffective level of performance

scoring guidelines: also called *rubrics* are sets of guidelines for giving scores to student work; a typical scoring guide states the assessment criteria, contains a scale, and helps the educator rate given work according to the scale (PATT, 2000)

scrapbook: a collection of artifacts that are compiled over time

server: a computer that stores information for use on the Web or by other computers that are connected to it

standards: a description of what students should understand or be able to do; standards may be listed or placed within categories (PATT, 2000)

standards-based reforms: educational reforms that have been prompted by assessment and accountability based on content and professional standards

structured reflection: reflection that is guided by prompts, questions, or activities intended to help elicit deeper thought in students (Skills4Study, 2008)

summative: the final stage or end result of a process, similar to the summary or events adding up to a whole; a final or overall evaluation or product

thumb drives: *see* USB flash drive

traditional exam: a method of examination that does not rely on authentic artifacts but on answering open-ended or multiple-choice questions about a specific topic to assess proficiency or competence

USB flash drive: a small, portable, removable, and rewritable devise for storing electronic data; also called thumb drive, stick drive, or pen drive

Web address: the universal resource locator (URL) of a Web site, usually starting with "http://," which is the method of retrieval, which then is followed by the type of page (e.g., "www"); then comes the Internet domain name—two examples are *http://www.microsoft.com* or *http://www.firefox.com*

Web-based: an electronic portfolio uploaded to an online server, then accessible from a Web site

Web browser: a program used to view Web pages (e.g., Internet Explorer, Firefox, Safari)

Word: Microsoft's word processor software program; for more information, see www.microsoft.com

WYSIWYG: "What You See Is What You Get"; a common user interface where what is viewed on the screen is what will be on the final product

zoom: zooming in magnifies the content of a document on a computer; the opposite, zooming out, shrinks the content

References

American School Counselor Association. (n.d.). *National standards for school counseling programs*. Alexandra, VA: Author. Retrieved February 24, 2009, from www.jeffcityschools.org/pdf files/ASCA Standards.pdf

ARC CAS. (2008). *Writing reflections*. Retrieved September 2, 2008, from http://arccas.tripod.com/id32.html

Astin, A. (1993). *What matters in college: Four critical years revisited*. San Francisco: Jossey-Bass.

Banks, J. A. (2006). *Race, culture & education: The selected works of James A. Banks*. New York: Routledge.

Bargal, D. (2006). Personal and intellectual influences leading to Lewin's paradigm of action research: Towards the 60th anniversary of Lewin's "Action research and minority research problems" (1946). *Action Research 4*(4), 367–388

Bargal, D. (2008, February). Action research: A paradigm for achieving social change. *Small Group Research, 39*, 17—27.

Barnes, P., Clark, P., & Thull, B. (2005). Web-based digital portfolios and counselor supervision. *Journal of Technology in Counseling, 3*(1). Retrieved May 2, 2005, from http://jtc.colstate.edu/V03-1/Barnes/Barnes.htm

Barnett, B. (1992). Using alternative assessment measures in educational leadership preparation programs: Educational platforms and portfolios. *Journal of Personnel Evaluation in Education, 6*, 141–151.

Barrett, H. (2001). *Electronic portfolios = multimedia development + portfolio development: The electronic portfolio development process*. Arlington Heights, IL: Skylight.

Bartell, C. A., Kaye, C., & Morin, J. A., (1998a, Winter). Guest editors' introduction: Teaching portfolios and teacher education. *Teacher Education Quarterly, 25*(1), 5–8.

Bartell, C. A., Kaye, C., & Morin, J. A. (1998b). Portfolio conversation: A mentored journey. *Teacher Education Quarterly, 25*(1), 129–139.

Barth, R. S. (1990). *Improving schools from within: Teachers, parents, and principals make a difference*. San Francisco: Jossey-Bass.

Barton, J., & Collins, A. (1997). *Portfolio assessment: A handbook for educators*. Menlo Park, CA: Addison-Wesley.

Baskerville, R., & Myers, M. (2004). Special issue on action research in information systems: Making research relevant to practice—Foreword. *MIS Quarterly, 28*(3), 329–335.

Bateson, D. (1994). Psychometric and philosophic problems in "authentic" assessment: Performance tasks and portfolios. *Alberta Journal of Educational Research, 40*(2), 233–245.

Bloom, B. S. (1956). *Taxonomy of educational objectives, handbook I: The cognitive domain*. New York: David McKay.

Bradbury, H., & Reason, P. (2003, June). Action research: An opportunity for revitalizing research purpose and practice. *Qualitative Social Work, 2*, 155–175.

Brown, G., & Irby, B. J. (2000). *The career advancement portfolio* (2nd ed.). Thousand Oaks, CA: Corwin Press.

Brown, G., & Irby, B. J. (2001). *The principal portfolio* (2nd ed.). Thousand Oaks, CA: Corwin Press.

Brown, J. D., & Wolfe-Quintero, K. (1997). Teacher portfolios for evaluation: A great idea or a waste of time? *The Language Teacher Online*. Retrieved on February 16, 2009, from http://www.jalt-publications.org/tlt/files/97/jan/portfolios.html

Brydon-Miller, M., Greenwood, D., & Maguire, P. (2003, July). Why action research? *Action Research, 1,* 9–28.

Burgess, J. (2006, December). Participatory action research: First-person perspectives of a graduate student. *Action Research, 4,* 419–437.

Burke, K. (1997). *Designing professional portfolios for change.* Thousand Oaks, CA: Corwin Press.

California State University, Charter College of Education. (2004). *Single subject credential: Directed teaching/demonstration of competencies evaluation rubric.* Los Angeles: Author. Retrieved March 7, 2009, from www.calstatela.edu/academic/ccoe/studserv/ss_rubric.pdf

Campbell, D. M., Cignetti, P. B., Melenyzer, B. J., Nettles, D. H., & Wyman, R. M., Jr. (2001). *How to develop a professional portfolio: A manual for teachers.* Boston: Allyn & Bacon.

Campbell, D. M., Cignetti, P. B., Melenyzer, B. J., Nettles, D. H., & Wyman, R. M., Jr. (2004). *How to develop a professional portfolio: A manual for teachers* (3rd ed.). Boston: Allyn & Bacon.

Campbell, D. M., Melenyzer, B. J., Nettles, D. H., & Wyman, R. M., Jr. (2000). *Portfolio and performance assessment in teacher education.* Boston: Allyn & Bacon.

Campus Compact. (2008). *Using structured reflection to enhance learning from service.* Retrieved September 4, 2008, from http://www.compact.org/disciplines/reflection/

Cassell, C., & Johnson, P. (2006, June). Action research: Explaining the diversity. *Human Relations, 59,* 783–814.

Charles, C. M. (2005). *Building classroom discipline* (8th ed.). Boston: Allyn & Bacon.

Clark, D. R. (2007). *Learning domains of Bloom's Taxonomy.* Retrieved March 16, 2009, from http://www.nwlink.com/ ~ Donclark/hrd/bloom.html

Coghlan, D., & Brannick, T. (2004). *Doing action research in your own organization* (2nd ed.). Thousand Oaks, CA: Sage.

Cook, T. (2006). Collaborative action research within developmental evaluation: Learning to see or the road to myopia? *Evaluation, 12*(4), 418–436.

Council of Chief State School Officers. (1996, November 2). *Interstate School Leaders Licensure Consortium standards for school leaders.* Retrieved July 19, 2004, from http://www.ccsso.org/projects/Interstate_School_Leaders_Licensure_Consortium/

Council of Chief State School Officers. (2007). *Educational leadership policy standards: ISLLC 2008.* Washington, DC: Author.

Covey, S. (1990). *The 7 habits of highly effective people: Powerful lessons in personal change.* New York: Simon & Schuster.

Danielson, C., & Abrulyn, L. (1997). *An introduction to using portfolios in the classroom.* Alexandria, VA: Association for Supervision and Curriculum Development.

Danielson, C., & McGreal, T. L. (2000). *Teacher evaluation to enhance professional practice.* Alexandria, VA: Association for Supervision and Curriculum Development.

Dehler, G. E., & Edmonds, R. K. (2006, October). Using action research to connect practice to learning: A course project for working management students. *Journal of Management Education, 30,* 636—669.

Dickens, L., & Watkins, K. (1999, June). Action research: Rethinking Lewin. *Management Learning, 30,* 127—140.

Dietz, Mary E. (2008). *Designing the school leader's portfolio* (2nd ed.). Thousand Oaks, CA: Sage.

Dollase, R. H. (1996). The Vermont experiment in state mandated portfolio program approval. *Journal of Teacher Education, 47*(2), 85–98.

Drummond, J. S., & Themessi-Huber, M. (2007, December). The cyclical process of action research: The contribution of Gilles Deleuze. *Action Research, 5,* 430—448.

Evans, S., Daniel, T., Mikovch, A., Metze, L., & Norman, A. (2006). The use of technology in portfolio assessment of teacher education candidates. *Journal of Technology and Teacher Education, 14*(1), 5–27.

Ferrance, E. (2000). *Themes in education: Action research.* Providence, RI: Laboratory at Brown University.

Fisher, K., & Phelps, R. (2006, June). Recipe or performing art? Challenging conventions for writing action research theses. *Action Research, 4,* 143–164.

Forgette-Giroux, R., & Simon, M. (2000). Organizational issues related to portfolio assessment implementation in the classroom. *Practical Assessment, Research & Evaluation, 7*(4). Retrieved July 19, 2004, from http://PAREonline

Funderstanding. (2009). *Authentic assessment.* Retrieved February 24, 2009, from www.funder standing.com/content/authentic-assessment

Gathercoal, P., Love, D., Bryde, B., & McKean, G. (2002). On implementing Web-based electronic portfolios: A webfolio program lets instructors and students use the Web to improve teaching and learning. *Educause Quarterly, 2,* 29–37.

Gay, G. (2000). *Culturally responsive teaching: Theory, research, and practice.* New York: Teachers College Press.

Georgi, D., & Crowe, J. (1998, Winter). Digital portfolios: A confluence of portfolio assessment and technology. *Teacher Education Quarterly,* 73–84.

Goodrich, H. (1997). Understanding rubrics. *Educational Leadership, 54*(4), 14–17.

Grant, G., & Huebner, T. (1998, Winter). The portfolio question: A powerful synthesis of the personal and the professional. *Teacher Education Quarterly,* 33–43.

Greenwood, D. J., & Levin, M. (2007). *Introduction to action research: Social research for social change* (2nd ed.). Thousand Oaks, CA: Sage.

Hartnell-Young, E., & Morriss, M. (2007). *Digital portfolios: Powerful tools for promoting professional growth and reflection.* Thousand Oaks, CA: Corwin Press.

Hill, A. (1999). *Developing a teaching resume: Guidelines especially for student teachers or recent graduates.* Retrieved March 6, 2009, from http://www.mcpherson.edu/careers/resource_center/Teaching%20Resume.doc

Hurst, B., Wilson, C., & Cramer, G. (1998, April). Professional teaching portfolios: Tools for reflection, growth, and advancement. *Phi Delta Kappan,* 578–584.

Huxham, C., & Vangen, S. (2003, July). Researching organizational practice through action research: Case studies and design choices. *Organizational Research Methods, 6,* 383–403.

International Society for Technology in Education. (2007). *NETS for students.* Washington, DC: Author.

International Society for Technology in Education. (2008). *NETS for teachers.* Washington, DC: Author. Retrieved March 7, 2009, from http://www.iste.org/

Interstate New Teachers Assessment and Support Consortium. (1992). *Model standards for beginning teacher licensing, assessment and development: A Resource for state dialogue.* Washington, DC: Council of Chief State School Officers.

Irvine, J. J. (1990). *Black students and school failure: Policies, practices, and prescriptions.* New York: Greenwood.

Johnson, R. S. (2002). *Using data to close the achievement gap: How to measure equity in our schools.* Thousand Oaks, CA: Corwin Press.

Johnson, R. S., & Bush, V. L. (2005). Leading the culturally responsive school. In F. English (Ed.), *Sage handbook of educational leadership* (pp. 269–296). Thousand Oaks, CA: Sage.

Johnson, R. S., Mims-Cox, J., & Doyle-Nichols, A. (2006). *Developing portfolios in education: A guide to reflection, inquiry, and assessment.* Thousand Oaks, CA: Sage.

Kerka, S. (1995). *Techniques for authentic assessment: Adult, career, and vocational education brief (ACVE).* Retrieved from http://www.cete.org/acve/docgen.asp?tbl+archieve&ID+A032

Kitchen, J., & Stevens, D. (2008, March). Action research in teacher education: Two teacher-educators practice action research as they introduce action research to preservice teachers. *Action Research, 6,* 7–28.

Klecka, C. L., Donovan, L., & Fisher, R. (2007). In their shoes: Teacher educators' reframing portfolio development from the students' perspective. *Journal of Computing in Teacher Education, 24*(1), 31–36.

Krathwohl, D. R., Bloom, B. S., & Bertram, B. M. (1973). *Taxonomy of educational objectives: The classification of educational goals. Handbook II: Affective domain.* New York: David McKay.

Ladson-Billings, G. (1994). *The dreamkeepers: Successful teachers of African American children.* San Francisco: Jossey-Bass.

Ladson-Billings, G. (2003). New directions in multicultural education: Complexities, boundaries, and critical race theory. In J. A. Banks & C. A. McGee Banks (Eds.), *Handbook of research on multicultural education* (2nd ed., pp. 50–65). San Francisco: Jossey-Bass.

Landau, S. I., & Bogus, R. J. (1975). *The Doubleday dictionary for home, school, and office.* New York: Doubleday.

Lazear, D. (1998). *The rubrics way: Using MI to assess understanding.* Tucson, AZ: Zephyr.

Lee, C. D. (1997). Bridging home and school literacies: A model of culturally responsive teaching. In J. Flood, S. B. Heath, & D. Lapp (Eds.), *A handbook for literacy educators: Research on teaching the communicative and visual arts* (pp. 330–341). New York: Macmillan.

Levin, B. B., &. Rock, T. C. (2003, March). The effects of collaborative action research on preservice and experienced teacher partners in professional development schools. *Journal of Teacher Education, 54,* 135–149.

Lindsey, R. B., Robins, K. N., & Terrell, R. D. (2005). *Cultural proficiency: A manual for school leaders* (2nd ed.). Thousand Oaks, CA: Corwin Press.

McKinney, M. (1998, Winter). Preservice teachers' electronic portfolios: Integrating technology, self-assessment and reflection. *Teacher Education Quarterly,* 85–103.

McNiff, J. (2003). *Action research: Principles and practices* (3rd ed.). London: Routledge.

McNiff, J., & Whitehead, J. (2006). *All you need to know about action research.* Thousand Oaks, CA: Sage.

Merriam-Webster. (2009). *Merriam-Webster* Online. Retrieved March 14, 2009, from www.merriam-webster.com.

Mertler, C. (2009). *Action research: Teachers as researchers in the classroom* (2nd ed.). Thousand Oaks, CA: Sage.

Mid-Continental Research for Education and Learning. (2008). *Asking the right questions: A school change toolkit* (Sponsored by U.S. Deptartment of Education). Retrieved September 1, 2008, from http://www.mcrel.org/toolkit/res/reflect.asp-

Mills, G. E. (2003). *Action research: A guide for the teacher researcher.* Upper Saddle River, NJ: Merrill/Prentice Hall.

Miskovic, M., & Hoop, K. (2006). Action research meets critical pedagogy: Theory, practice, and reflection. *Qualitative Inquiry, 12,* 269–291.

Montgomery, K. (1997). Student teacher portfolios: A portrait of the beginning teacher. *The Teacher Educator, 32*(4), 216–225.

Montgomery, K., & Wiley, D. (2008). *Building e-portfolios using PowerPoint: A guide for educators.* Thousand Oaks, CA: Sage.

Morris, W. (Ed.). (1976). *The American heritage dictionary.* Boston: Houghton Mifflin.

Morsch, L. (2009). *10 ways to get your résumé tossed.* Retrieved March 16, 2009, from www.careerbuilder.com/Article/CB-597-Cover-Letters-and-Resumers-10-Ways-to-Get

Mosely, C. (2004-2005). The value of professional teaching portfolios to prospective employers: School administrators' views. *The Professional Educator, 27,* 58–72.

Mueller, J. (2008). *Authentic assessment toolbox.* Retrieved March 6, 2009, from http://jonathan.mueller.faculty.noctrl.edu/toolbox/rubrics.htm

National Board for Professional Teaching Standards. (1999). *General information about the NBPTS standards.* Retrieved March 5, 2009, from http://www.nbpts.org/standards/stds.cfm

National Board for Professional Teaching Standards. (2009). Elegibility polices. *Become a candidate.* Retrieved March 5, 2009, from http://www.nbpts.org

National Commission on Teaching and America's Future. (1996). *What matters most: Teaching for America's future.* New York: Columbia University, Teachers College.

Newman, J. M. (2000, January). Action research: A brief overview. *Forum Qualitative Sozialforschung [Forum: Qualitative Social Research;* online journal], *1*(1). Retrieved February 5, 2005, from http://qualitativeresearch.net/fqs

Nielsen, E. (2006). But let us not forget John Collier: Commentary on David Bargal's "Personal and intellectual influences leading to Lewin's paradigm on action research." *Action Research, 4*(4), 389–399.

No Child Left Behind Act, Pub. L. 107–110 115, Stat. 1425H.R.1 (2002). Retrieved March 7, 2009, from www.ed.gov/nclb/landing.jhtml

Oosterhof, A., Conrad, R., & Ely, D. (2008). *Assessing learners online.* Columbus, OH: Merrill/Prentice Hall.

Painter, S., & Wetzel, K. (2005). School administrators' perceptions of the use of electronic portfolios in K–8 teacher hiring. *Journal of Computing in Teacher Education, 22,* 23–29.

Pennsylvania Assessment Through Themes. (2000). *Portfolio implementation guide.* Retrieved March 9, 2009, from http://www .pde.state.pa.us/fam _consumer/lib/fam_consumer/20/23/portig.pdf

Polansky, H. B., & Semmel, M. (2006, September) Hiring the best and retaining them. *The School Administrator.* Retrieved March 6, 2009, from http://www.aasa.org/publications/

Popham, W. (1997). What's wrong and what's right with rubrics? *Educational Leadership, 55*(3), 72–75.

Post, A. (2009). *My sample resume.* Retrieved March 16, 2009, from www.AtoZTeacherStuff.com

Reason, P. (2006, June). Choice and quality in action research practice. *Journal of Management Inquiry, 15,* 187–203.

Reason, P., & Bradbury, H. (Eds.). (2004). *A handbook of action research: Participative inquiry and practice.* Thousand Oaks, CA: Sage.

Riding, P., Fowell, S., & Levy, P. (1995). An action research approach to curriculum development. *Information Research, 1*(1). Retrieved February 5, 2005, from http://InformationR.net/ir/1–1/paper2.html

Robins, K. N., Lindsey, R. B., Lindsey, D., & Terrell, R. D. (2002). *Culturally proficient instruction: A guide for people who teach.* Thousand Oaks, CA: Corwin Press.

Sagor, R. (2003). *Action research guidebook: A four-step process for educators and school teams.* Thousand Oaks, CA: Sage.

Salend, S. J. (2001). Creating your own professional portfolio. *Intervention in School and Clinic, 36*(4), 195–201.

Salzman, S. A., Denner, P. R., & Harris, L. B. (2002). *Teacher education outcomes measures: Special study survey.* Washington, DC: American Association of Colleges of Teacher Education.

Sankaran, S. (2005). Notes from the field: Action research conversations. *Action Research, 3*(4), 341–352.

Satterthwaite, F., & D'Orsi, G. (2003). *The career portfolio workbook: Using the newest tool in your job-hunting arsenal to impress employers and land a great job.* New York: McGraw-Hill.

Schmuck, R. (1997). *Practical action research for change.* Thousand Oaks, CA: Corwin Press.

Sewell, M., Marczak, M., & Horn, M. (2005). *The use of portfolio assessment in evaluation. Cyfernet Evaluation.* Tucson: University of Arizona. Retrieved July 14, 2004, from http://ag.arizona .edu/fcs/cyfernet/cyfar/Portfo ~ 3.htm

Shade, B. J., Kelly, C., & Oberg, M. (2004). *Creating culturally responsive classrooms.* Washington, DC: American Psychological Association.

Shaklee, B. D., Barbour, N. E., Ambrose, R., & Hansford, S. J. (1997). *Designing and using portfolios.* Boston/New York: Allyn & Bacon.

Simpson, E. J. (1972). *The classification of educational objectives in the psychomotor domain.* Washington, DC: Gryphon House.

Skills4Study. (2008). *Structured reflection.* Retrieved March 6, 2009, from www.palgrave.com/skills 4study/pdp/structured/index.asp

Snyder, J., McKelvey, T., & Edwards, D. (1998). *Constructing your portfolio for the teacher interview.* A report funded by The Middle Atlantic Association for School, College and University Staffing. Slippery Rock University: Office of Career Services.

Southwest Educational Development Laboratory. (2000). *Using reflection to promote instructional*

coherence. Retrieved 9/1/08 from http://www
.sedl.org/pubs/1001/welcome.html and http://
www.sedl.org/pubs/1001/reflection.pdf

Steele, C. (2002). Stereotype threat and student
achievement. In T. Perry, C. Steele, & A. Hillard,
III (Eds.), *Young, gifted and black: Promoting high
achievement among African-American students*
(pp. 109–130). Boston: Beacon.

Stiggins, R. (2008). *An introduction to student-
involved assessment for learning* (5th ed.).
Columbus, OH: Merrill/Prentice Hall.

Stone, B. (1998, Winter). Problems, pitfalls and benefits of portfolios. *Teacher Education Quarterly,*
105–114.

Strawhecker, J. Messersmith, K. & Balcom, A. (Winter
2007–2008). The role of electronic portfolios
in the hiring of K–12 teachers. *Journal of
Computing in Teacher Education, 24,* 65–71.

Strijbos, J., Meeus, W., & Libotton, A. (2007). Portfolio
assignments in teacher education: A tool for self-
regulating the learning process? *International
Journal for the Scholarship of Teaching and
Learning, 1*(2), 1–16.

Stringer, E. (2004). *Action research in education.*
Upper Saddle River, NJ: Pearson Education.

Strudler, N., & Wetzel, K. (2005). The diffusion of electronic portfolios in teacher education: Issues of
initiation and implementation. *Journal of Research
on Technology in Education, 37*(4), 411–433.

Taggart, G. L., & Wilson, A. P. (2005). *Promoting
reflective thinking in teachers: 50 action research
strategies* (2nd ed.). Thousand Oaks, CA: Sage.

Theel, R. K. (2001). *Teacher selection and the interview
portfolios: Principals' perspectives.* Retrieved
March 6, 2009, from www.dissertation.com/
library/1121482a.htm

Villegas, A. M., & Lucas, T. (2002). Preparing culturally
responsive teachers: Rethinking the curriculum.
Journal of Teacher Education, 53(1), 20–32.

Wetzel, K., & Strudler, N. (2006). Costs and benefits of
electronic portfolios in teacher education:
Student voices. *Journal of Computing in Teacher
Education, 22*(3), 99–108.

Whitehead, J., & McNiff, J. (2006). *Action research:
Living theory.* Thousand Oaks, CA: Sage.

Wiggins, G. (1999). *Educative assessment. Designing
assessments to inform and improve student performance.* San Francisco: Jossey-Bass.

Wiggins, G., & McTighe, J. (2000). *Understanding
by design* (Rev. ed.). Alexandria, VA: Association of Supervision and Curriculum
Development.

Wilcox, B., & Tomei, L. (1999). *Professional portfolios
for teachers.* Norwood, MA: Christopher-Gordon.

Wilkerson, J. R., & Lang, W. S. (2003, December 3).
Portfolios, the Pied Piper of teacher certification
assessments: Legal and psychometric issues.
Education Policy Analysis Archives, 11(45).
Retrieved March 25, 2004, from http://epaa.asu
.edu/epaa/v11n45/

Wilkins, R. (1999). *Curriculum, instruction, and
assessment.* Harrisburg, PA: Pennsylvania
Assessment Through Themes.

Winsor, P., & Ellefson, B. (1998, Winter). Professional
portfolios in teacher education: An exploration
of their value and potential. *Teacher Education
Quarterly,* 68–81.

Wolf, K. (1999). *Leading the professional portfolio process
for change.* Thousand Oaks, CA: Corwin Press.

Wolf, K., & Dietz, M. (1998). Teaching portfolios:
Purposes and possibilities. *Teacher Education
Quarterly, 25*(1), 9–22.

Wright, V. H., Stallworth, B. J., & Ray, B. (2002).
Challenges of electronic portfolios: Student perceptions and experiences. *Journal of Technology
and Teacher Education, 10*(2), 49–61.

Wyatt, R. L., III, & Looper, S. (1999). *So you have to
have a portfolio: A teacher's guide to preparation
and presentation.* Thousand Oaks, CA: Corwin
Press.

Wyatt, R. L., III, & Looper, S. (2004). *So you have to
have a portfolio: A teacher's guide to preparation
and presentation* (2nd ed.). Thousand Oaks, CA:
Corwin Press.

Yancey, K. (2001). Introduction: Digitalized student
portfolios. In Barbara Cambridge (Ed.), *Electronic*

portfolios: Emerging practices in student, faculty, and institutional learning (pp. 15–30). Washington, DC: AAHE.

Zeichner, K. M. (1993, February.) *Educating teachers for cultural diversity* (NCRTL special report). East Lansing, MI: National Center for Research on Teacher Learning. (ERIC Document Reproduction No. ED 359 167).

Zeichner, K. M. (2003). The adequacies and inadequacies of three current strategies to recruit, prepare, and retain the best teachers for all students. *Teachers College Record, 105*(3), 490–519.

Zeichner, K. M., & Wray, S. (2001). The teaching portfolio in U.S. teacher education programs: What we know and what we need to know. *Teaching and Teacher Education, 17,* 613–621.

Index

About the Authors

Ruth S. Johnson is a professor emeritus at California State University, Los Angeles. She has served in a variety of educational settings in New Jersey and California. At the K–12 level, she has been a classroom teacher, an instructional consultant, a director of elementary education, an analyst, an assistant superintendent of schools in the areas of curriculum and business, and a superintendent of schools. She was a compensatory education consultant for the New Jersey Department of Education. Her major scholarly interests and publications focus on processes related to changing the academic culture of urban schools, with an emphasis on access and equity. Her second book, *Using Data to Close the Achievement Gap: Measuring Equity in Our Schools*, published in 2002, has been designated a best seller by Corwin Press. In addition to her two published books, she has written numerous book chapters, articles, editorials, research reports, and manuscript reviews. She serves as a consultant to schools and districts and as a recognized speaker, she has presented nationally to scholarly and professional audiences.

J. Sabrina Mims-Cox is currently professor of education at California State University, Los Angeles, and director of the Los Angeles Accelerated Schools Center. Her primary areas of research and interest include multilingual–multicultural education, emergent literacy, new models of teacher education in a global community, and school transformation. She has authored several children's reading textbook series in both Spanish and English, along with numerous articles in professional journals. She is on the editorial board of *Teacher Education Quarterly*. She has presented nationally and internationally on the topics of school transformation and reform and serves as an educational consultant for a variety of organizations, including Rotary International, the International Reading Association, the American Egyptian Master Teacher Exchange Program, and Intel Teach to the Future.

Adelaide Doyle-Nichols is a professor in instructional technology at California State University, Los Angeles. Recognizing the need to integrate technology into the curriculum as a fundamental piece of teacher education, she enjoys teaching teachers to use technology in the classroom. Her primary areas of research and interest include technology integration in education, computer anxiety, distance education, and computer-based instruction.

All three authors have been actively engaged in portfolio development with teacher and administrator candidates at California State University, Los Angeles.